CP 12^{50}

Diplomacy and Revolution

Diplomacy and Revolution

G. V. CHICHERIN
AND SOVIET FOREIGN AFFAIRS,
1918–1930

TIMOTHY EDWARD O'CONNOR

Iowa State University Press, Ames

TIMOTHY EDWARD O'CONNOR received his B.A. and M.A. from Creighton University and his Ph.D. from the University of Minnesota. He is an Associate Professor of History at the University of Northern Iowa.

Library of Congress Cataloging-in-Publication Data

O'Connor, Timothy Edward.
    Diplomacy and revolution.

    Bibliography: p.
    Includes index.
    1. Chicherin, Georgii Vasil'evich, 1872–1936.
2. Soviet Union—Foreign relations—1917–1945.
3. Diplomats—Soviet Union—Biography.   I. Title.
DK254.C57036   1988   327.47'0092'4 [B]   87–16785
ISBN 0–8138–0367–5

To Maureen A. O'Connor
with the sincere hope that her generation
will better understand the USSR

Contents

Preface

A major concern of any revolutionary government must be the creation of institutions and policies to deal with other governments to consolidate and maintain power. After the 1917 November Revolution in Russia the Bolsheviks had to resolve such a problem: they had to determine the relations of the new Soviet government with foreign governments, many of which were hostile toward the Soviets, at least in the beginning. This difficult task was further complicated because Russian Marxists had not explicitly elaborated the role of diplomacy for a postrevolutionary government; thus there were few guidelines on which to construct policies. After having acquired power in Russia the Bolsheviks expected that socialist revolution would spread throughout Europe. But to their chagrin and dismay, revolution did not sweep across the continent. During the 1920s the Bolsheviks debated the role of diplomacy for a revolutionary government and had to devise policies for their foreign relations. Therefore, Soviet foreign affairs were largely a product of the interaction of diplomacy and revolution.

The first commissar of foreign affairs for the new Soviet government was L. D. Trotskii. He intended, as he put it, "to issue a few revolutionary proclamations to the people and close up shop." This attitude was typical of many Bolsheviks immediately after the November Revolution, and in general they believed that diplomacy was unnecessary for their revolutionary government. In March 1918 the Treaty of Brest-Litovsk with Germany officially took Russia out of World War I and served to remind the Bolsheviks that foreign governments expected them to engage in traditional diplomacy. That same month, with civil war impending, Trotskii resigned as chief of the Commissariat of Foreign Affairs (Narkomindel) to take up the post of commissar for military and naval affairs. The leader of the Bolshevik party and the chairperson of the Council of People's Commissars (Sovnarkom) of the Soviet government, V. I. Lenin, selected G. V. Chicherin to succeed Trotskii at Narkomindel. Using Chicherin, commissar of foreign affairs from 1918 to 1930, as a case study, this book investigates the efforts of the Soviet government to establish diplomatic relations with foreign governments during the first decade after the Bolshevik Revolution.

Chicherin's appointment as chief of Narkomindel was the result of his knowledge of European diplomatic history, his experience in the Tsarist Ministry of Foreign Affairs, and his commitment to socialist revolution. He came from an old aristocratic family that could trace its lineage back to the fifteenth century and which had been active in diplomatic service to the Tsarist government. He received a splendid education, traveled extensively in Western Europe, and was fluent in several European languages. In 1904 Chicherin joined the revolutionary movement against Tsarism and decided to emigrate to study revolutionary literature in the West. Between the 1905 Revolution and the November Revolution he was affiliated with the Mensheviks, although he had initially sided with the Bolsheviks. He returned to Russia after the November Revolution, rejoined the Bolshevik party, and was recognized as one of the leading Bolshevik experts on diplomacy and international relations. He channeled all his energies into his work; he never married and for relaxation turned to music, particularly Mozart. Chicherin came to be regarded as one of the leading diplomats in Europe, and his colleagues in Western diplomatic circles admired him for his erudition, keen memory, superb literary expression, and enormous abilities. Even though he did not create policies for Narkomindel, which Lenin and the other members of the Politburo established, he set the style for and contributed to the prestige of Soviet diplomacy during the 1920s. Thus Chicherin added respectability to and helped legitimize the Soviet government in Russia.

Since Western scholars—notably George F. Kennan, *Russia and the West under Lenin and Stalin*; Richard K. Debo, *Revolution and Survival: The Foreign Policy of Soviet Russia, 1917–1918*; and Teddy J. Uldricks, *Diplomacy and Ideology: The Origins of Soviet*

Foreign Relations, 1917–1930—have already analyzed Soviet foreign affairs during the first decade after the November Revolution, this work is not conceived as a comprehensive diplomatic history. Rather it is a biography of Chicherin that examines his role in the formulation, articulation, and explanation of Soviet conduct and policies in foreign affairs. While Soviet historians have written some books on Chicherin—primarily S. V. Zarnitskii and N. N. Sergeev, *Chicherin*; I. Gorokhov, L. Zamiatin, and I. Zemskov, *G. V. Chicherin: Diplomat leninskoi shkoly*; and I. M. Khovratovich, *Georgii Vasil'evich Chicherin*—Western scholars have not produced a study that focuses on him (Debo's Ph.D. dissertation, "George Chicherin: Soviet Russia's Second Foreign Commissar," has not been published). Even though the specific thrust of this work is on the revolutionary process in Soviet Russia, for it investigates the interaction between diplomacy and revolution, the questions raised apply to other countries and different epochs. Thus the book has a place within the wider framework of scholarship on revolution in the modern world.

Acknowledgments

MOST of the research for this book was accomplished in the Soviet Union. I served as the resident director of the American Council of Teachers of Russian (ACTR) 1983–1984 language study program at the Pushkin Institute in Moscow. I am deeply grateful to my colleague and friend, Dan E. Davidson, director of ACTR's USSR Programs Group, for his constant encouragement and support of my professional development. I have thoroughly enjoyed my association with ACTR and appreciate the opportunities it has given me to conduct research in the Soviet Union. In addition, the Graduate College of the University of Northern Iowa provided research and travel grants that facilitated the completion of this project. I would like to express my gratitude to ACTR and the University of Northern Iowa; without their assistance and support this book would not have been written.

I am particularly grateful to the Chief Archive Administration of the USSR for access to important materials on Chicherin located in archives in Leningrad and Moscow. I received a great deal of cooperation and help from Soviet archivists who were sincerely interested in my work on Chicherin. Furthermore, the administrative staff of the Pushkin Institute deserves special mention, as they obtained permission from the Chief Archive Administration for me to use the archives. The librarians of the Saltykov-Shchedrin Library and the Library of the Academy of Sciences of the USSR in Leningrad and the Lenin Library in Moscow provided invaluable assistance in locating journals and newspapers that were essential for my research. I would like to extend my appreciation to the librarians; without their expertise and willingness to find journals, memoirs, and newspapers, and the goodwill they showed a foreign scholar working in the Soviet Union, this project would have been impossible to conceive and complete.

A number of people have contributed to the preparation of this book. My friend and colleague Irina H. Corten read and critiqued the manuscript in the early stages of its development. As always, her comments were incisive and useful, even though the topic of this book differs substantially from her own area of specialization. Irina's parents, Henry and Ludmilla Shapiro, originally suggested that I pursue research on Chicherin and Soviet foreign affairs. They gave me a great deal of pertinent information about Chicherin and Soviet Russia during the 1920s. I am indebted to them for their insights into Russian history and Soviet society. I would also like to thank Alfred E. Senn, who was in Moscow during the 1984 spring semester and who took time away from his own research to discuss the conceptualization of my study of Chicherin. My graduate assistant, Steven V. Moravec, helped considerably with the preparation of the manuscript, cheerfully reading and evaluating several drafts before it reached its final form. I owe a special debt of gratitude to Ruth M. Petersen, now retired, and particularly to Patricia L. Murphy of the Word Processing Center of the University of Northern Iowa. Patricia patiently typed several revisions of the entire manuscript, willingly making changes and expertly dealing with the transliteration of Russian names and words into English. Suzanne C. Lowitt of the Iowa State University Press expertly edited the manuscript. Finally, I would like to thank my colleagues in the Department of History and Robert E. Morin, former Dean of the College of Social and Behavioral Sciences at the University of Northern Iowa, for their encouragement of and interest in this project. I especially appreciate the understanding of my colleagues and the administration of my need to conduct research in the Soviet Union. Responsibility for errors of fact and interpretation, of course, is mine alone.

I am extremely fortunate in the devotion and love of my family. My parents faithfully encourage and support my interest in Russian Studies, and I am most grateful that they were able to travel with me to the Soviet Union in May 1983. My wife, Nancy, and my oldest daughter, Katie made the best of a difficult situation when they remained in the United States while I was in the Soviet Union in

1983–1984. Nancy patiently endured numerous lonely evenings when I was preoccupied with this, my second book, just as she did with the first. And I fervently hope that Katie, and her younger sister, Maureen, will continue to develop and thrive in spite of a father who frequently travels abroad.

Cedar Falls, Iowa   TIMOTHY EDWARD O'CONNOR
April 1986

Note on Dates and Transliteration

FOR THE SAKE of consistency all dates are given according to the "New Style" Gregorian calendar the Soviet government adopted in 1918. In some cases, however, in order to be precise, dates are also given according to the "Old Style" Julian calendar used in Russia from 1700 to 1918.

There is no easy solution to the problem of transliterating Russian names and words into English. Once again, for the sake of consistency, I have strictly adhered to the Library of Congress system. Therefore, I have retained the Russian soft sign, represented in English by an apostrophe, and have allowed the Library of Congress system to prevail over customary English usage: thus, Trotskii rather than Trotsky, and Pavlov-Sil'vanskii rather than Pavlov-Silvansky.

Abbreviations and Acronyms

ABBREVIATION	ENGLISH MEANING
Arkos	Soviet Trading Company in Britain
BSP	British Socialist Party
Comintern	Communist International
CPSU	Communist Party of the Soviet Union
KBE	Committee of Nonparty Émigrés
KDRSGL	Committee of Delegates of Russian Socialist Groups in London
KOPPSP	Relief Committee for Political Exiles and Deportees
KOPRPSP	Russian Political Prisoners, Exiles, and Deportees Relief Committee
KPPK	Relief Committee for Political Prisoners
LKRE	London Committee for the Repatriation of Emigrants
Narkomindel	People's Commissariat of Foreign Affairs
Narkompros	People's Commissariat of Enlightenment
NEP	New Economic Policy

Okhrana	Tsarist Secret Police
RSDRP	Russian Social Democratic Workers Party
Sovnarkom	Council of People's Commissars
SPD	German Social Democratic Party
SR	Socialist Revolutionary Party
Tsentrosoiuz	All-Russian Union of Consumer and Cooperative Societies
ZB	Foreign Bureau
ZTsB	Central Foreign Bureau

Diplomacy and Revolution

1

Chicherin Family Heritage

IT is interesting and perhaps ironical that Georgii Vasil'evich Chicherin, Soviet commissar of foreign affairs from 1918 to 1930, came from an old and distinguished aristocratic Russian family whose members had made a significant contribution to Muscovite and Tsarist government and society. The founder of the family was Afanasii Chicherini, who came to Muscovy from Italy in 1472, a servitor in the suite of Zoe Paleologue, the niece of the last Byzantine emperor, Constantine XI. After the Turkish conquest of Constantinople in 1453 Constantine's family fled to Rome, and the Vatican, in an attempt to influence the course of political and religious developments in Muscovy, proposed that Zoe Paleologue marry Grand Duke Ivan III. Moscow was receptive to this idea; for after the fall of Constantinople to the Turks, it perceived itself as the repository of true Christianity and was anxious to consolidate its cultural and religious links with Byzantium.[1] Zoe Paleologue had been brought up as a Catholic, but she converted to Russian Orthodoxy in order to marry Ivan III, thus becoming the Grand Duchess Sof'ia, consort of the Grand Duke of Muscovy.

Even though Afansii Chicherini is best remembered as the founder of the Chicherin family, he must have had a relatively important position in the retinue of Zoe Paleologue, for his descendants, who changed the name Chicherini to Chicherin, occupied significant posts in the governments of the Grand Dukes of Muscovy and the Tsars of Russia.[2] Many of the most prominent members of the family lived in the nineteenth century. Georgii

3

Vasil'evich's paternal grandfather, Nikolai Vasil'evich (1801–1860), who was well known within aristocratic circles for his erudition and liberal views, purchased the estate of Karaul in Kirsanov *uezd* (district) in Tambov *guberniia* (province) in 1837. Under the direction of Nikolai Vasil'evich, Karaul became one of the intellectual centers of the Tambov *guberniia*. He had seven sons and one daughter, the eldest of whom was Boris Nikolaevich (1828–1904), probably the most famous member of the Chicherin family during the nineteenth century.

Boris Nikolaevich inherited Karaul from his father and continued to administer the estate as a center of intellectual life for the aristocracy of Tambov. In addition, Boris Nikolaevich became one of the outstanding representatives of nineteenth-century Russian liberalism. He was a professor of public law at Moscow University, but he resigned his position in 1868, declaring that his philosophical and political disagreements with the government of Tsar Aleksandr II made teaching intolerable.[3] In 1882–1883 he served as lord mayor of Moscow, but, once again, his liberal views clashed with the reactionary policies of Tsar Aleksandr III. After his retirement from Moscow University, Boris Nikolaevich spent most of his time at Karaul, where he became active in the Tambov *zemstvo* and devoted his energy to writing articles and treatises on law and philosophy.

Georgii Vasil'evich's father, Vasilii Nikolaevich (1829–1882), while certainly not as famous as his illustrious brother, was also a distinguished member of the nineteenth-century Russian aristocracy. Like all of the sons of Nikolai Vasil'evich, Vasilii Nikolaevich received an excellent education. After graduating from Moscow University in 1849, he decided to enter the diplomatic service. This seemed to be a brilliant choice, for other members of the Chicherin family had been active in diplomacy. Furthermore, Vasilii Nikolaevich spoke French fluently and had excellent connections in aristocratic and government circles. His sister, Aleksandra Nikolaevna, was married to Emmanuel Dmitrievich Naryshkin, a descendent of one of the principal *boyar* families of Muscovy. Vasilii Nikolaevich served in various capacities in Russian missions abroad and was quickly promoted for his ability and dedication. In 1859, as secretary of the Russian mission in Piedmont during the Italian war, he married Baroness Zhorzhina Egorovna Meiendorf (1836–1897), a member of one of the oldest and most respected aristocratic Russian families, which was noted for its service in the

Tsarist diplomatic corps. Baroness Meiendorf had influential relatives and friends close to the imperial throne in St. Petersburg, and it
seemed that with the help of his wife Vasilii Nikolaevich would rise
even more rapidly through the diplomatic ranks. In 1862 he became
councilor (*sovetnik*) of the Russian embassy in Paris, and three years
later their first child, Nikolai, was born. But even though Vasilii
Nikolaevich had proved to be an accomplished diplomat, just at the
height of his career in 1869 when he had been selected to become
Russian ambassador to the United States he resigned from the diplomatic service.

Vasilii Nikolaevich left government service because of an
incident involving one of his wife's relatives. Baron Rudol'f
Kazimirovich Meiendorf, a mentally unbalanced cousin of Baroness Meiendorf, insulted Vasilii Nikolaevich and tried to provoke
him to fight a duel. Vasilii Nikolaevich refused to succumb to the
provocation, which many friends and acquaintances interpreted as
an act of cowardice, and decided to resign his position in Paris and
return to the family estate in the Tambov *guberniia*. Although the
event disgraced and humiliated Vasilii Nikolaevich, he was not a
coward and rejected dueling for religious reasons. He and his wife
had become devout adherents of an evangelical sect, the
"Radstokisty," founded by the third Lord Radstock, an English
evangelical who enjoyed greater popularity in Russia than in
England. Lord Radstock's main Russian disciple was V. A. Pashkov,
who led what came to be known as the Pashkovite movement. Pietism, during the last part of the nineteenth century, stressing an
emotional, personal relationship between God and Christians,
advocating the brotherhood of humanity and pacifism, and
renouncing dueling, gained increasing success among the Russian
aristocracy and gentry. Pietism deeply influenced the personal and
religious development of Georgii Vasil'evich's parents, and consequently the evangelical views of the Radstokisty also had a
considerable impact on his own upbringing.[4]

After leaving Paris in 1869 Vasilii Nikolaevich and his family
returned to the Tambov *guberniia* to take up residence on their
estate of Pokrov in the Kozlov *uezd*, which was not far from Boris
Nikolaevich who lived at Karaul. During the summer and autumn
of 1872 Vasilii Nikolaevich and his family visited Boris Nikolaevich
at Karaul, and there on November 12 (O.S. [Old Style]), a second
son, Georgii, was born. Like most of the aristocracy of the Tambov
guberniia, the Chicherin family spent the winter in Tambov and

lived on their estate during the summer. In addition, Georgii frequently visited his uncle at Karaul, in part because of the excellent library there consisting of more than four thousand titles in Russian and foreign languages on art, diplomacy, history, law, and philosophy. But life in Tambov and the surrounding countryside was vastly different from the diplomatic service in Paris to which the Chicherins had been accustomed.[5]

Zhorzhina Egorovna tried to compensate for the isolation of provincial existence by giving her three children—in addition to his older brother, Georgii also had a younger sister, Sof'ia—a broad, comprehensive education. Zhorzhina Egorovna was well suited to the task, for she enjoyed teaching, was well educated, and appreciated the fine arts, particularly painting. Even though she was concerned about the education of her children, much of her time was taken up with philanthropic and religious activities in the village of Pokrov. She and her husband were determined to spread the pietistic teachings of the Radstokisty among the peasants; they established a village school (which their daughter later administered), a library, and a medical clinic in an effort to improve the quality of life and the standard of living of the peasants in Pokrov.[6] The village school was an especially successful venture, and eventually Georgii's brother's wife, Natal'ia Dmitrievna, became a teacher there. Although Nikolai was seven years older than Georgii, the two brothers maintained a close relationship, and Georgii corresponded regularly with him and Natal'ia Dmitrievna throughout his years as a student at St. Petersburg University, in service in the Ministry of Foreign Affairs, and in emigration in Western Europe.[7]

Life in Tambov *guberniia* isolated the Chicherins from aristocratic society in Moscow and St. Petersburg, but provincial existence did not retard Georgii's intellectual development. His outstanding abilities were apparent from early childhood, and his parents anticipated a brilliant career for him in government service. He was a precocious child who read voraciously, using the extensive libraries available to him at Pokrov and Karaul. History especially appealed to him, and Georgii spent a great deal of time perusing the diplomatic documents in his mother's possession. He also devised games in which he would draw up diplomatic agreements between states reflecting territorial acquisitions and losses as a result of diplomacy and war. In addition to an aptitude for history, even as a child Georgii exhibited a remarkable facility for foreign languages. He studied English in childhood, which he spoke and wrote fluently, and he also knew French, German, Italian, Polish, and Serbian. Yet in spite of his intellectual pursuits, Georgii experienced a lonely childhood with only limited contact with the outside world; he entered the Tambov Gymnasium in 1884 when he was twelve years old, but he was introverted and shy and had difficulty developing friendships with his classmates.[8]

Georgii's father contributed to his son's restricted upbringing and isolation from other children. Vasilii Nikolaevich had never recovered from the humiliating experience of 1869 when he refused to fight a duel with his wife's cousin; as a result he avoided aristocratic society, fearing that he would not be able to undo his reputation as a coward. In an effort to restore his honor he voluntarily joined the Russian Red Cross during the Russo-Turkish war of 1877–1878, undertaking the dangerous task of removing wounded soldiers from the battlefields. Although he did not perish during the campaign, the war undermined his health, and, following a long illness which exacerbated the difficulties of the family, he died of tuberculosis in 1882.[9]

Georgii sought consolation for his lonely childhood and the death of his father by increasing his attention to intellectual endeavors. He developed a strong interest in music, a fascination that continued throughout his life. He became an accomplished pianist, a talent he displayed even after he became Soviet commissar of foreign affairs, and he also enjoyed the flute. Together with his brother, Georgii composed music and studied the lives of musicians and the history of music theory. His favorite composers were Beethoven, Mozart, and Wagner, and the brothers often performed the works of these great artists at home to entertain and to relax.[10]

Georgii Vasil'evich spent only two years at the Tambov Gymnasium; after the death of this father, his mother moved the family to St. Petersburg in 1886. Zhorzhina Egorovna was well connected with the aristocracy of the capital, and she wanted to provide a better education for her children. Georgii enrolled in the fourth class of the Eighth Gymnasium (Aleksandr Lyceum) of St. Petersburg, and he quickly discovered that the cultural and intellectual interests of his classmates were richer and more diverse than in Tambov. But at least at the outset he still experienced problems forming friendships with his peers, largely because of his introverted personality. While the Chicherins associated with their relatives in St. Petersburg, Georgii was uncomfortable in the company of his aunt, Aleksandra Nikolaevna Naryshkina, who was much wealthier than the

Chicherin family, and he visited her infrequently and primarily out of a sense of obligation. In contrast, Georgii enjoyed his visits to his maternal grandmother, who regaled him with intriguing stories of early nineteenth-century European diplomacy.[11]

Even though Georgii had difficulty making the transition from Tambov to St. Petersburg, he found the capital a more exciting place to live and continued to excel at the gymnasium, graduating with a gold medal in 1891. His family had raised him with the expectation that he would attend the university, and he immediately enrolled in the historical-philological faculty of St. Petersburg University, a logical choice given his interests and predilections since childhood. He was determined to pursue a broad, general education and registered for courses covering a wide range of subjects, including lectures from such prominent scholars as I. M. Grevs, N. I. Kareev, and S. F. Platonov. Georgii was especially impressed with the great Russian historian V. O. Kliuchevskii, praising him for his brilliant lectures and sound analytical methodology.[12] Georgii was sympathetic toward the student disturbances of 1895, but his role in these events was insignificant, as his name was not listed in the police records. In May of that year he passed his examinations with distinction in the historical-philological faculty and graduated from St. Petersburg University with highest honors.[13]

Georgii Vasil'evich had clearly demonstrated his intellectual abilities at St. Petersburg University, but graduation did not alleviate his feelings of failure, inadequacy, and despondency about a lack of specific goals and positive ideals to give his life direction and meaning. During his university career he experienced considerable emotional and intellectual torment and uncertainty, and his spiritual searchings led him away from the pietism of his parents to total self-abnegation.[14] He absorbed a tremendous amount of literature, much of it devoted to philosophy and political theory, in his attempt to find answers to questions about his role in society that continued to plague him. He turned briefly to the works of the reactionary writer B. V. Nikol'skii, finding there a response to his own pessimism and self-torment. In Nikol'skii's writings Chicherin discovered individual anarchism and contempt for human existence, which reinforced his own feelings of self-doubt.[15] Nikol'skii's ideas led Chicherin to spiritual despair, yet he continued to search for values that would give his life a sense of purpose. Poor physical health aggravated Georgii Vasil'evich's mental anguish, and in the autumn of 1895 he left Russia for Western Europe, hoping that rest and travel would improve his condition. His mother's critical illness forced Chicherin's return to Russia in 1897, although he still had not resolved the basic philosophical issues that would permit him to establish goals and give direction and meaning to his life.

Despite the opposition of his relatives and friends, Chicherin entered government service as a junior official in the Department of the Archives of the Ministry of Foreign Affairs in St. Petersburg in January 1898. It had seemed obvious to those who knew him well that he would choose a career in the diplomatic corps, but few people understood or accepted his decision to work in the archives. Chicherin's choice in part was based on his love for history, and he was especially fond of nineteenth-century European diplomacy; but even more important was his sense of alienation from aristocratic and government circles and his inability to remove the doubts about the direction that his life should take.[16] His immediate superior in the archives was the respected historian of European diplomacy N. P. Pavlov-Sil'vanskii, a left-wing member of the Constitutional Democrats, with whom Chicherin quickly established cordial relations. The two historians, with the assistance of several colleagues, collaborated on a history of the Ministry of Foreign Affairs for the centenary of the Ministry, celebrated in 1902.

Chicherin was particularly knowledgeable about foreign policy during the reign of Aleksandr II, the period when his father had been active in the diplomatic service. In addition, Chicherin prepared a massive biography, consisting of more than 500 pages in manuscript (never published) of the famous Russian diplomat, A. M. Gorchakov, who served as minister of foreign affairs from 1856 to 1883.[17] Chicherin divided his work into three parts. He devoted the first section to Gorchakov's experiences at the celebrated Imperial Lyceum in Tsarskoe Celo and especially his association with the writer A. S. Pushkin, a study of Gorchakov's diplomatic activity up to 1863, with special emphasis on the Crimean War and the Peace of Paris of 1856, and relations between Russia and the United States between 1861 and 1869. In the second portion, the longest part of the manuscript, Chicherin concentrated on Russia's relations with the great European powers—Austria, Britain, France, and Prussia—from 1856 to 1870. Finally, in the last unit of his biography Chicherin focused on Gorchakov's reactions to Aleksandr II's internal reforms.[18]

An examination of Chicherin's manuscript provides an understanding of his work as a professional historian and also gives some insights into his philosophy of diplomacy, for he admired Gorchakov and eventually used the great diplomat as a reference for his own activities and policies as Soviet commissar of foreign affairs. In this respect, the last part of the first section dealing with relations between Russia and the United States during the American Civil War, is especially interesting. According to Chicherin, Gorchakov tried to establish cordial and friendly relations with other states, regardless of their system of government and even if their political structure clashed with Tsarist autocracy. Only in this manner could Russia preserve its status as a great power and successfully complete sweeping domestic reforms without being distracted by crises in foreign affairs.[19] Borrowing this idea from Gorchakov, Chicherin modified it to fit the circumstances of the 1920s; in his view, Soviet Russia needed peaceful relations with other nations to survive in a hostile environment and which would give the Soviet government the necessary time to restore the economy and consolidate its political position. Furthermore, Chicherin's history of Russo-American relations put a great deal of emphasis on the support Gorchakov rendered to Washington in its struggle with the Confederacy. Moscow did not grant diplomatic recognition to the Confederacy; according to Chicherin, educated Russian society was clearly in sympathy with Washington.[20]

The last portion of the manuscript, an analysis of Gorchakov's attitude toward the internal reforms of Aleksandr II, also casts additional light on Chicherin's understanding of Soviet foreign affairs. Chicherin argued that Gorchakov was determined to create a propitious foreign policy for Russia so that the Tsarist government could effectively introduce domestic reforms.[21] And Chicherin attempted to perform a similar service for the Soviet government in his conduct of foreign policy during the twenties. By studying Gorchakov, Chicherin concluded that foreign affairs had to complement and support a government's domestic policies since the strength of a state's international position was directly related to its economic resources and political stability. Chicherin would not forget this valuable lesson when the opportunity came for him to direct the Soviet Commissariat of Foreign Affairs.

Chicherin's work as a historian in the archives of the Ministry of Foreign Affairs brought him a measure of professional satisfaction, but his choice of career did not end his philosophical searchings, which continued to be a source of considerable personal discontent. His initial flirtation with the student rebellions of 1895, his travels throughout Western Europe from 1895 to 1897, and the student disturbances and industrial strikes of 1899 intensified his quest for a body of doctrines and a meaningful political and social cause to which he could channel his energies. Chicherin's activities in the Ministry of Foreign Affairs, by an unusual coincidence, led him even closer to radicalism, as Pavlov-Sil'vanskii openly supported opposition to Tsarism and encouraged his young associate in the same direction. The increasing radicalization of Chicherin's intellectual and political views can be deduced in part by his choice of residence in St. Petersburg. He persistently shunned his aristocratic relatives and lived alone, taking a small room not far from the Tsarskoe Celo railway station, certainly humble quarters for a man of his background and status. It was here that Chicherin began his first serious contacts with the revolutionary movement, which would ultimately lead to his renunciation of Tsarism and emigration abroad in order to become more closely involved with the efforts to overthrow the government.[22]

During his tenure at St. Petersburg University Chicherin had become acquainted with a young neuropathologist, V. M. Narbut, who was active in revolutionary circles. Gradually Chicherin began to perform services for Narbut and his colleagues, usually of a "technical nature," which primarily involved the use of his lodging as a safe place to store manuscripts and typographical materials.[23] In this fashion Chicherin became associated with other radicals, most of whom were Socialist Revolutionaries (SRs), who collaborated with Narbut. Although Georgii Vasil'evich was not yet ready to make a complete break with his past, he accomplished valuable services for St. Petersburg radicals without arousing the suspicion of the authorities, for police registers at the turn of the century did not include him in their records. Continuing his historical work at the Ministry of Foreign Affairs, in his free time he increasingly engaged in a study of revolutionary literature, particularly the writings of Marx and Engels, which had become more readily available in Russia since the formation of G. V. Plekhanov's Liberation of Labor Group (*Osvobozhdenie truda*) in Switzerland in 1883. As Chicherin's commitment to radicalism grew, he resolved to travel abroad to undertake a more thorough examination of the latest revolutionary writings in Western Europe; in addition, he feared that the police might discover his activities and that he would be arrested.[24] In the spring of 1904, after informing Pavlov-Sil'vanskii of his intentions and having resolutely committed himself to revolution, Chicherin left Russia for Western Europe with a legal passport and still officially a colleague of the Ministry of Foreign Affairs on a temporary leave of absence for reasons of health. He went abroad with the assumption that he would soon return to Russia better prepared to participate in the revolutionary movement. He miscalculated considerably, for he would not return to his homeland until January 1918.

The year 1904 was a watershed for Chicherin. He had followed a difficult and tortuous path to radicalism, but once he embraced the revolutionary movement, he renounced his aristocratic heritage and devoted himself unsparingly to socialist revolution. Unlike revolutionaries of poor social origins, his adherence to radicalism meant a significant change in life-style. According to Bessie Beatty, a writer who knew him well:

> Materially he had nothing to gain for himself by revolution. He was one of the few who already had all there was worth having in Russia, of place and power and the fruits of empire. . . . A monk eschewing the world, the flesh, and the devil could make no more thorough job of renunciation for his faith than George Chicherin has done.[25]

Yet in spite of the apparent incongruity between Chicherin's aristocratic background and commitment to revolution, his upbringing influenced his decision to become a revolutionary and unwittingly encouraged him in this direction. His parents, strict adherents to the Pashkovite movement, increasingly ignored aristocratic society after returning to Russia from Paris in 1869. Their philanthropic activities in the village of Pokrov occupied most of their time and represented a means of religious salvation for them. In addition, they nurtured their beliefs—pacifism, the brotherhood of humanity, and the value of philanthropy—in their children. Since childhood Chicherin had been taught to champion social justice, for the pietism of Radstock evangelicalism contained a strong message of humanitarian reformism and urged Christians to ignore social distinctions, considering all people equal before God. Even though Georgii Vasil'evich eventually rejected the Christian pietism of his parents, he remained devoted to many of the principal ideals of Pashkovism for the rest of his life.[26]

Chicherin's upbringing and training also contributed to his decision to support socialist revolution by fostering unorthodox intellectual views. His parents' religious nonconformism permitted Georgii Vasil'evich to grow up "undisciplined and eccentric."[27] His philosophical searchings led him to question traditional authority and, in particular, eventually to challenge political institutions he regarded as anachronistic and oppressive. Although to his contemporaries, even his fellow revolutionaries, it seemed unusual that such a committed and inspired champion of socialist revolution would come from the aristocracy, in view of his childhood, education, and personality, Chicherin's decision in favor of radicalism was consistent and logical. He came from a family of distinguished diplomats, and his parents prepared him to enter government service, but they were also religious nonconformists, and in him nonconformism, which led to a rejection of Tsarism, triumphed.[28]

Yet neither Chicherin's upbringing nor the religious nonconformism of his parents adequately explains the fanaticism with which he accepted socialist revolution. Beginning in 1904 he devoted himself exclusively to the revolutionary movement, sacrificing everything for the cause he embraced with so much zeal. In this respect he compares favorably with the Populists of an earlier generation, especially the *Narodniki* of the 1870s—the young men and women from aristocratic families and the gentry who went to the countryside determined to serve the peasants by sparking an agrarian rebellion and in the process hoping to identify with those from whom they were so clearly separated by birth and education.[29] Like the *Narodniki*, Chicherin, too, was overwhelmed by feelings of guilt for his privileged position in society; he sought to atone for these privileges before suffering humanity by renouncing his birthright and pledging his total support for the elimination of social injustices in Russia. By the 1890s Populism had lost much of its former popularity among educated Russians, and young radicals increasingly turned to Marxist socialism for guidance and inspiration. But, just as with the Populism of the seventies, Marxism also demanded unswerving commitment to revolution. Like their Populist predecessors, for the generation reaching adulthood in the nineties, Marxist revolution meant personal fulfillment through service to the masses by resisting political oppression and social injustices, particularly when the government was distrustful of the educated people whom it needed to modernize the economy. By analogy with the *Narodniki* of the seventies in their infatuation with Populism, even though Chicherin's thinking was logical and rational, his approach to Marxism was highly emotional. Marxism enabled him to identify with the downtrodden masses and to assist them in the task of liberation from autocracy, a goal that ultimately held out the promise of the brotherhood of humanity without class or social distinctions. Chicherin had followed an arduous path to Marxist socialism, but by 1904 he was ready to leave Russia for Western Europe, determined to break definitively with his aristocratic heritage.

2

Emigration and Radicalism

AFTER leaving Russia in the spring of 1904, Chicherin traveled to Germany where he first settled in Bonn. Even though he had frequently associated with the SRs when he worked for the Department of the Archives of the Ministry of Foreign Affairs in St. Petersburg, one of the principal reasons for emigration was his determination to become more familiar with Marxist socialism. He also wanted to investigate the frequent internal disagreements, culminating in the split between the Bolsheviks and the Mensheviks at the Second Congress in 1903, that were disrupting the Russian Social Democratic Workers Party (RSDRP). He attended courses at Bonn University and came under the influence of Karl Liebknecht's German Socialist Youth Movement. Chicherin believed he could become well acquainted with Western revolutionary literature in Germany.

There was a sizeable community of Russian émigrés in Berlin and its surrounding suburbs. Because of its close proximity to Russia and the strength of the powerful German Social Democratic Party (SPD), Berlin proved attractive to many revolutionaries seeking refuge from the Tsarist secret police (Okhrana).[1] But the Tsarist regime, through its connections with the government of Imperial Germany, was able to dispatch a considerable number of agents to Berlin and other German cities to observe closely the activities of Russian émigrés. Generally the Prussian state police were quite cooperative in dealing with the Tsarist authorities.

In 1905 Chicherin moved from Bonn to Berlin and joined the Berlin section of the Bolshevik wing of the party. At this point he chose the Bolsheviks over the Mensheviks primarily because he was convinced that the former's interpretation of the acquisition of political power in a bourgeois-democratic revolution was correct; he argued that the Mensheviks would obstruct the revolutionary process by refusing to take power, even if circumstances and events offered them the opportunity. In essence, he opted for the more militant approach of the Bolsheviks and, with the outbreak of revolution in Russia that same year, prepared to return to his homeland illegally to participate in the revolutionary movement. But his generally poor health prevented him from undertaking such an arduous task. He remained in Berlin during the Revolution of 1905, where he continued to support the German Socialist Youth Movement and was active in the collection of funds for the RSDRP, serving as the secretary for the Russian Marxist university students.[2]

Chicherin became quite effective at raising money for the RSDRP, for with his aristocratic connections he appealed to liberal-minded aristocrats in Berlin for donations. In addition, Boris Nikolaevich Chicherin died in 1904, and he bequeathed his estate, Karaul, to his nephew. Georgii Vasil'evich also received an inheritance from his parents. But he renounced his legal rights to Karaul and used most of his inheritance to replenish the depleted coffers of the RSDRP.[3] In particular, he was active in financing the Fifth Congress of the RSDRP in London in 1907, donating 12,000 marks to the party to pay the expenses of delegates at the Congress. Chicherin used part of his inheritance to provide for his own personal needs during emigration, but on the whole he lived quite modestly and tried to make funds available to the party whenever they were needed. In this respect he was one of the founders of a Social Democratic publication written in German and produced in Berlin, *Der Russische Bulletin*, the purpose of which was to attack the Tsarist government in the Western European press. Obviously, Chicherin's commitment to the revolution was sincere, since he refused to accept Karaul and used a substantial portion of his inheritance in the service of the party.[4]

In addition to a growing reputation as a financial promoter for the RSDRP, Chicherin also became well known among Russian émigrés for his organizational abilities. Like other revolutionaries engaged in extensive journalistic and publishing endeavors, he increasingly used the pseudonyms "A. Ornatskii" and "Batalin," partly to conceal his identity from the Okhrana.[5] Even though he had originally joined the Bolshevik wing of the party, he disapproved of factionalism and made an effort to promote the unity of the RSDRP, particularly after the Fourth ("Unity") Congress of 1906 in Stockholm. And in general members of the party tried to achieve greater cohesion after the Fourth Congress. To realize this goal, the Central Committee established in January 1907 an organizational center in Berlin for émigré Social Democratic groups—the Central Foreign Bureau (*Zagranichnoe Tsentral'noe Biuro*, or ZTsB). One of the main purposes of the ZTsB was to promote cooperation and unity among the various factions of the party and to provide information for émigrés about the revolutionary movement in Russia.

Chicherin was elected secretary of the ZTsB and did a great deal of the preliminary, preparatory work for the Fifth Congress of the RSDRP in London in May. He had been relatively successful in hiding his activities from the Tsarist government until 1907, but as secretary of the ZTsB he received greater attention from agents in Berlin. On June 16 (O.S.), the Okhrana dispatched a directive warning border guards and customs officials to watch for him should he attempt to return to Russia, with further instructions to conduct a thorough search and take appropriate action if he should be apprehended with illegal, revolutionary materials.[6] But it is interesting that the Tsarist authorities had not yet issued an order for his arrest, and it seems there was still some doubt or hesitation about his activities in Germany, which was probably an indication that he had been somewhat successful in avoiding police agents.

In 1907–1908 Chicherin gradually moved away from the Bolsheviks toward an affiliation with the Menshevik wing of the RSDRP. He attended the Fifth Congress of the party, but he was not an official delegate and did not play an active role in its proceedings. Yet the Congress was extremely important for his revolutionary career. Chicherin had been concerned about party unity, which was one of the principal reasons he was so zealous in the performance of his duties as secretary of the ZTsB. In spite of the resolutions on unity of the Fourth Congress of 1906, it became increasingly clear a year later that factionalism was still rampant within the party. Chicherin primarily blamed the Bolsheviks, led by V. I. Lenin, whom he met for the first time at the London Congress, for this development.[7] At this point the principal disagreement between Chicherin and Lenin centered on the organizational structure of the RSDRP.

Lenin was in favor of a tightly knit, highly disciplined core of professional revolutionaries functioning as the party vanguard who would lead the proletariat to political consciousness, especially in the aftermath of the failure of the Revolution of 1905. In his view a new revolutionary wave might not emerge for a long period, and the Tsarist government was recovering its nerve under the vigorous leadership of Prime Minister P. A. Stolypin. The Mensheviks, however, led by F. I. Dan, Iu. O. Martov, and Plekhanov, advocated revolutionary spontaneity, which for them essentially meant a program of agitation and propaganda among the workers to broaden as much as possible the popular base of the party. Since the SPD had developed and thrived as a mass political party and because of the influence which it exerted on Chicherin, he gravitated toward the Mensheviks, perceiving that they were closer to the policies and tactics of German Social Democracy than the Bolsheviks.[8] Furthermore, the Mensheviks began to have a greater emotional appeal for him; in their interpretation of the party organization he sensed a closer association and identification with the masses and felt that the Bolshevik approach smacked of revolutionary elitism.

A second, equally significant reason for Chicherin's break with the Bolsheviks was his disagreement with them on revolutionary tactics. And indeed he was not the only member of the RSDRP concerned about tactics after the Revolution of 1905. One of the main problems of the party was a constant lack of resources, which hindered operations and made existence for revolutionaries precarious and uncertain. Lenin, along with his chief associates A. A. Bogdanov and L. B. Krasin, had resorted to "expropriations," or "exes," as they were called, to provide funds for the party, especially the Bolshevik faction. The Mensheviks increasingly criticized these expropriations—involving robberies of Tsarist banks and post offices by highly secret Bolshevik "fighting squads"— particularly after they gained control of the Central Committee at the Fourth Congress.

At this Congress the Bolsheviks established an organization called the Bolshevik Center. While operating as the expanded editorial board of the paper *Proletarii* (*Proletarian*), it functioned as the Bolsheviks' own central committee within the RSDRP primarily for the purpose of executing expropriations and managing factional affairs. Although it is difficult to ascertain the exact membership of the Bolshevik Center, it certainly included Lenin, Bogdanov, and Krasin. While Lenin directed general policy for the expropriations, Krasin, who was a professional engineer and factory manager, brilliantly organized their technical operations, which occurred most frequently in the Urals and the Caucasus. A precise calculation of

the money supplied to the Bolshevik exchequer by these expropriations is impossible to document, but the total amount was undoubtedly "several hundred thousand rubles" from 1906 to 1908.[9]

Even though most factions of the RSDRP had generally
accepted expropriations during the Revolution of 1905, by the
fourth Congress they aroused considerable debate and discontent
within the party. The Mensheviks, supported by the Jewish Bund,
the Poles, and even some Bolsheviks, used their majority to pass a
resolution on partisan activities designed "to combat the actions of
persons or groups aimed at seizing money in the name of or using
the slogans of the Social Democratic Party." The Congress considered "that a very important element in revolution is its moral and
political effect on the revolutionary masses, on society," and pushed
through a ban on expropriations because it believed that they were
having a demoralizing effect on members of the RSDRP and dis-
crediting the party among its supporters abroad, particularly within
the SPD.[10] But the Bolshevik Center refused to obey the resolution,
and Bolshevik fighting detachments continued to carry out expropriations until at least 1910.

The Fifth Congress of the RSDRP also dealt with the issue of
expropriations. Even though Lenin managed to gain a majority at
the Congress, primarily because the Polish and Latvian Social Democrats tended to vote with the Bolsheviks, there was still substantial
opposition even within the Bolshevik faction against expropriations. Therefore, the Congress passed another resolution on partisan activities, which declared "that party organizations must
conduct an energetic struggle against . . . expropriations . . ." and
"that party members are forbidden to participate in any way at all in
the partisan activities and expropriations, or to give them assistance." In addition, in a strongly worded statement, the Congress
resolved "that all specialized fighting squads attached to party organizations are to be disbanded."[11]

Despite the resolutions against expropriations of the Fourth
and Fifth Congresses, the Bolshevik Center refused to disband its
fighting squads. Shortly after the Fifth Congress had adjourned in
May 1907, the newly enlarged Bolshevik Center carried out one of
its most spectacular expropriations. On June 13 (O.S.), the secret
Bolshevik fighting unit in the Caucasus, led by the legendary bandit
Kamo, robbed a government shipment of more than 250,000 rubles
in Erevan Square in Tiflis, which was enroute to the Tiflis branch of
the St. Petersburg State Bank.[12] Even though Kamo was responsible

for the robbery, I. V. Stalin played a directing role in Bolshevik expropriations in the Caucasus. Nearly all of the money obtained in the Tiflis operation consisted of 500-ruble notes. About a month after the holdup, Kamo took the money to Lenin and Bogdanov who were in Finland. At this point Lenin arranged for one of his associates living in Berlin, Dr. Jacob Zhitomirskii who also happened to be a Tsarist police spy, to coordinate the exchange of the 500-ruble notes into foreign currency in banks all over northwestern Europe. The exchange was set for December 1907. Zhitomirskii supplied the Okhrana with a list of the Bolshevik agents who were to undertake the transactions. Since the authorities already had the serial numbers of the 500-ruble notes, it was a relatively easy matter to arrest these agents at the banks where they attempted to exchange the stolen money. In addition, Zhitomirskii facilitated Kamo's arrest in Berlin.

With the help of information provided by Zhitomirskii the Prussian state police also conducted raids on Bolshevik addresses in Berlin, resulting in the seizure of weapons, ammunition, and fresh bank-note paper. It seems that Krasin, who worked for the Allgemeine Elektrische Gesellschaft, intended to use the bank-note paper to counterfeit three-ruble notes.[13] He had ingeniously arranged for the SPD daily, *Vorwarts*, to ship much of the bank-note paper to Lenin in Finland. The German Social Democrats, who believed that they were involved in the transfer of bank-note paper necessary for the production of revolutionary literature for distribution in Russia, were outraged when they learned that it was actually intended for counterfeiting. Thus, after the discovery of Krasin's scheme to counterfeit rubles, the scandal within the RSDRP became international.

The Mensheviks demanded that the Central Committee investigate the expropriations conducted by the Bolshevik Center, banned by resolutions of the Fourth and Fifth Congresses. The investigation occurred on two levels: first, since the Mensheviks controlled the party apparatus in the Transcaucasus, they were anxious to undertake a local inquiry in Georgia on the Tiflis robbery; second, the Central Committee ordered the ZTsB to make a general study of expropriations and the role of the Bolshevik Center in their execution. In this fashion, serving as the secretary of the ZTsB, Chicherin directed the overall investigation into the question of expropriations, which had become a highly emotional issue within the RSDRP and even for Social Democracy in Western Europe.

The Mensheviks were furious that the Bolshevik Center had ignored the resolutions against expropriations passed by two party congresses. But ultimately the discord focused on tactics after the 1905 Revolution. The Mensheviks were convinced that armed expropriations disrupted the more important work of conducting agitation and propaganda among the masses and cost the RSDRP support both at home and abroad. Lenin and his associates, particularly Bogdanov and Krasin, rejected this view and insisted that the party needed revenue to purchase arms and ammunition to prepare for another armed uprising. Thus the dissension over tactics reflected starkly different appraisals of the course that the revolution ought to follow in the radically changed political circumstances after 1905.

The scandal caused by Bolshevik expropriations—especially the Tiflis robbery—and the investigation conducted by Chicherin as secretary of the ZTsB compelled Lenin to alter his tactics in the face of mounting criticism by the Mensheviks. More significantly, as an astute political organizer and strategist, Lenin realized that the revival of reaction and the Tsarist government's counterattack against revolutionaries necessitated a new, more flexible approach to revolution after 1905. By gaining control of the Central Committee from the Mensheviks, he succeeded in taking the investigation into expropriations out of the hands of Chicherin's ZTsB.

The August 1908 plenum of the Central Committee met in Geneva, and Chicherin received an invitation to attend to give an account of his investigation. At the last session of the plenum on 25 and 26 August he presented his findings to the Central Committee, which detailed breaches of party discipline by the Bolshevik Center on the basis of resolutions of the Fourth and Fifth Congresses. The Bolsheviks, however, repudiated his evidence, claiming that he had collected a mass of information not germane to the topic under scrutiny and which served only to cast aspersions on and damage the reputations of Lenin, Bogdanov, Krasin, and indeed the entire RSDRP. With the support of the Poles and the Latvians, Lenin arranged to have the inquiry removed from the ZTsB and turned over to a new investigatory commission of the Central Committee, chaired by his colleague G. E. Zinov'ev, who effectively stifled further action on the issue.[14] The Central Committee also discharged the Menshevik-dominated ZTsB and replaced them with a ten-person board consisting of four Bolsheviks, four Mensheviks, and two German Social Democrats. The task of representing the interests of the Central Committee among the émigré party organizations, the responsibility for all intelligence activities conducted abroad, and the job of maintaining contact with members of the Central Committee in Russia became the main assignment of a new three-member body, headed by Zinov'ev, called the Foreign Bureau (*Zagranichnoe Biuro*, or ZB) of the Central Committee. Furthermore, the ZB clearly dominated the new ZTsB, and a member of the Central Committee attended the sessions of the latter with an absolute veto over its actions. On the whole the Central Committee severely curtailed the functions of the new ZTsB. According to Okhrana reports the ZB delegated tasks to the new ZTsB, and, just as significantly, 85–90 percent of the latter's revenues had to be turned over to the Central Committee.[15]

The Central Committee's decision to dismiss the old Menshevik-controlled ZTsB led to an open rupture between the two organizations, specifically, between the latter and the Bolsheviks, for Chicherin and the other Mensheviks on the old ZTsB refused to submit to the Central Committee and did not disband. Neither the Bolsheviks nor the Mensheviks wanted to take the initiative for a complete and permanent rift in the RSDRP. Both groups continued to call for adherence to the principles of the Fourth ("Unity") Congress, but the issues of party organization and tactics were leading to a definitive separation. In reaction to the Bolshevik action at the August plenum, members of the old ZTsB demanded the convocation of a congress of RSDRP émigré organization's intending to use their influence among these groups to reverse the Central Committee's decision.[16] The Mensheviks counted on their numerical superiority over the Bolsheviks in emigration, for most of the Mensheviks' sympathizers, after stubbornly attempting to maintain legal factional organizations in Russia, had been compelled to flee abroad in the wake of renewed government repression. Moreover, the Mensheviks believed that they could rely upon the SPD to support them against the Bolsheviks. While the Mensheviks were stronger in emigration, the Bolsheviks dominated the remaining RSDRP groups in Russia, largely because the latter had realized the futility of adhering to a legal party framework and once again had gone underground. The Bolsheviks also controlled the Central Committee from the middle of 1908, and as a result of expropriations commanded much larger financial resources than the Mensheviks.

The Mensheviks assiduously prepared for the congress of RSDRP émigré groups. On 9 and 10 October (O.S.), in a session Chicherin primarily financed, the old ZTsB, dominated by the Mensheviks but including some Bolsheviks and German Social Democrats, met in Leipzig to discuss the outstanding problems between it and the Central Committee. The Mensheviks, as expected, refused to submit to the Bolsheviks and demanded that the ZTsB turn over only 5–10 percent of its revenues to the Central Committee, allocating the rest to *Golos sotsial-demokrata* (*Voice of Social-Democracy*), the official newspaper of the Menshevik wing of the party. The Bolsheviks, realizing that they could not expect the support of the SPD, left the meeting without coming to an agreement with the Mensheviks. Undaunted, the Mensheviks elected an Organizational Commission, which on 5 November (O.S.) convened in Basel to plan the forthcoming congress of party émigré organizations. Both factions campaigned to control the congress. The Bolsheviks, fearing that they would be swamped, began to create their own independent émigré groups; therefore, the split between the old ZTsB and the Central Committee widened to include the establishment of competing émigré organizations of the RSDRP in several major cities of Western Europe— Berlin, Brussels, Geneva, Paris, and Zurich.[17]

The congress of the RSDRP émigré groups finally convened in Basel in late November (O.S.), but in reality it was a gathering of Menshevik organizations, since the Bolsheviks for the most part refused to attend. The congress, consisting of about thirty delegates, discussed relations between the Central Committee and the ZTsB and criticized the former for its "unwarranted attacks" upon the latter; in addition, the congress resolved to terminate the ZTsB's function as an agency subordinate to the Central Committee. But this did not mean that the Menshevik-controlled ZTsB ceased to exist. New elections reaffirmed Chicherin as its secretary, and the congress called upon it once again to arrange activities and resolve administrative problems for RSDRP émigré groups in Western Europe.[18]

Chicherin also continued to negotiate with the Central Committee for a settlement of the issues dividing the two organizations. In late December (O.S.) the Fifth All-Russian Conference of the RSDRP met in Paris and immediately before and after the conference the party held a plenum of the Central Committee. Chicherin's ZTsB appealed to the Central Committee in an effort to normalize relations. But the Central Committee, now firmly controlled by the Bolsheviks, refused to grant concessions. The conference passed a resolution which stated that "the Central Committee can work with complete success only if its minority will submit to party discipline and work loyally within the framework of a single institution and through its executive organs." The conference also confirmed the decision about the ZTsB made at the August plenum of the Central Committee, passing a resolution calling the existence abroad of the ZB "useful and necessary."[19] There were other attempts, later in 1909 and 1910, to regularize relations between the Central Committee and the Menshevik-dominated ZTsB. These efforts, however, all ended in failure, as neither organization was willing to make substantive concessions.

For Chicherin, who had begun to drift toward the Mensheviks by the beginning of 1907, the scandal caused by the Tiflis robbery and his subsequent investigation into expropriations by the Bolshevik Center intensified his disenchantment with Bolshevik tactics, led to a closer association with the Menshevik wing of the party by the end of the year, and resulted in a formal rift with the Bolsheviks at the August 1908 plenum of the Central Committee. While he was embroiled in this dispute with the Bolsheviks, the Berlin authorities subjected him to greater surveillance. On 2 January 1908 the Prussian state police arrested him for the first time in Charlottenburg, a suburb of Berlin, in the apartment of a prominent German Social Democrat. The arrest was made when he was attending a secret meeting of some members of the RSDRP, probably to discuss the police raids on Bolshevik addresses in Berlin a month earlier. The police charged the group with unlawful assembly and fined Chicherin 30 marks for giving a fictitious name and for carrying a false passport; in addition, on 6 January for using false identification and for participating in an unlawful assembly, the authorities ordered him to leave Prussia.[20] Even though he was legally prohibited from residing in Berlin, he managed periodically to enter the city illegally from his new residence in Saxony.

It is interesting to note the reaction of the Ministry of Foreign Affairs to Chicherin's arrest in Charlottenburg. The ministry initially took a rather lenient attitude toward Chicherin and his activities in Berlin, possibly because of the influence of Pavlov-Sil'vanskii. In a document dated 31 December 1907 (O.S.) the director of the ministry's Second Department (in charge of personnel) informed the Okhrana that he would withhold action against

Chicherin pending a thorough investigation of the circumstances of his arrest. Furthermore, in a memorandum dated 7 January 1908 (O.S.) the Second Department provided the Okhrana with some information about Chicherin it had received from the German Ministry of Internal Affairs. Finally, as a result of his revolutionary activities, in an order dated 22 January (O.S.) the director of the Second Department officially removed Chicherin from his position in the Department of the Archives.[21] Chicherin had succeeded in concealing his involvement in the revolution from the Okhrana for a period, but his growing prominence among émigrés in Germany and especially his role as secretary of the ZTsB aroused the suspicion of the authorities and led to his arrest in 1908. Henceforth, the Okhrana's agents abroad closely watched his movements in anticipation that he might attempt a return to Russia.

Chicherin's split with the Bolsheviks was not the only, nor the most significant, personnel problem Lenin encountered after the 1905 Revolution. In 1908–1909 Lenin broke with his two principal associates in the Bolshevik Center, Bogdanov and Krasin, who were primarily responsible for financial affairs and the technical operations of expropriations. Bogdanov and Krasin continued to advocate expropriations as a means of generating funds to purchase arms for a new revolutionary uprising and wanted to use the remaining money from the Tiflis holdup to engineer Kamo's release from prison. In April 1908 Bogdanov resigned from the editorial board of *Proletarii*; in August, at Lenin's behest, the Bolshevik Center replaced Bogdanov and Krasin with a new financial commission headed once again by Zinov'ev.[22]

The culmination of this disagreement over money and tactics within the Bolshevik Center occurred in 1909. In February, Bogdanov and Krasin were effectively expelled from the Bolshevik Center when they were charged with misappropriating party funds. So far, however, these personnel changes within the Bolshevik Center had been kept secret. Public disclosure of the break came in June at a meeting of the expanded editorial board of *Proletarii*. The conference condemned the Recallers and Ultimatists (*otzovisty* and *ul'timatisty*) and expelled Bogdanov from the Bolshevik faction, removing him from the editorial board he had already left over a year earlier; there was no mention of Krasin, possibly because Lenin valued his organizational acumen and hoped to persuade him to unite against Bogdanov with whom Vladimir Il'ich had serious ideological and philosophical disagreements.[23]

Although the split within the Bolshevik faction of 1908–1909 was to some extent the result of different interpretations of the value of expropriations in revolutionary work and the question of control over these funds, of greater importance was the disagreement on tactics after the Revolution of 1905. Lenin had initially advocated a RSDRP boycott of the elections to the First Duma in 1906. But as the extent of the government counterattack became apparent to him, at the Fourth Congress of the party he reversed his position and henceforth supported Social Democratic participation in the Duma elections. He felt that the party had no recourse but to use legal means, including participation in the Duma, to harass the government and expose the weakness of constitutionalism. Bogdanov and the other Recallers and Ultimatists refused to accept RSDRP participation in the Duma. In addition, they opposed other legal methods in the struggle against Tsarism, urging that conspiratorial agitation and propaganda and illegal organizations among the workers would be the best means of preparing for the coming revolution they continued to believe was inevitable.[24]

Bogdanov and his supporters formed their own faction within the RSDRP on the island of Capri in December 1909, uniting on the basis of their opposition to participation in the Duma and their insistence on illegal party work, organizing the paper *Vpered* (*Forward*) against *Proletarii*, which Lenin and the Bolshevik Center controlled. Even though the Recallers and Ultimatists came together in the *Vpered* group, they were not in complete agreement on all political issues. Both stressed conspiratorial, illegal party activities to promote political consciousness among the workers and spark a revolution as quickly as possible. But the more militant Recallers, renouncing any legal work, demanded the removal of Social Democratic deputies from the Duma, while the Ultimatists, although critical of RSDRP representation in the Duma, held that the party might be able to radicalize Duma politics if Social Democratic delegates were subject to strict control and discipline by the Central Committee.[25]

Lenin reacted to the formation of the *Vpered* group and its establishment of a party school—"The First Higher Social Democratic Propagandist-Agitator School for Workers"—on Capri in August 1909 and a second version in Bologna in 1910 by attempting to achieve a reconciliation with Plekhanov and other Mensheviks who advocated RSDRP representation in the Duma and who were willing to adjust revolutionary tactics to meet legal opportunities.

Lenin hoped that he and Plekhanov could unite in a center coalition against pressure from both the extreme left and the extreme right within the party. The Recallers and Ultimatists attacked Lenin and his supporters for their lack of militancy; within Bolshevism he was clearly in the minority, and even Stalin's sympathies lay more with Bogdanov than with Lenin between the summer of 1908 and December 1910.[26] Plekhanov, too, was induced to make common cause with Lenin, for just at the time that the Bolsheviks were plagued by dissension within their ranks, the Mensheviks were also divided by a new wave of factionalism. The Liquidators (*likvidatory*), as they were called, led principally by Dan, P. B. Aksel'rod, and A. N. Potresov, rejected the use of illegal organizations and conspiratorial tactics during a period when the revolution had undoubtedly subsided, preferring to concentrate on legal activities in their belief that the advance of modern industry in Russia would culminate in the emergence of a legal workers' political party.[27]

The issue of revolutionary tactics caused serious discord among the Mensheviks and prevented them from taking advantage of a similar rift among the Bolsheviks. Plekhanov, like Lenin, was willing to resort to legal devices—the Duma, trade unions, and workers' cooperatives and clubs—to engender political consciousness among the masses, but the Menshevik leader also insisted that all legal organizations had to be conducted "under the guidance" of the illegal party apparatus. On this basis Lenin and Plekhanov made an attempt to achieve unification at the January 1910 plenum of the Central Committee in Paris. To appeal to Plekhanov and his supporters, Lenin agreed to disband the Bolshevik Center, to close down his factional paper *Proletarii*, and to turn over his factional funds to three SPD trustees—Franz Mehring, Klara Zetkin, and Karl Kautsky. In return, Lenin wanted to expel the *Vperedists* and Liquidators from the party; the Central Committee, in an effort to preserve a facade of unity, refused to take this step and instead merely reprimanded those who deviated from the orthodox formula of functioning in both legal and illegal organizations under the jurisdiction of the illegal party.[28]

Chicherin's role in the disputes and intrigues of the RSDRP is not always clear. On the whole he strongly disapproved of factionalism, regretting that precious energy and time had to be squandered on intraparty dissension. On the basis of the available evidence in Okhrana records it seems that he repudiated the Liquidators, although he did not completely support Plekhanov within the Mensheviks.[29] Chicherin had accepted armed rebellion as a prerequisite for the establishment of socialism in Russia; and even though the revolutionary momentum of 1905 had passed, he was not willing to discard illegal, underground party activities and organizations in order to embrace exclusively legal political action. In essence, he was too deeply committed to socialist revolution to compromise on the issue of revolutionary tactics. Yet Chicherin was also practical enough to realize that legal devices, as long as they were under the strict supervision of the illegal party, could have a positive impact on the emergence of a new revolutionary uprising in Russia. It is highly probable that among the Menshevik leaders he was closely aligned with Martov, who also favored a combination of legal and illegal actions to promote revolution.[30]

While attacking the Liquidators, Chicherin's worst fears about party unity were realized in 1910–1912. The cooperation between Lenin and Plekhanov at the January 1910 plenum of the Central Committee was only temporary, for their efforts did not lead to a lasting settlement of outstanding problems. In spite of the threat from the extreme right and extreme left of the RSDRP, there was little genuine agreement between the two leaders, as each side attempted to control the Central Committee. This failure to resolve disagreements and reach an accord by the two most influential party leaders did extensive damage to the RSDRP in Russia. Okhrana records contain reports from local party committees and organizations complaining about and criticizing the émigré leadership for a lack of understanding of political conditions in Russia, which continued to deteriorate as the government repression gained momentum. In particular, party members in Russia had little information about the ideological-philosophical disputes that divided the émigré groups, and many party leaders had lived abroad for so long that they had little knowledge of and appreciation for contemporary political affairs inside the country.[31] Moreover, it became increasingly difficult to conduct conspiratorial agitation and propaganda in Russia: membership in local committees declined; with the reimposition of strict government censorship, it was virtually impossible to print, receive, and distribute revolutionary literature; and in general local party organizations were weak and suffered from ineffective leadership from abroad.[32]

Ironically, many Social Democrats in Russia were demanding that the Bolsheviks and Mensheviks overcome their differences and unite to save the party from Stolypin's counteroffensive just at the time when the two factions abroad concluded their decisive and final separation.[33] Lenin organized the Sixth All-Russian Conference of the RSDRP in Prague in January 1912. This conference completed the process begun at the Second Congress of the party nine years earlier. The Prague conference was almost an all-Bolshevik meeting for Lenin did not invite the Mensheviks, and the result was a formal rift between the two factions; thus the conference foreshadowed future congresses of the Communist Party of the Soviet Union (CPSU) by the uniformity of its composition.

During the culmination in the split between the Bolsheviks and Mensheviks, Chicherin did not deviate from his support of the latter. Although he condemned the Liquidators and applauded Lenin's eventual rejection of expropriations and his break with Bogdanov and Krasin, Chicherin was still rankled by his clash with Vladimir Il'ich in 1907–1908. Most importantly, Chicherin steadfastly refused to accept Bolshevik principles of party organization. Lenin and the Bolsheviks advocated strict party centralism—a policy involving the subordination of local organizations in Russia and émigré groups to the Central Committee in finances, ideology, and tactics.[34] In contrast, the Mensheviks repudiated Bolshevik centralism and maintained that RSDRP organizations in Russia and émigré groups should have considerable autonomy from the Central Committee. Chicherin had gradually shifted from the Bolsheviks to the Mensheviks largely because he was unwilling to give the Central Committee complete control over local organizations and émigré groups, especially in the area of finances.[35] And neither Chicherin nor Lenin would compromise on this issue. At the Prague conference of 1912 the Bolsheviks passed a resolution which stated "that groups abroad which do not submit to . . . the Central Committee are not able to use the name of the Russian Social Democratic Labour Party," a policy Chicherin did not accept and which continued to separate him from Lenin and the Bolsheviks until the outbreak of World War I.[36]

In the years before World War I Chicherin lived primarily in Paris, where he moved from Germany in 1908, not long after his arrest in Charlottenburg. Greater surveillance by the German authorities induced him to change residence, and he also wanted to be close to the editorial board of *Golos sotsial-demokrata*, which had recently relocated the paper in Paris. From his new location Chicherin continued to serve as the secretary of the ZTsB; he was still active as the secretary for Russian Marxist student organizations in Western Europe. While maintaining a hectic schedule, he found time to keep up his study of Western European socialism and made a lasting impression on French socialists. He frequently associated with the Montparnasse branch of the French Socialist Party, usually visiting there after midnight to present in leisurely fashion his ideas on socialism and the revolution in Russia.[37] Chicherin thoroughly enjoyed his discussions of the theoretical intricacies of socialism with French socialists and Russian Social Democrats residing in Paris. But his principal endeavor involved working for the ZTsB.

As the secretary of the ZTsB Chicherin was responsible for administrative and organizational problems that the RSDRP émigré groups encountered. He was an indefatigable worker on behalf of the émigrés, unselfishly sacrificing his energy, money, and time in their interests. He planned official visits of representatives of one émigré organization to another, occupying himself with the smallest details, such as train and ship schedules, to avoid confusion and uncertainty and in part attempting to restore some semblance of unity among party factions abroad. Most importantly, Chicherin succeeded in raising money for the émigrés, who were almost always in need of funds, especially those who had just arrived from Russia. He solicited revenues from Western European socialists, calling upon them to make donations to the ZTsB so that it could supplement the income of impoverished émigrés. He proved to be an able financial manager, and his organizational skills were well known within the RSDRP.

To raise large sums of money, Chicherin arranged a lecture circuit for which he recruited prominent party members who were sympathetic to the plight of the émigrés to travel around Western Europe addressing socialist groups on political topics. He used the donations from these lectures to finance the operations of the ZTsB. Two leading members of the RSDRP, A. M. Kollantai and I. M. Maiskii, participated on Chicherin's lecture program. They praised him for its success, indicating that he was primarily responsible for providing a livelihood for many émigrés and marveling at the extent to which he was concerned about organization, supplying the usual transportation schedules, and also reserving auditoriums and securing lodging for the speakers.[38] Thus before World War I Chicherin's reputation within the RSDRP was based largely on his role as secretary of the ZTsB.

Although Chicherin essentially associated with RSDRP émigré groups in Western Europe, he also had connections with organizations trying to alleviate the plight of political prisoners in Russia. In January 1910 the prominent revolutionary V. N. Figner founded the Relief Committee for Political Prisoners (*Komitet pomoshchi politicheskim katorzhanam*, or KPPK) in Paris. As originally established, it collected funds for Russians sentenced to prison for political offenses; for example, in 1911 Figner published a pamphlet entitled *Les Prisons Russes* which called attention to political prisoners in Russia and which was part of a larger effort to solicit money on their behalf. But the demands on the limited resources of the KPPK were substantial, and in May 1912 Figner expanded its activities to include Russians sent to Siberia for political crimes, founding the Relief Committee for Political Exiles and Deportees (*Komitet dlia okazaniia pomoshchi politicheskim ssyl'no-poselentsam*, or KOPPSP), with its own staff and treasury. According to Okhrana records, during the first eight months of its existence the KOPPSP collected over 7,000 francs for distribution among political deportees in Siberia, hoping to aid them particularly during their initial six months of exile, giving them an opportunity to find employment and become accustomed to conditions there. Furthermore, to the amazement of the Tsarist authorities, the KOPPSP correctly estimated the number of exiles in Siberia—approximately 2,500 people, a figure that was increasing despite those who managed to escape abroad.[39] Paris was a convenient headquarters for Figner's organizations, in part because of the cooperation rendered by Chicherin and the ZTsB. While Chicherin was principally involved with the émigré groups, he also actively supported the KPPK and the KOPPSP.

At the outbreak of World War I Chicherin was in Lille working with the French Socialist Youth Movement. He had left Paris to study socialism in northeastern France; moreover, beginning in 1913 he curtailed his activities as secretary of the ZTsB, for he was increasingly disillusioned with the lack of unity among RSDRP émigré groups. Chicherin was on the verge of an ideological-philosophical crisis, which the war would exacerbate but whose origins were clearly connected with his experiences in emigration. Early in his revolutionary career he had been deeply impressed with the SPD, admiring its powerful organization and popular appeal for German workers. His conversion from Bolshevism to Menshevism was in part the result of a close identification in policies and tactics

between the Mensheviks and the SPD. Yet as secretary of the ZTsB
Chicherin became critical of the German Social Democrats, attacking them for a lack of militancy, a tendency to compromise
principles too easily, poor communication between the leaders and
the rank and file, and an alarming growth of bureaucracy in the
party.[40] His disagreement with Lenin and the Bolsheviks, originally
involving questions of tactics and organization, eventually focused
almost exclusively on the latter, for Chicherin did not abandon his
commitment to armed rebellion and militancy. In his view, therefore, the SPD seemed to be undermining socialist revolution, its
members content with mere economic gains rather than concentrat-
ing on the acquisition of political power.

Chicherin's disenchantment with Western European Social
Democracy had intensified when he moved to France, for he discovered problems among French socialists similar to those he had
encountered in Germany. And to some extent he found the situation
even more deplorable in France, since the French workers were not
nearly as well organized or as united as their German counterparts.
This growing criticism of Western European Social Democracy had
important ramifications for his association with the Mensheviks.
Chicherin had disapproved of his faction's treatment of the
Liquidators; he felt that the Menshevik leaders had been too willing
to compromise with them and had not taken sufficient measures to
discipline them for lack of militancy.[41] Hence even though he was
not yet ready to join ranks with the Bolsheviks, still disagreeing with
Lenin on he issue of party centralism and the autonomy of local
organizations vis-à-vis the Central Committee, he nonetheless was
slowly moving away from Menshevism to a position that would
eventually result in accommodation with Bolshevism. World War I
proved to be the precipitant reuniting Chicherin irrevocably with
the Bolsheviks.

In the summer of 1914 Chicherin, who had been in Lille when
hostilities began, moved to Brussels. He did not stay in Belgium for a
long period, however, for he managed to flee across the English
Channel to Britain just ahead of the rapidly advancing Germany
army. He took up residence in London, renting a room at 12 Oakley
Gardens, where he lived until the British government imprisoned
him in August 1917.[42]

As a result of the war Chicherin's ideological-philosophical
views were undergoing a radical transformation. He experienced

considerable anxiety, self-doubt, and an intense scrutiny of previously held political suppositions during the autumn and winter of 1914–1915. He was not alone in this endeavor, as World War I compelled socialists to examine anew their political and philosophical beliefs. For a brief time Chicherin rejected the arguments of the principal leaders of both Bolshevism and Menshevism. He was unwilling to accept Lenin's call for a program of "revolutionary defeatism," that is, a concerted effort by socialists to turn the imperialist war of nation against nation into a revolutionary civil war of class against class. But Chicherin also repudiated Plekhanov's appeal for "social patriotism," which held that interests of national defense were greater than and should receive priority over international socialism. Chicherin vacillated between the two extreme positions, trying to find an appropriate approach to the war.

During the early stages of the war Chicherin adhered to the idea, originally developed by Kautsky, of "ultraimperialism." According to Chicherin, capitalism had not yet outlived its usefulness and especially in democratic, progressive countries like Britain and France could still engender a society that would expunge elements of feudalism, promote pacifism, and stress flexibility and compromise over force and violence. In his view, moreover, there was a qualitative difference between the imperialism of the Western democracies on the one hand and German imperialism—which was aggressive and feudal—on the other.[43] Although Chicherin insisted that his position was not identical with Plekhanov's, the former's elaboration of ultraimperialism brought him increasingly closer to social patriotism and defensism.

Ultimately Chicherin was arguing that since German imperialism presented a greater menace to social progress, the proletariat should support the Western democracies. Thus in refusing to adhere to Lenin's interpretation of the war as primarily a conflict between capitalism and socialism, Chicherin initially regarded it as a struggle between two competing forms of capitalism, Britain and France representing the lesser evils. But Chicherin's position on the war became untenable when he attempted to apply his ideas to Russia. He argued that the necessary preconditions for socialism did not exist, neither in Western Europe nor in Russia, and therefore that it was essential for all countries, but especially Russia, to pass through a period of capitalism developed to its fullest capacity—ultraimperialism. He urged socialists to work for the complete democratization of society as a prerequisite for the establishment of socialism and advocated peace without forced annexations. His views on peace where complicated, for Chicherin had always been a pacifist, and indeed his pacifist inclinations in part had originally led him to the RSDRP. But he did not advocate peace at any price, as did Martov, for example. Instead, Chicherin maintained that Russia would have to defend itself from attack making a distinction between an offensive and a defensive war.[44] In this fashion he tried in vain to reconcile the coalition of "progressive, democratic" Britain and France and "backward, autocratic" Russia.

By early 1915 Chicherin had fundamentally altered his stance on the war. He repudiated defensism, depicting it as the capitulation of the proletariat to capitalism, and reversed his earlier description of the Western democracies as progressive countries.[45] He joined the ranks of the internationalists, arguing that only the destruction of capitalism and the triumph of socialism could bring an end to the conflict. Beginning in September Chicherin became the London correspondent for the internationalist newspaper *Nashe slovo* (*Our Word*), which was based in Paris under the editorial leadership of Bolshevik and Menshevik internationalists, including Trotskii. *Nashe slovo* began to appear in January 1915, after the Parisian authorities shut down the newspaper *Golos* (*Voice*). By the summer Trotskii virtually dominated the editorial board, and he respected Chicherin's writings that were published in the paper on an average of twice a month, usually with the pseudonyms "Ornatskii," "Orn," or simply "O."[46] In September 1916 Trotskii was expelled from France, which meant the closing of *Nashe slovo*. But the internationalists in Paris quickly established a new newspaper, *Nachalo* (*Beginning*), which operated from September to March 1917. Chicherin was also a regular contributor to it.

Chicherin's conversion from defensism to internationalism led to an intensification of his revolutionary activities in Britain. The self-doubt and vacillation that characterized his actions at the outset of the war were gone. Once again he devoted all his energies to socialist revolution. Chicherin's colleagues within the RSDRP had never questioned his commitment to socialism, but even they were amazed by his fanaticism and ascetic life style, qualities that revealed a sense of self-discipline few revolutionaries could match. Chicherin concentrated exclusively on his work, traveling throughout Britain to participate on committees and in programs against the war. He was rarely at home, usually only in the morning, for in London he developed the habit of returning to his room at

12 Oakley Gardens quite late and then reading and writing until well past midnight. He cared little for personal comfort, as his room was quite small and most of the furniture was buried under piles of books, newspapers, and pamphlets Chicherin used as references to write articles and letters.[47] Other émigrés active in the RSDRP, particularly Maiskii, have left amusing and interesting accounts of Chicherin's eccentric behavior in London:

> Chicherin has become a fanatic who rules all his actions, thoughts and behaviour with rigour. Before he had liked to dress elegantly, now he wore only cheap workingman's clothes. Before he had liked good food, been a connoisseur of good wines, now he was a vegetarian and a tee-totaller. Before he had loved the theatre, opera, ballet, now he allowed himself no recreation. Before he had been a musician and played the piano well, now he never went near the piano. . . .
>
> Before Chicherin, who was amply supplied with money, had spent it on himself freely, now he began to love a Spartan life and give his money to the Party. As a Social-Democrat he believed that every moment of his time belonged to the revolution and to it alone. He was busy from morning until late into the night with all kinds of public duties—talks, meetings, the writing of articles and proclamations.[48]

Thus Chicherin's devotion to internationalism made him one of the most influential Russian émigrés in London, and his services were constantly in demand by committees and organizations within both the RSDRP and British socialism.

Shortly after his arrival in London Chicherin became a member of the Communist Club and joined the British Socialist Party (BSP). Following the example of Figner's efforts in Paris to aid Russian political prisoners and exiles, he was one of the founders of the Russian Political Prisoners, Exiles, and Deportees Relief Committee (*Komitet dlia okazaniia pomoshchi russkim politkatorzhanam i ssyl'no-poselentsam*, or KOPRPSP) in London in June 1915. Chicherin was elected secretary of the KOPRPSP, and he supervised its activities for more than two years, collecting funds to be dispatched to Russia on behalf of revolutionaries in Tsarist prisons and Siberian exile. But just as with Figner's organizations in Paris, he did not limit the KOPRPSP to the solicitation of money for Russian political prisoners and exiles. Chicherin used it for political purposes, calling attention to the plight of revolutionaries in Russian prisons and in exile in Siberia and thus attacking the Tsarist government, appealing to British liberals, radicals, socialists, and trade unionists for support. His principal collaborator was Mrs. Bridges-Adams, a militant suffragette, who, according to Maiskii, functioned as the "soul" of the KOPRPSP, and the committee's headquarters was her house at 96 Lexham Gardens, Kensington.[49]

Furthermore, under Chicherin's direction, the KOPRPSP became a center of antimilitarist propaganda; espousing internationalism, he conducted an energetic campaign against conscription, which the British government was considering in 1915.[50] He expanded the KOPRPSP to include other cities in Britain, notably Liverpool and Glasgow. But in October the police closed the Liverpool branch of the committee and arrested its members. According to Chicherin the authorities accused the KOPRPSP of working to aid the Central Powers and therefore to bring about the defeat of the Allies.[51] He rejected this accusation, indicating that the KOPRPSP was opposed to the war in general and did not favor one side over the other; its goal was the development of political consciousness among the workers to promote socialist revolution and end the conflict, since a termination of hostilities could only occur through the leadership of the proletariat and by the destruction of capitalism.[52] This message became the central theme of Chicherin's writings for the duration of his residence in Britain. Although he opposed the introduction of conscription in Britain, he refused to accept the idea that he was conducting propaganda exclusively against the Allied war effort. He attacked all the belligerents in the conflict and called upon the workers of Europe to resist conscription—a question which for him was part of the class struggle—and to rebel against the capitalist governments for their imperialist, militarist policies.[53] He hoped to persuade the proletariat to abandon their participation in the war and to convince them that patriotism benefited only the capitalists who used conscription to deceive the workers and distract them from socialism.

In his writings about the war Chicherin sharply criticized the leaders of socialist parties in Western Europe. His rejection of defensism in favor of internationalism can best be explained by his disillusionment with Social Democratic leadership. His attacks on the leaders of the BSP and the Menshevik defensists were similar to his criticism of the French socialists and the German Social Democrats before the war. But it introduced a new dimension in his writing about social democracy. For Chicherin the war increased the gap, apparent to him before the outbreak of hostilities, which separated the leadership from the rank and file. He argued that Social Democratic leaders both in Russia and abroad, by urging the workers to support the war, had joined forces with capitalism against socialism; for him the defensism of most socialist leaders was counterrevolutionary and an outgrowth of their persistent lack of militancy, general conservatism, and obsequiousness before established capitalist authorities.[54] Therefore, in his view the proletariat had to ignore the Social Democratic leadership and call for a program favoring the immediate termination of hostilities and the promotion of socialist revolution. His internationalist thinking on the war brought him close to Lenin's position—revolutionary defeatism—and while there was still no open collaboration between them, by early 1916 the two revolutionaries were essentially in agreement on many political issues.

Chicherin's renunciation of socialist leaders who espoused defensism and his advocacy of internationalism were especially evident in his criticism of the BSP and the antimilitarist campaign of the KOPRPSP. The committee's radicalism increasingly antagonized the British government, and on 20 December 1915 the police raided the London headquarters of the KOPRPSP and searched Chicherin's room at 12 Oakley Gardens.[55] Although the police only held him briefly and then released him, the government clearly wanted to thwart his efforts to agitate against conscription. Two days after the incident in London, Scottish authorities arrested P. M. Petrov, a member of the RSDRP who was active in the BSP and the KOPRPSP in Scotland, charging him with conducting agitation and propaganda against the Allied war effort, which was construed as a violation of the Defense of the Realm Act.[56] Chicherin responded by organizing a massive campaign in support of Petrov, giving speeches, writing articles and letters, and calling on members of Parliament for his release. Chicherin explained that Petrov's arrest was symbolic of government repression and of the increasingly difficult position of the Russian émigrés in Britain. Chicherin ridiculed the BSP leadership for failing to defend Petrov adequately and for its reluctance to form a mass political party, contending that the BSP existed primarily on paper and was designed to serve the narrow interests of its small clique of leaders.[57] The arrest of Chicherin and Petrov reflected the government's growing impatience with the KOPRPSP and its fight against conscription.

Although Chicherin continued to urge the British, and in general European, workers to resist conscription throughout 1915 and the first part of 1916, he recognized that the proletariat on the whole were loyal to their governments. The British introduced conscription in January 1916, and even though Chicherin and the militant members of the BSP hoped for rebellion among the workers, socialist revolution did not threaten Britain. He maintained his criticism of the leaders of trade unions and the BSP, continuing to argue that they used nationalism to dupe the workers into supporting the war effort that in his view was clearly contrary to the latter's class interests. Moreover, he soon had to contend with the issue of conscription as it related to Russian political émigrés residing in Britain. Shortly after the introduction of conscription for British citizens, the government, after consultation with its ally Imperial Russia, began to consider the possibility of somehow requiring military service for the thousands of Russian émigrés who had sought political asylum in Britain. The prospect of entering the service, either for Russia or with the British, created a crisis for the émigré community and added a significant new dimension to the general problem of conscription.

In early 1916 the British government announced its consideration of a plan either to conscript Russian political émigrés of military age into the armed forces or to deport them to Russia to serve in the Tsarist army if they refused to comply. The government, realizing that most of the émigrés would undoubtedly oppose repatriation, hoped that many of them would join the British army, thus making a contribution to the Allied war effort and virtually eliminating anti-Tsarist propaganda in Britain. The socialist émigrés, incensed about the possibility of military service, responded to the threat by forming the Committee of Delegates of Russian Socialist Groups in London (*Komitet delegatov russkikh sotsialisticheskikh grupp v Londone*, or KDRSGL) on 3 March 1916. Chicherin was elected secretary of the committee; once again he was tireless in the performance of his duties, writing articles and pamphlets, delivering speeches, addressing appeals to sympathetic members of Parliament and heads of trade unions, and organizing demonstrations and meetings throughout the country against the proposed conscription of Russian émigrés.[58] The KDRSGL selected him as its secretary because of his considerable experience with émigré organizations and his strong internationalist stance against the war. Moreover, the government's plan had implications well beyond Britain, for later that year the French declared that if the British went ahead with conscription, they, too, would conscript Russian political émigrés located in France.[59]

Chicherin and the KDRSGL insisted on the right of political asylum, which the British government had honored for centuries. He construed the idea either to conscript émigrés or deport them to Russia for noncompliance as a violation of this right and held that if the government could violate British custom and tradition with such impunity during a period of war, then it would not hesitate to act in a similar fashion in peacetime.[60] He also warned that British citizens would be indirectly threatened by this violation of the right of asylum, for their political liberties to a considerable extent were based on the observance of established traditions.[61] Chicherin explained that according to international law foreigners could not be compelled to enter the military service of a country in which they sought political asylum, since they had no legal rights—they were not naturalized citizens—and thus could not be forcibly conscripted.[62] He was opposed to compulsory naturalization to conscript foreigners legally. Most importantly, he argued that the British government was functioning as a coercive agent of the Tsarist regime. In his view:

Those who advocate compulsion for Russians, endeavor to justify this breach of International Law, by pointing out that Russia is now at war as England's ally. Thus, if they succeed in their proposal and Russians are conscripted, it would be not because of residence in England, but because they are Russian subjects. Conscription then would be based not upon obligations on their part towards England, but on their presumed obligation towards the Tsarist Government. It would mean compelling them to serve the Tsarist Government, only technically to do it on British soil and under British command. It would mean enforcing upon them the Tsarist Government's will and its decisions regarding them. The refugees, who when coming here thought that they would now be immune from the action of Tsarism's authority, would be submitted to it by the British Government. It would be a veiled form of deliverance to Russia. . . . The British authorities in this case would merely act as substitutes for the Tsarist authorities, deriving their power in this case from the supreme power of the Tsar over his Russian subjects. . . .

If the British authorities assume the role of agents of the Tsar, the inevitable result will be that the Russian emigration to all countries will consider them as such. It would be more than an alliance of Britain with Tsarism, it would be an amalgamation, or shall we say, an absorption?[63]

Furthermore, Chicherin insisted that the socialist émigrés would resist conscription, given the extent of their animosity toward Tsarism, their disdain for "capitalist patriotism," and their efforts to end World War I. He questioned the reliability of émigrés pressed involuntarily into the military and serving without patriotic inspiration, asking: "Does the British government hope to get willing soldiers from these refugees? Is there not a danger that it might be preparing the possibility of some trouble?[64]

Chicherin's campaign against the conscription of Russian political émigrés was also intended to radicalize and increase the political consciousness of British workers and to appeal to intellectuals and political figures who supported socialism and were sympathetic toward the revolutionary movement in Russia. He called for the proletariat to close ranks with the émigrés, joining them in a common struggle between capitalism and socialism.[65] On the whole his program was highly effective, as he ridiculed the British government for professing liberal ideas, regard for individual liberties, and a respect for constitutionalism and the rule of law at the same time in which it was contemplating the denial of political asylum to Russians.[66]

Throughout the late spring and early summer of 1916 Chicherin and the KDRSGL intensified their attacks on the British government. Consequently, the government began to reconsider its position, since the issue was generating heated debate in Britain. In late June Home Secretary Herbert Samuel announced a subtle change in his government's plan. He acknowledged that it would be difficult to conscript aliens into the army, but he continued to hope that many émigrés would either voluntarily enter the service or, instead, that they would return to Russia to join the Tsarist armed forces. Sensing a weakening in the government's position, Chicherin kept up an unrelenting campaign against conscription. He maintained that voluntary enlistment was only a facade to mask the real intentions of the government and that obligatory enlistment, that is, conscription under the threat of repatriation, would follow shortly thereafter.[67]

As criticism of the government mounted, on 22 August the Home Secretary announced that the question of conscription would be left in abeyance while Parliament recessed (from 25 August to 10 October) and in the interim the government would launch a program of recruitment and voluntary enlistment of Russian émigrés into the army. The results of the campaign would influence the government's future actions. Chicherin, having achieved a temporary victory, responded by calling for the émigré community to stand united against the government, not to compromise with it or succumb to the threat of deportation to Russia, for voluntary enlistment would essentially mean acceptance of the violation of the right of political asylum. Furthermore, he was convinced that regardless of the outcome of the voluntary recruitment campaign the government would institute conscription and repatriation for noncompliance.[68] The KDRSGL used the postponement to gather additional support for its program. During the summer it had attempted to organize the nonparty émigrés in Britain, hoping to augment the number of émigrés speaking out against conscription and in opposition to the government. On 23 September the initial meeting of the Committee of Nonparty Émigrés (*Komitet bezpartiinikh emigrantov*, or KBE) was held in the Communist Club in London; although Chicherin was not elected secretary, he participated in its organization and worked to coordinate activities and events between it and the KDRSGL.[69]

Largely through the efforts of the KDRSGL and the KBE, the government's campaign of voluntary enlistment of Russian émigrés ended in failure. Writing in *Nachalo* on 25 November Chicherin reported that out of more than 30,000 émigrés in Britain only 400 had volunteered for service in the British army by 1 October. In London, which was the residence of the largest émigré community in the country, 320 had joined the armed forces by 25 October.[70] The government's inability to persuade the émigrés to enter the military service voluntarily in large numbers meant a victory for Chicherin and the internationalists. He deplored compromising with the government and refused to capitulate, hoping that British society, especially the proletariat, would actively oppose the repatriation of émigrés and that the crisis might spark a socialist revolution in Britain. But it became increasingly apparent that the government, too, was determined to resolve the dilemma in its favor. On 27 February 1917 the Home Office proclaimed that an agreement had been reached with the Tsarist government whereby all émigrés of military age refusing to enlist in the British army would be repatriated to Russia. Chicherin promised resistance to this decision, and he prepared the KDRSGL for a new round of skirmishes with the government, even taking the precaution of bringing British citizens onto the committee in case the Home Office would order the arrest of its Russian members.[71]

The March Revolution in Russia drastically changed the political situation, for with the fall of Tsarism and the creation of the Provisional Government the émigrés now demanded to return to their homeland as quickly as possible. To expedite the process of repatriation the socialist émigrés in London organized yet another committee—the London Committee for the Repatriation of Emigrants (*Londonskii komitet po repatriatsii emigrantov*, or LKRE). Once again, Chicherin was elected secretary, Maiskii, his friend and fellow internationalist, served as chair, and M. M. Litvinov, another prominent revolutionary, played a leading role on the committee. The LKRE attempted to negotiate with the British government for the speedy repatriation of the thousands of émigrés in Britain. Similar committees throughout Western Europe also burdened the London committee with requests for assistance, since given the military situation at that time, the best and safest way to reach Russia from the West was the northern route—from Britain through the North Sea to Norway.[72] This course, too, was fraught with peril, as German submarine warfare made crossing the North Sea a dangerous venture. By 1917, however, the grouping of ships in convoys by the Allies had greatly reduced the effectiveness of the German submarines. Thus, émigrés from France, Italy, and Switzerland began to pour into London, demanding that they be repatriated along with those who had been residing in Britain.

As soon as the Russian émigrés indicated their desire to be repatriated as quickly as possible, the British government changed its tactics dramatically. It was difficult for the government to proceed with repatriation as rapidly as the LKRE wanted: the organization of the undertaking was complicated, the large number of Russians from Western Europe who considerably augmented the size of the émigré community in London exacerbated the problem, and the government had to devote precious personnel and resources to the task while it was conducting war against the Central Powers. Just as importantly, the British were concerned about the political ramifications of returning to Russia thousands of revolutionaries who were opposed to the war. According to Chicherin and Maiskii, the government was willing to assist with the repatriation of defensists, for it believed that they would have a positive impact on the war effort of the Provisional Government; but the British proved to be extremely reluctant to repatriate the internationalists, many of whom were Bolsheviks.[73] Specifically, the LKRE demanded permission to send émigrés on the British ship *Jupiter* which, under the protection of minesweepers and fighting vessels, traveled between Aberdeen, Scotland, and Bergen, Norway, approximately once every ten days, carrying government mail, diplomats, and soldiers. After several weeks of appealing to the government for access to the *Jupiter* and becoming increasingly dissatisfied with its unwillingness to aid internationalists in their attempt to return to Russia, the LKRE decided to petition the Russian embassy in London for support.

In April Chicherin and Maiskii went to see the Russian chargé d'affaires in London, K. D. Nabokov, who promised to intercede for the LKRE with the British government to help repatriate émigrés, particularly on the *Jupiter*. At approximately the same time Nabokov received a message from the Provisional Government instructing him to assist with the repatriation of émigrés.[74] According to Maiskii, relations between the LKRE and Nabokov were initially cordial, but the chargé d'affaires quickly developed a strong dislike for Chicherin, whom he described as a "graphomaniac" and a "specimen of degenerate fanaticism."[75] Nabokov became alarmed because Chicherin and Maiskii accorded priority to the internationalists in their efforts to repatriate the émigrés.

With Nabokov's help, the British government finally agreed to allocate the LKRE a specific number of places on each voyage of the *Jupiter*, and Chicherin and Maiskii insured that preference was given to the internationalists. In Nabokov's view, this policy was detrimental to the interests of the Provisional Government:

> It soon became apparent that the Bolshevik section on the Emigres' Committee was getting the upper hand, and that Chicherin, Litvinov and others were straining every nerve in order that as many 'defeatists' as possible be given the opportunity of slipping in and getting to Russia. Also, the Embassy had every reason to believe that the extensive funds allotted by the Provisional Government to the Emigres' Committee to control were being recklessly squandered and unevenly distributed ... according to Chicherin's personal inclination.[76]

The Provisional Government provided a great deal of financial support for the repatriation of the émigrés; Nabokov estimated that "it certainly amounted to several million rubles." Furthermore, although Nabokov tried to obstruct Chicherin's work in the LKRE, the latter eventually gained the upper hand, primarily by constantly dispatching letters and petitions to the Petrograd Soviet. As its power and authority grew, it put pressure on the Provisional Government with orders for Nabokov to cooperate with the LKRE. Much to Nabokov's chagrin and dismay, Chicherin was even able to send messages in code through the embassy to the Petrograd Soviet.[77]

The British government became increasingly uneasy about Nabokov's reports detailing the deleterious effect that Chicherin and the LKRE were having on the Russian conduct of the war. Furthermore, Chicherin's antiwar agitation and demonstrations in Britain had not abated. At this point the government informed Chicherin that if he did not agree to repatriation, he would be arrested. He refused to succumb to the threat, preferring to remain in Britain until the task of repatriation had been accomplished and thus, by sacrificing his own personal welfare for the internationalist émigrés, placing the government in a difficult position.[78] On 7 August the Home Office responded by issuing an order for his arrest under regulation 14 B of the Defense of the Realm Act, charging:

1. That he is of hostile associations by reason of his association with Germans and pro-Germans at the Communist Club . . . [and]
2. That, having regard to his anti-ally and pro-German activities and sentiments, he is a danger to the public safety and the defence of the Realm.[79]

Chicherin immediately filed a protest against the government's allegations. First, he pointed out that the Communist Club was a "legally registered Working Men's Club" and that the Germans who were previously members had already been interned. Second and most importantly for him, he rejected the accusation that international socialism was "anti-ally and pro-German," stating that "We, the International Socialists, oppose imperialism in its totality, alike in its German, British and other representations." Finally, Chicherin claimed that the real reason for his arrest, in addition to his actions against the war, involved his investigation by order of the Provisional Government conveyed in a telegram he received on 3 August into the activities of the Okhrana in Britain, especially in connection with Scotland Yard.[80]

Although the order for Chicherin's arrest was issued on 7 August its execution was delayed for two weeks. Thus on 22 August he became prisoner No. 6027 in Brixton gaol, where he would spend the next four months. It is conceivable that he might have been incarcerated until the end of World War I if not for the November Revolution in Russia. After the Bolsheviks came to power, Trotskii, the first commissar of foreign affairs (Narkomindel), initiated a campaign to free Chicherin, Petrov (who had been in prison since 1915), and other international socialists interned in Britain and Western Europe. Trotskii instructed Litvinov, who had replaced Chicherin as secretary of the KDRSGL in London, to secure the liberation of the two revolutionaries. The British government, however, refused to negotiate on the subject. Undaunted and undeterred, Trotskii on 28 November sent a note to George Buchanan in Petrograd, the former British ambassador to the Provisional Government, demanding the immediate release of Chicherin and Petrov and adding that "Russian democracy would not . . . tolerate the imprisonment of two innocent fellow countrymen and allow British subjects who were carrying on active propaganda in favour of a counter-revolution to go unpunished."[81] When the British persisted in holding Chicherin and Petrov, Trotskii dispatched a second note to Buchanan on 3 December reiterating his demand and warning that no British citizens, including the former ambassador himself, would be permitted to leave Soviet Russia as long as the British government continued to imprison the two Russians.[82] In the face of this pressure the government of David Lloyd George relented. On 14 December the British announced that Chicherin and Petrov would be repatriated as soon as safe passage across the North Sea could be arranged; Trotskii in turn authorized the free exit of British citizens from Soviet Russia.[83] On 3 January 1918 Chicherin was released from Brixton gaol and transported to Aberdeen, from where he made the voyage across the North Sea to Bergen. From Scandinavia he traveled to Soviet Russia, arriving in Petrograd on 19 January. The Soviet government extended him a hero's welcome, and he and Petrov (who had arrived at the same time) addressed the Third All-Russian Congress of Soviets, describing their experiences and commenting about the possibility of socialist revolution in Britain.

Chicherin had not been in Russia since he left the country to participate in the revolutionary movement in the spring of 1904. When he first went abroad he had been unsure of his ideological-philosophical convictions and had vacillated between the Bolsheviks and the Mensheviks before finally deciding to join the latter. He had opposed Lenin on questions of organization and tactics, even though he criticized the Mensheviks and Western European Social Democrats for their lack of militancy and insufficient commitment to socialist revolution. World War I led to a definitive break between Chicherin and Menshevism; for, after some initial hesitations, he supported the internationalists against the defensists and social patriots. By 1916 his strong stance against the war meant that he and Lenin were basically in agreement on essential political issues. In the spring of 1917 Chicherin confided to Maiskii that he had severed his ties with the Mensheviks and thus his sympathies were entirely with the Bolsheviks, although he had not yet formally rejoined the party.[84] In the end Chicherin sided with the Bolsheviks because of Lenin's uncompromising revolutionary position and superior leadership, especially in comparison with the Mensheviks and Western European socialists. In January 1918 Chicherin arrived in Petrograd and rejoined the Bolshevik party, ready to offer his services to the Soviet government as it proceeded with the enormous task of consolidating the revolution in Russia.

3

The Making of a Soviet Diplomat

AFTER the Bolsheviks acquired power in the November Revolution, it took them about a decade to achieve full political control. They established a new Soviet government despite bitter opposition from their opponents, the Whites, during the Russian Civil War from 1918 to 1921. Foreign intervention seriously complicated the Bolsheviks' task, and in the initial months after the revolution it often seemed as if the Soviet government was about to collapse. In addition, the new regime faced enormous economic difficulties—World War I, the 1917 Revolutions, and the Civil War had devastated the country. Extremism and revolutionary fervor, referred to as War Communism, dominated the Civil War period. The years from 1921 to 1928, known as the New Economic Policy (NEP), witnessed economic recovery and political compromise and consolidation.

Bolshevik political objectives were unclear in November 1917, but the foundations of the highly centralized Soviet government were laid during the Civil War. Lenin was the unquestioned leader of the party who had led it to victory in 1917, but he was not a dictator. Before the revolution the Central Committee had directed party policies, but after 1917 the Politburo became increasingly significant. In 1919 the Eighth Congress of the party created the first operating Politburo with five full members (Lenin, Trotskii, Stalin, L. B. Kamenev, and N. M. Krestinskii) and three candidates (Zinov'ev, N. I. Bukharin, and M. I. Kalinin), which constituted Bolshevism's general staff.

In January 1918 the Third Congress of Soviets drafted a constitution for the new government. The 1918 Constitution outlined a centralized political structure with virtually all power concentrated in top government and party bodies. Between congresses of Soviets, a Central Executive Committee, consisting of about 200 members, was to exercise authority and appoint the executive of the government, the Council of People's Commissars (Sovnarkom). As the foremost leader of the Bolsheviks, Lenin became the chairperson of Sovnarkom. Yet real political power remained with the Bolshevik party, and it had to find qualified personnel to serve in the Commissariats of the new Soviet government.

Even before Chicherin's arrival in Petrograd on 19 January 1918, Lenin and Trotskii indicated that he should serve in the Commissariat of Foreign Affairs. Chicherin's aristocratic heritage, excellent education, extensive knowledge of several foreign languages, and experience in the Tsarist Ministry of Foreign Affairs provided the foundation for a career in diplomacy. On 21 January Sovnarkom appointed Chicherin acting deputy commissar of Narkomindel. The Central Committee endorsed the decision the next day.

Although Trotskii was commissar of foreign affairs, Chicherin immediately assumed considerable responsibility. Trotskii was away from Petrograd negotiating peace with the Germans at Brest-Litovsk. Actually, he did not want the post as he considered diplomatic activity insignificant. Like most of the Bolsheviks he believed that the socialist revolution in Russia would soon expand to Western Europe and eventually spread throughout the entire world, thus rendering diplomacy irrelevant for the future. He advised other Bolsheviks to work in more interesting and important Commissariats; in his view the party should direct its efforts toward revolution, not diplomacy. Trotskii is even quoted as having said that as chief of Narkomindel he would merely "issue a few revolutionary proclamations to the people and close up shop."[1] His relative unconcern about Narkomindel was apparent, and his failure to organize it thoroughly should not be surprising. In his defense it must be noted that most of the Bolsheviks shared this attitude.

With civil war impending in early 1918, the Bolsheviks needed Trotskii's services in military and political affairs and did not keep him at Narkomindel for long. On 8 March he became commissar of military and naval affairs, resigning his post at Narkomindel. With a "sigh of relief" he turned over the responsibility for Soviet diplomacy to Chicherin, who became acting commissar of foreign affairs.[2] Sovnarkom officially designated Chicherin commissar of Narkomindel on 30 May only a few months after he had returned to Russia from Britain.

Chicherin's appointment came as a surprise to many Bolsheviks, who remembered his aristocratic background and long association with the Mensheviks in emigration. Initially they questioned his political reliability and speculated about the sincerity of his decision to rejoin the party. But Lenin did not hesitate in selecting Chicherin to direct Narkomindel. Even though the two revolutionaries had disagreed on party organization and tactics after the 1905 Revolution, during World War I Chicherin's internationalist stance was close to Lenin's position on the war. And Lenin had welcomed Chicherin's decision to rejoin the Bolsheviks in 1918.

More importantly, although Lenin valued Trotskii's fighting spirit and dedication to international socialist revolution, Vladimir Il'ich quickly realized that Chicherin was the best choice to manage Narkomindel. Trotskii acted much too independently to be Lenin's commissar of foreign affairs. Lenin needed a subordinate in that position who would follow his directives and orders unquestioningly and without hesitation; in this respect, Chicherin was an ideal candidate.[3] Events proved Lenin correct in his assessment of the respective strengths and weaknesses of Chicherin and Trotskii, especially as it became increasingly apparent that socialist revolution would not spread rapidly to Europe and that the fledgling Soviet government would have to implement a defensive foreign policy to consolidate power in Russia. Trotskii performed brilliantly as commissar of military and naval affairs, organizing the Red Army and leading the Bolsheviks to victory against the Whites in the Russian Civil War. Chicherin also played a key role in the establishment of Soviet power in Russia, for he became one of the leading diplomats of his era, but he did not attempt to initiate foreign policy independently of Lenin and the Politburo.

In the first months of the new Soviet regime the Central Committee and Politburo freely debated issues of foreign policy. But gradually the Politburo, under Lenin's guidance, became the principal policymaking body in foreign affairs, transmitting its decisions to Narkomindel for implementation. Given the circumstances of the Civil War and the highly centralized structure of the Soviet government and the Bolshevik party, Narkomindel's role was largely to execute policies already determined by the Politburo. Furthermore, the Politburo frequently bypassed or ignored Narkomindel in deciding foreign policy matters. Lenin usually acted as his own foreign commissar, for he was an astute negotiator and provided the basic theoretical concepts of Soviet foreign policy. While Chicherin enjoyed an extensive association with Lenin, he had only limited contacts with the other members of the Politburo and was virtually isolated from its policymaking procedures when Stalin came to power.

From 1918 until 1921, when Lenin's health deteriorated to the point that he was no longer actively involved in the daily operations of the Soviet government, he and Chicherin were in frequent communication with each other over issues of foreign policy. Chicherin did not question Lenin's authority, deferring to Vladimir Il'ich's superior leadership and prestige within the party, and Lenin often provided detailed instructions for and even drafted the outlines of diplomatic correspondence.[4] Because of their close working relationship, a genuine friendship developed between the two men. Chicherin liked and respected Lenin and did not hesitate to give Vladimir Il'ich credit for the overall direction of Soviet foreign affairs. Lenin, too, appreciated Chicherin's contribution to the consolidation of the Soviet government in Russia. In 1918 Lenin commented: "Chicherin is an excellent, conscientious, intelligent, knowledgeable worker. It is necessary to value such people. His weakness—insufficient 'bossiness'—is not a misfortune. There are many people in the world with the opposite weakness!"[5]

Yet it would be a mistake to construe Chicherin as a mere functionary or technician, simply executing policies developed by Lenin while he was alive, and then Stalin after he acquired power in the late 1920s. Although Chicherin did not create Soviet foreign policy, he set the style for and contributed to the prestige of Soviet diplomacy during the twenties. He earned the admiration and respect of the Bolsheviks, for on the whole they came to recognize and appreciate his commitment to socialism and his devotion to the consolidation of the Soviet government in Russia. During the middle of the decade when the party leaders were preoccupied with a struggle for power after Lenin's death, the Politburo, although deciding foreign policy issues collectively and then transmitting its decisions to Chicherin for implementation, nevertheless sometimes consulted with the latter about foreign affairs. Thus while Chicherin was not a political leader—he was never a member of the Politburo and was elected to the Central Committee rather late in his career at the Fourteenth Congress in 1925 and the Fifteenth Congress in 1927—he played a significant role in the conduct of Soviet foreign policy during the twenties.

Lenin's decision to appoint Chicherin commissar of foreign

affairs was also made on the basis of other, essentially nonpolitical considerations. In his last writings shortly before his death, Lenin expressed great concern about cultural progress in Soviet Russia and seemed to identify the success of the revolution with cultural transformation. He cited culture, politeness, and toleration as the prerequisites of governing and designated them as the ultimate goal of socialism.[6] His respect for Chicherin was based in part on Georgii Vasil'evich's erudition and training, his impeccable manners, and politeness—in short on his personal attributes and characteristics associated with cultural distinction. Chicherin represented the finest tradition of nineteenth-century Russian culture, for he had received a splendid education and during his years in emigration had become well acquainted with Western Europe. Furthermore, his aristocratic background enabled him to feel at ease in dealing with the diplomats of the European powers, who were often the scions of old aristocratic families. Therefore Chicherin's education and cultural sophistication were just as important to Lenin as Georgii Vasil'evich's political reliability and commitment to socialism.

Even though Chicherin did not play a leading role in party affairs, he was respected by officials who worked in Narkomindel. He impressed everyone with his energy and virtually unlimited capacity for work. Even Lenin, who also was known to spend long hours in his own office, commented in 1920 that Chicherin was working too hard, "killing himself," and not taking the time to rest properly.[7] Chicherin continued the habit he had first developed as an émigré of working through the night, usually making appointments to receive foreign diplomats and correspondents after midnight, retiring at an hour when most people were getting up and sleeping until the middle of the afternoon.[8] He was so devoted to his work that he had no hobbies except for music, particularly Mozart, and few if any social relations outside of the Commissariat. Chicherin never married, and he preferred to sleep in a barren room adjacent to his office at Narkomindel. A Swiss couple cleaned his room and took care of his few personal needs. Chicherin insisted on living next to Narkomindel's offices so he could be awakened during the day when the Commissariat received an important telegram or message requiring his attention.

Along with his peculiar work schedule, which he maintained in spite of the Central Committee's efforts to prevent him from receiving official visitors after midnight, Chicherin's reputation for

eccentricity was also accentuated by his appearance. He was completely unconcerned about the way he dressed, an unusual trait for a
diplomat but one which was characteristic of him. According to R.
H. Bruce Lockhart, who described Chicherin in 1918, "He was
dressed in a hideous yellow-brown tweed suit, which he had brought
with him from England, and during the six months of our almost
daily contact I never saw him in any other."[9] Other memoirs have
substantiated Lockhart's evaluation of Chicherin's attire. For
example, after an interview with Chicherin in 1920, Marguerite E.
Harrison commented that "Around his neck was a woolen muffler
which almost concealed his chin. During the entire winter and well
into the spring I never saw him without it."[10] Yet despite the somewhat amusing impression he made on others, Chicherin remained
unperturbed about his appearance, refusing to be distracted from
his work by matters he considered insignificant.

Physically Chicherin was a rather tall man, but he seemed much
shorter, for he was stoop shouldered, the result of long hours behind
a desk. Although thin as a young man, he became thickset—even
slightly portly—as he grew older, largely because he refused to exercise. He rarely ventured out of Narkomindel, except to travel to the
Kremlin and attend official diplomatic and government functions
or occasionally to visit book stores to buy musical notes. Clare
Sheridan, who had an interview with Chicherin on 25 October 1920,
made the following amusing observation of him:

> To-day was a particularly unfortunate one for me. It happened to be
> the first day for months that Tchitcherin had gone out. He went to
> the dentist. Someone watching him from an office window
> described to me the phenomenon of Tchitcherin in the street. He
> did not go in a car, but on foot. He stood at the corner of the kerb,
> looked at the street hesitatingly, much as one might look into a river
> on a cold day before plunging in. When he did finally decide to get
> across, he got half way and then ran back. What with the traffic, the
> fresh air, and the dentist, it must have been a thoroughly unnerving
> day for him. . . .[11]

Chicherin's eyes, which were round and a pale, greenish blue,
attracted the greatest attention, for they were perpetually red
rimmed from overwork and insufficient sleep. He had sandy, red-
dish brown hair, thin around the temples, and a bald spot on top of
his head. His high forehead seemed to protrude slightly, probably
because of his receding hairline. Finally, Chicherin wore a mustache

and a small, wispy, pointed, sandy beard, which emphasized his elongated face.[12]

Chicherin was aloof, introverted, modest, and shy, and he did not like diplomatic receptions or large public gatherings, preferring private conversations, quiet diplomacy, and an austere life-style. His deputy commissar, Litvinov, was chiefly responsible for entertaining foreign dignataries. Entertainment usually took place at Narkomindel's guest house—the so-called Sugar King's Palace and the former home of an Ukrainian sugar magnate, Kharitovenko, which eventually became the British embassy— directly across from the Kremlin on the right bank of the Moskva river. Yet Chicherin was an emotional, excitable, nervous, and sensitive man.[13] His high, thin voice and delicate, gentle manners belied his determination and resolve, for he steadfastly held opinions and pursued goals. In keeping with his refined tastes and cultural sophistication, he expressed great compassion toward others and was considerate and tactful in dealing with diplomats, journalists, and subordinates at Narkomindel.

Chicherin's unusual work schedule meant that his secretariat had to conform to irregular hours and insure that a complete staff was available twenty-four hours a day. Even though Chicherin was polite and exhibited exemplary manners, he often failed to realize that his staff had personal lives outside of Narkomindel. Sheridan commented that "He has no idea of time and does not realise that other people live differently. He will ring up a comrade on the telephone at 3 or 4 o'clock in the morning for the most trivial information."[14] Although this characteristic of Chicherin's personality was irritating to Narkomindel officials, they generally accepted his eccentric behavior with good humor and remained loyal to him, for they appreciated his dedication to the Soviet government. Bessie Beatty correctly observed:

> It takes a stout hearted communist to be a member of Chicherin's secretariat. He spares them little more than he spares himself. . . . But I knew what the frailest and hardest worked of them all meant when he said, with utter devotion in his eyes, "Chicherin is one great man who does not diminish as you come closer to him."[15]

To some extent Chicherin's greatest attribute—his ability to work long hours—was also the source of one of his most exasperating weaknesses. He seemed utterly incapable of delegating responsibility, doing almost all of his own work, which included drafting diplomatic correspondence, sealing envelopes, sharpening pencils, and delivering messages to departments within the Commissariat.[16] He often exhausted himself with unnecessary tasks that should have been performed by members of his secretariat. Yet he insisted on actively participating in all of its operations. Chicherin in particular needed several stenographers because of his habit of writing long, tedious, and intricate notes which he dictated in several languages. According to Beatty, who observed him at work:

> He goes from one to the other dictating in French or English, German, or Russian, equally at home in all of them. One of his stenographers told me she could tell the mood he was in by the language he used. . . . Everything else that is done by the foreign office, Chicherin does. Every paper passes through his hands, and the passing is no mere formality. His is not a rubber stamp signature. He knows the first word and the last and all the in-between ones on every written page submitted to him.[17]

Besides his inability to delegate authority, Chicherin's work habits were complicated by disorganization. Given the difficulty of recruiting a reliable staff and the numerous tasks he himself felt obligated to perform, some degree of disorder was probably inevitable. But part of the problem was his insistence that he keep many important documents in his own office, refusing to allow his secretaries to file them away, contending he might need them as a reference to draft diplomatic communications. Louise Bryant wrote a memorable description of Chicherin's office at Narkomindel:

> The confusion of the Foreign Minister's desk is a national scandal. In mid-winter I have seen his summer hat still lying there, crushed under a pile of papers. I have seen papers piled high on all the chairs and sofa and gray with the dust of months. He has a fearful habit of misplacing important telegrams and then sending out a search call. These were terrible moments in the Foreign Office. All other work stops. After everything is turned upside down some subordinate gets the courage to ask, "Comrade Tchicherin, perhaps it is on your own desk." And there it invariably is, almost on his nose, like grandmother's proverbial spectacles.
>   It was his habit to give a short talk about once a month to the personnel of the Foreign Office. We would meet about eight o'clock

in the Foreign Office Club. Tchicherin was persistently late, sometimes one, sometimes two or even three hours. From time to time
someone would whisper, "He has lost another telegram!"[18]

Chicherin's intellectual abilities, especially his remarkable memory,
also contributed to his disorganization. His memory was so keen
and retentive that he seemed incapable of distinguishing between
important matters and trivial details, for he remembered virtually
everything that he read. Among the numerous memoirs about
Chicherin, William H. Chamberlin's description of Georgii
Vasil'evich's memory is among the best:

> An American woman correspondent from Seattle, meeting
> Chicherin at a diplomatic function, observed that she presumed he
> had never heard of her native city. Thereupon, to her amazement,
> the Foreign Commissar launched into a little lecture on the history,
> settlement, population, and resources of Seattle, containing many
> facts of which she herself was ignorant. There was formerly a Rus-
> sian consulate in Seattle, and Chicherin had apparently memo-
> rized its reports verbatim.[19]

Chicherin's irregular work habits, austere life-style, and lack of
concern about his own personal comfort had a deleterious effect on
his health. But he was also a hypochondriac, often exaggerating the
gravity of his illnesses and traveling frequently to Germany to consult with German physicians. However, by the end of the 1920s he
suffered from diabetes and polyneuritis.

In addition to his idiosyncrasies, Chicherin's reputation among
foreign diplomats was based on his knowledge of the history of
European diplomacy and his ability to communicate well. He spoke
English, French, and German fluently and was a gifted writer,
especially adept at conveying irony and sarcasm in his notes and
correspondence with the diplomatic ministers of the European
powers. Chicherin earned the grudging respect of his rivals in diplomatic circles, for they were forced to acknowledge his superb literary
style. According to Beatty, who was familiar with his writings:

> His general and specific knowledge is staggering in its extent and
> precision. Most of his notes, masterpieces of political ingenuity
> and fearlessness, would be the better for a liberal blue-penciling,
> but Chicherin adds to the Russian inclination toward circumlocu-
> tion a passion for exactitude. His mind is an encyclopaedic of
> historic, geographic, and biographic data.[20]

In summary, Chicherin's rare intellectual talents, erudition, unsurpassed knowledge of European diplomatic affairs, tact, refined tastes reflecting cultural distinction, devotion to the ideals of the Communist state, and personal loyalty to Lenin made him in spite of his eccentricity and weaknesses an outstanding choice to be the chief of Narkomindel.

One of Chicherin's principal assignments was to organize Narkomindel, which included the difficult task of recruiting and training personnel. The Ministry of Foreign Affairs under the Tsarist regime and the Provisional Government had maintained a large staff. For example, the Ministry employed 689 officials in 1913.[21] Most of them supported the Provisional Government after the March Revolution. On the whole they sympathized with the Constitutional Democrats (Cadets) and wanted to continue the war against Germany. Thus they were opposed to Lenin's policy of "revolutionary defeatism" and generally refused to cooperate with the Bolsheviks after the November Revolution.

Under the Provisional Government the civil servants formed their own union—the Union of Unions of State Employees—which announced a general strike against the Soviet government. The Foreign Ministry staff joined the strike, prompting Sovnarkom to dismiss them from their posts on 13 November. When Trotskii arrived at the Ministry headquarters on 27 November he found only a few minor officials willing to serve the Soviet government. Up to that time he had carried out operations at the Smolny Institute, close to Sovnarkom offices, for he and Lenin together formulated foreign policy. Gradually, however, Trotskii was able to build up a reliable staff. A few former Ministry officials agreed to work for Narkomindel, the Petrograd party organization dispatched some Bolsheviks to serve in the Commissariat, and workers from the Siemens-Schuckert factory provided a unit of guards for military protection; by the end of December, Narkomindel employed 126 officials, and it was the first Commissariat to be fully operational.[22]

Yet when Chicherin joined Narkomindel he discovered that it was more adept at propaganda than diplomacy. The expectation among the Bolsheviks that socialist revolution would soon engulf Europe accounted for this development, and Chicherin had to establish regular bureaucratic procedures in the Commissariat. Furthermore, he oversaw the transfer of Narkomindel from Petrograd to Moscow, which, along with the rest of the Soviet government, was completed on 25 March 1918. To complicate the situation, the initial headquarters of the Commissariat in Moscow in a former private residence on the corner of Spiridonovka, proved inadequate. In early July Sovnarkom authorized its relocation to the top floors of the Metropol' hotel, then converted into a government office building and called the Second House of the Soviets. But the Metropol', too, did not have sufficient space to accommodate the growing Commissariat, and in December 1921 it moved to a large office building on the corner of Lubianka and Kuznetskii Most, where it remained until 1952.

Apart from organizing the staff of Narkomindel, Chicherin was also responsible for the establishment of a number of publications it sponsored. For example, on 20 June 1919 Narkomindel initiated the publication of *Vestnik NKID* (*NKID Herald*), which continued until 1922 when it was replaced by the journal *Mezhdunarodnaia zhizn'* (*International Life*). From 22 February 1920 to 13 March 1922 Narkomindel issued an information bulletin entitled *Biulletin' NKID* (*NKID Bulletin*). Chicherin played an active role in these publications, contributing articles and commentaries and to the newspapers *Izvestiia* and *Pravda* (*Truth*). Many of his articles, especially in *Izvestiia* and *Pravda*, were written under pseudonyms, although different from those he had used in emigration, such as "Mikhail Sharonov," "Osvedomlennyi," "Byvshii Diplomat," "V.D.," "Marko Polo," and "Liutsifer." He wrote a great deal about foreign policy, serving as one of the principal spokespersons for Narkomindel, and his writings articulated and explained Soviet conduct in foreign affairs.

Like other Commissariats, a collegium that included the commissar and the most important assistants directed Narkomindel. The collegium, which came into existence during the summer of 1918, was to advise Chicherin on significant issues, although he could act unilaterally, obliged only to inform it of his decisions. Even though he was theoretically the most powerful person in the Commissariat, he was actually outranked in party power and prestige by several of his nominal subordinates. This was especially true of Litvinov, who joined the collegium of Narkomindel in April 1919 and became the deputy commissar.

Chicherin's relations with Litvinov were complicated, and there was considerable rivalry between the two men. Litvinov was ambitious and coveted Chicherin's position, particularly since Georgii Vasil'evich was a virtual nonentity within the party. Nor could Litvinov forget Chicherin's ties with Menshevism before World War I and his involvement in the Central Committee's investigation of Bolshevik expropriations after the Revolution of 1905. According to Chamberlin, who knew both men well, "They kept the Political Bureau busy with the complaints which they lodged against each other and it was a byword in the Commissariat that if Chicherin would say, 'Yes,' Litvinoff would say 'No,' and vice versa."[23]

As the Bolsheviks eventually realized that revolution would not sweep across Europe and therefore accorded increasing importance to diplomacy, Narkomindel gradually became a professional organization. Chicherin deserves much of the credit for this development. He oversaw the growth of the Commissariat so that it employed between 450 and 550 people during the mid-1920s.[24] Even though some women, such as Kollontai, worked in the Commissariat during the period from 1917 to 1930, about 96 percent of Narkomindel staff in the upper grades were men while only 4 percent were women.[25] Yet Chicherin's organization of Narkomindel had to proceed slowly, for the Soviet government possessed few resources or trained personnel it could offer the Commissariat during the Civil War.

Chicherin's diplomatic skills and loyalty to Lenin were tested soon after he became acting deputy commissar of foreign affairs. Lenin needed someone he could trust to negotiate with the Germans at Brest-Litovsk beginning in December 1917. Trotskii had been unwilling to capitulate to the Germans, an attitude Lenin understood but which he regarded as increasingly unrealistic in view of the limited military capabilities of the Soviet government. Trotskii's famous "no peace, no war" statement, that the Soviets would neither accept a dictated peace from nor continue to fight the Germans, had seemed at first like a brilliant solution to the German military threat. But the Germans, encountering no resistance from the Soviets, refused to abide by conventional conditions of war and pushed farther into the territory of the former Russian Empire. The Bolsheviks became thoroughly alarmed, and led by Bukharin many of them advocated a "revolutionary war" against Germany that they hoped would lead to a general European socialist revolution. Lenin, however, was convinced that such a war would end in the destruction of the Soviet state, as the peasants were exhausted from more than three years of fighting, and at this point his government could not compete militarily with Germany.

Lenin's decision to make peace with the Germans, even if terms were dictated and therefore extremely unfavorable to the Soviet government, aroused considerable opposition among the Bolsheviks. Like many Bolsheviks, Chicherin's initial reaction was to fight, to call for a "revolutionary war" against the German invaders, and he admitted that it was difficult for him to accept the necessity of signing the "obscene treaty."[26] Although he did as Lenin requested—traveling to Brest-Litovsk to reach a settlement with the Germans signed on 3 March 1918—it was not an easy task for him. But in the end he acquiesced to Lenin's judgment. Only Lenin's unquestioned authority within the party enabled him to persuade the Bolsheviks that signing a dictated peace was the sole means of saving the Soviet government. Chicherin also took part in the negotiation of three supplementary agreements to the treaty, which were signed in Berlin on 27 August. The Soviets were forced to make further territorial concessions and pay a large indemnity to Germany.

Chicherin objected to the Treaty of Brest-Litovsk primarily because it was not a negotiated agreement but a dictated peace. He argued it was vaguely written, it failed to guarantee the inviolability of the territory left to the Soviets, and it did not specify future Soviet relations with Germany, leaving the opportunity for German penetration farther into Soviet Russia.[27] His evaluation of German intentions was correct. The separation of the Ukraine from the rest of Soviet Russia was one of the conditions of the treaty, and its subsequent occupation by German troops gave the Germans a base from which to expand farther into the territory of the former Russian Empire. The Germans pushed into the Crimea, occupied the Donets Basin, and even reached into the Caucasus. Chicherin dispatched a steady stream of protests to Berlin as the Germany army advanced deeper into Soviet Russia.[28]

Chicherin also attempted to counteract the growing German threat by appealing to commercial and industrial interests in Germany. He pointed out that the colonization of Russia would not be economically profitable for Germany. Using the Ukraine as an example, he argued that German military occupation would engender guerilla warfare by the native population, making it virtually impossible to conduct normal agricultural and commercial activities.[29] In his view Germany could profit only by cooperating with the Soviets; otherwise, it would encounter such stubborn resistance that German troops would be needed to maintain order and the countryside would be devastated by warfare. His appeal produced a sympathetic response in the German business community, but the general staff largely ignored such arguments and pushed farther into Soviet Russia. The continuing German military threat during the spring and summer of 1918 increased Chicherin's criticism of the Treaty of Brest-Litovsk, for he realized that while saving the Soviet government from imminent disaster, it had failed to lead to a normalization of relations between the two countries.

In addition to diplomatic pressure on the German government and appeals to German business leaders, Chicherin continued to call for an end to World War I in his effort to stabilize relations between Imperial Germany and Soviet Russia. Even though the prospect that the European proletariat would compel their governments to terminate hostilities remained slim, his criticism of the socialist patriots did not abate. Chicherin's internationalist stance against the war continued even after Soviet Russia had withdrawn from the conflict. He refused to abandon the hope that the European proletariat would soon come to their senses and realize that a speedy termination of the war would best serve their interests.[30] Chicherin remained adamant in his position up to the armistice of November 1918, and it was difficult for him to accept that nationalism evoked greater loyalty than socialism from most workers in Europe.

German aggression after the Treaty of Brest-Litovsk was not the only military threat the Bolsheviks faced in 1918. The Allies, especially France, rejected the November Revolution because it meant Russia's withdrawal from World War I. The Allies wanted to maintain a two-front war against Germany. They had exerted considerable pressure on the Soviet government not to sign a separate peace with Germany, fearing the Germans might be victorious before American troops could turn the tide. In late 1917 and early 1918 the German general staff transferred troops from Eastern Europe to the western front in anticipation of an offensive to win the war before the involvement of the United States could determine the outcome in favor of the Allies. Furthermore, Soviet revolutionary slogans and appeals to the workers of Europe to rise up against their governments aggravated relations between the Bolsheviks and all the great powers.

The Treaty of Brest-Litovsk was important for relations between the Allies and Soviet Russia. It ended any hope that the Allies might still have harbored about recreating the second front and bringing the Russians back into the war against Germany. Moreover, there was growing sentiment among some statesmen of

Western Europe that Bolshevism must be destroyed before its revolutionary appeals could jeopardize the existing economic and political system in Europe. Allied military intervention in Russian affairs, which the Supreme War Council formally initiated on 2 July 1918, was motivated by a confusing and complex combination of reasons, most of which were not well understood by the citizens of the countries involved. To complicate the situation further, the Allies had little reliable information about conditions and events in Russia, making it extremely difficult to formulate coherent policies toward the Soviet government. Intervention poisoned relations between Soviet Russia and Western Europe and compelled the Bolsheviks to articulate again the traditional question of Russia's association with the West.

Chicherin's interpretation of and reaction to Allied intervention reflected the manner in which the Bolsheviks attempted to resolve the problem. Although his writings on this subject were contradictory, probably because of his strongly emotional approach to the issues and differing views within the Bolshevik leadership, a distinct pattern clearly emerged. He initially accepted the official Allied explanation for intervention as an effort to reestablish a second front against Germany in desperate military circumstances. Chicherin realized that France's position was particularly difficult, since it confronted an enlarged German army. But his attitude changed after the Treaty of Brest-Litovsk. It became increasingly apparent to him that military concerns were only part of the question. He argued that a subtle change had occurred within the capitalist camp and that Britain and France on the one hand and Germany on the other were competing for the economic domination of Russia. The economic exploitation and colonization of Russia became for Chicherin the basic motive behind both German and Allied intervention.[31] In his view, while the European powers represented a formidable military threat, their struggle for economic supremacy in Soviet Russia was an indication of the continuing disintegration of capitalism.

As time passed, especially after the armistice of 11 November 1918 ending World War I, Chicherin indicated that the Allies had revealed their true intentions. It was no longer possible to justify Allied intervention on the basis of military needs, for Germany had been defeated even without the reestablishment of the second front. Henceforth, Chicherin attacked the Allies for supplying and supporting the Whites and for attempting to undo the November

Revolution and overthrow the Soviet government. But even during the bleakest moments of 1918 and 1919, when it seemed that the Soviet government was about to collapse, he did not abandon hope for a Bolshevik victory in the Civil War. He continued to predict the disintegration of the old capitalist world and the inevitable superiority of socialism; yet he also maintained that the survival of the Soviet state depended largely on the strength of the Red Army. Like the other Bolsheviks, Chicherin was extremely proud of the accomplishments of the party and the Soviet government during the intervention and Civil War. He pointed out that most statesmen of Western Europe had regarded Bolshevism as a temporary phenomenon and that his government had survived in a hostile environment against superior military forces.[32] For him the durability and resilience of the Soviet state was a clear indication of the correctness and historical inevitability of socialism.

As Allied intervention proceeded throughout 1918 and the Soviets found themselves in an especially precarious position in 1919, Chicherin put forward a number of peace proposals. His "peace offensive" was designed to persuade the Allied governments to end their military involvement in the Russian Civil War by appealing to the economic benefits that would accrue to them in trade and concessions if they would withdraw their troops and make peace with the Soviet government. He concentrated on the British, beginning with a proposal for an armistice on 3 November 1918, indicating that they would have to take the lead in removing the economic and military blockade of Soviet Russia if they wanted to restore normal trade relations.

Chicherin felt that economic incentives would eventually entice the British government, headed by David Lloyd George, to lift the blockade. Chicherin acknowledged that the Soviets were desperately in need of credits, loans, equipment, and machinery from Western Europe to reconstruct the war-torn economy, but he also believed that the Allies, particularly Britain, needed Soviet markets and raw materials to maintain and expand production.[33] In spite of his appeals for peace on the basis of trade agreements and concessions, Chicherin repeatedly warned about the possibility of deception by the Allied powers. He insisted that any peace agreement his government might consider would have to be mutually advantageous and that the Soviets would not capitulate to the Allies by making internal economic and political changes as a precondition

for a treaty; he demanded binding, long-term economic and diplomatic relations with the European powers, arguing that the Soviet
government was not an aberration or a temporary phenomenon and
that international affairs dictated stable relations between capitalist
governments and Soviet Russia.[34]

Chicherin's peace campaign laid the foundation of Soviet foreign policy during the 1920s. Soviet foreign-policy goals consisted
of two principal components: first, foreign policy was to help secure
and consolidate socialist revolution and the Soviet government in
Russia; and second, foreign relations were to contribute to the
defense of the Soviet state against economic, ideological, and military opposition from the capitalist powers that the Soviets believed
sought to undermine their government whenever the opportunities
presented themselves. The Bolsheviks did not immediately elabo-
rate these aims after they acquired power in 1917. They had
assumed that the question of Soviet relations with foreign governments would be solved by the coming international revolution,
which would sweep aside capitalist states and establish in their place
soviet governments modeled after the Russian Soviet government.
Therefore, the Bolsheviks placed enormous emphasis on revolutionary agitation and propaganda among the workers of Western
Europe to spark a world socialist revolution.

Immediately after his initial appointment to Narkomindel,
Chicherin had also been preoccupied with revolutionary propaganda. He, too, was caught up in the euphoria among the Bolsheviks
after the November Revolution, and his faith in the coming European socialist revolution was unshakable. But continued German
aggression and Allied intervention forced him to reconsider his
views. Following Lenin's lead, he quickly recognized the need for
traditional diplomacy. As long as the Soviet government was surrounded by powerful states opposed to its existence and in the
absence of a general European socialist revolution, there would be a
need for a defensive foreign policy. And Chicherin proved to be an
able and articulate defender of Soviet interests abroad, for he combined a fervent devotion to the Communist state with an appreciation of the need to protect traditional Russian national interests.
According to Ernest Hemingway, who knew Chicherin personally:

> He is an old Russian diplomat and he is soundest when he is fight-
> ing for the national aims of Russia. He sees that the problems of
> Soviet Russia, the territorial and national problems, are the same

as they were under the Russian Empire. The world revolution did
not come off and Russia faces the same problems she always faced.
Tchitcherin knows those problems.[35]

Yet Chicherin's understanding of power politics among nations
did not supercede his commitment to socialist revolution and the
Communist state. In his writings he urged his fellow Bolsheviks and
the proletariat of Soviet Russia to sacrifice themselves completely
for the revolution. In his view the revolution would be successful
only if the Bolsheviks were "merciless and strict" with themselves in
the performance of their duties.[36] For Chicherin a defensive foreign
policy and traditional great power diplomacy represented a call to
action to preserve the communist future, the only salvation for
humanity, until a time when the revolution would sweep across
Europe. The receding of the revolutionary wave after it was
unleashed in Russia was not a permanent occurrence for him but
rather a brief pause in the inevitable progression of humanity
toward communism.

Chicherin's efforts to establish normal relations with nations
along the Soviet border—especially with the newly independent
Baltic states, his criticism of the Treaty of Versailles, and his reaction to the League of Nations were evidence of his emphasis on
diplomacy to defend the Soviet state. He implemented a policy,
designed essentially by Lenin, of promoting divisions within the
capitalist camp. In 1919–1920 Chicherin was involved in negotiating peace with the border states—Estonia, Latvia, Lithuania,
Finland, and Poland. He recognized that friendly relations with
these nations would be beneficial to the Soviet government, for they
could provide a buffer against renewed intervention, about which
Chicherin often warned during the 1920s.[37] But he also understood
that it would be difficult to reach an agreement with these countries,
since they had been part of the former Russian Empire and were
deeply distrustful of the Soviet government. Moreover, even though
the Baltic had traditionally been Russia's "window to the West,"
Chicherin anticipated considerable competition with Britain and
France for influence over it.

Chicherin's peace offensive toward the border states was
designed to secure the Soviet western frontier and cause a split
between Britain and France. He hoped that the negotiation of peace
and the establishment of diplomatic relations with the border
nation would lead directly to the end of Allied intervention and the

blockade of Soviet Russia. He turned to traditional diplomacy instead of revolutionary appeals to the proletariat of Western Europe to save the revolution in Russia.

On 31 August 1919 Chicherin made a peace proposal to Estonia and a similar offer to Lithuania, Latvia, and Finland on 11 September. The latter states refused to negotiate with the Soviets, but Estonia agreed to initiate talks at Pskov, which began in September. Chicherin's initial optimism about the negotiations was dashed when they were broken off after a White army, under the command of General Nikolai Yudenich, launched an attack on Petrograd from Estonia. Although Trotskii wanted to pursue Yudenich into Estonia, Lenin supported Chicherin's policy not to dispatch the Red Army into the country, thus persuading the Estonians to resume the peace negotiations and demanding only that the White troops be disarmed. Chicherin's assessment of the situation proved correct, as talks between the Estonians and the Soviets were renewed in early December at Tartu. On 31 December an armistice was signed between the two countries; it was followed by a peace treaty on 2 February 1920, and Estonia and Soviet Russia concluded a trade agreement two months later. The Treaty of Tartu guaranteed nonintervention, nonrecognition of pretender governments, and nonaggression.[38]

The peace settlement with Estonia meant success for Chicherin's peace offensive. He attributed great importance to the treaty with Estonia, regarding it as a model for negotiations with the other border states and also for the establishment of diplomatic relations with the Allied powers; furthermore, it ended the diplomatic isolation of Soviet Russia.[39] Chicherin believed that the prospect of lucrative trade with Soviet Russia had induced the Estonians to come to the bargaining table, and he hoped that other states could be similarly persuaded.

In January 1920 Britain lifted the blockade and initiated trade negotiations with Soviet Russia. The two countries also reached an agreement on a prisoner of war exchange on 12 February that Litvinov had been discussing with the British in Stockholm since November 1919. The British government agreed to repatriate its Russian prisoners and to arrange for the transportation to Soviet Russia of Russians living in Belgium, Denmark, the Netherlands, and Switzerland who wished to return to their homeland.[40]

The Soviets concluded an armistice with Latvia to last for at least two months on 30 January 1920.[41] Although the Latvians would not yet agree to a peace treaty, Chicherin was optimistic that the armistice would eventually lead to a peace settlement. His peace offensive and the offer of favorable trade concessions were powerful incentives for the border states.

Soviet relations with Poland exerted considerable influence on Allied intervention and were instrumental in driving a wedge between Britain and France with respect to their policies toward Soviet Russia. The newly independent Polish government, under the leadership of Josef Pilsudski, posed a serious threat to the Soviet state. He was determined to recreate the "Poland of 1772," that is, to restore Polish frontiers to where they had been prior to the eighteenth-century partitions by Austria, Prussia, and Russia. Poland and Soviet Russia were involved in a sporadic, undeclared war in Eastern Europe throughout 1919. Chicherin, continuing his peace offensive, frequently dispatched peace proposals to Warsaw in the autumn of 1919 and the spring of 1920. His efforts were in vain, however, as Pilsudski did not want to negotiate a settlement of outstanding problems.

The Poles opened an offensive in the Ukraine west of Kiev on 25 April 1920, and they took the city on 6 May. Later that month the Soviets mounted a counterattack that pushed the Poles back from Kiev. The Polish retreat became a rout, and it seemed that the Red Army would quickly sweep into Warsaw, for it had reached the gates of the city by mid-August. Many Bolsheviks anticipated a Soviet victory over the Poles that could be used as a springboard to launch a socialist revolution in Germany. But just as the Reds were about to capture Warsaw, Pilsudski counterattacked on 16 August forcing them to retreat. By the end of the month the Reds had fled back across the Curzon Line—the Allied demarcation along roughly ethnic lines between Poland and Soviet Russia that British Foreign Secretary Lord Curzon had proposed on 12 July to end the war.

At this point it was apparent to Lenin that Red troops would not be able to take Warsaw. Soviet successes throughout the summer had seriously alarmed the Allied powers, who had cast Poland in the role of containing both Germany and Soviet Russia. Therefore, Lenin instructed Chicherin to renew his attempts to bring the Poles to the peace table. An armistice, which resembled the Estonian-Soviet armistice of a year earlier, was signed at Riga on 12 October; it contained the essential provisions of a future peace settlement, confirmed by the Treaty of Riga on 18 March 1921.[42]

For Chicherin the Polish-Soviet War and the Treaty of Riga

served as an example of the use of diplomacy to defend revolutionary Russia, since appeals to the Western European proletariat to revolt in support of the advancing Red Army did not spark an international socialist rebellion. The war with Poland brought the Soviets a number of diplomatic successes, for Chicherin effectively isolated the Poles during the conflict. In May, June, and July 1920 the Soviet government signed agreements with Hungary, Latvia, and Austria respectively, which provided for an exchange of prisoners of war. On 12 July and 11 August the Soviets signed peace treaties with Lithuania and Latvia respectively, thus terminating hostilities in the Baltic. The settlement with Lithuania in particular was a result of the Polish-Soviet War, for the Lithuanians feared the Poles as much as the Soviets. The treaty granted Lithuania considerable territory under dispute with Poland in return for which the Lithuanians allowed the Red Army to use this land as a base of operations in its campaign against Pilsudski. In August the Soviets negotiated an armistice with Finland that established the foundation for a peace treaty on 14 October.[43]

Pilsudski's military adventures had worked to the advantage of Soviet Russia, since the Baltic states sought accommodation with the Soviets in the face of the growing Polish threat. They attempted to plot an independent course in foreign affairs between Poland and Soviet Russia. But Pilsudski's blunders were not the only or even the principal reasons for Moscow's diplomatic successes. Chicherin's diplomatic skills were largely responsible for the peace treaties and trade agreements with the Baltic nations. He constantly presented the Soviet government as a champion of peace interested in preserving the independence and sovereignty of the border states with whom Soviet Russia wanted to develop mutually advantageous diplomatic and trade relations.[44]

The armistice and treaty with Estonia were particularly important, for they established Chicherin's reputation as a promoter of peace. His insistence that Trotskii not dispatch Red troops into Estonia in pursuit of Yudenich was a valuable lesson for the other Baltic states. Chicherin's negotiations with the governments of these nations reduced their fears and suspicions of Soviet Russia. His efforts to negotiate differences between Poland and Soviet Russia were initially unsuccessful, but he still achieved a great deal of good will for his country. By dispatching a steady stream of peace proposals to Warsaw he created a favorable impression of the Soviet government in contrast to Pilsudski's expansionist, militarist policies.

The Polish-Soviet War was a turning point in Soviet diplomatic history for other reasons as well. It effectively undermined Allied unity toward Soviet Russia and produced a split between Britain and France. After the Polish war and Soviet peace treaties with the Baltic states the British were no longer willing to support interventionist policy. They, too, had been attracted by Chicherin's peace offensive, and Lloyd George's government hoped to work out a trade agreement with the Soviets. Difficult problems still remained, but Britain resolved to retreat from active intervention, content with a zone of independent states bordering Soviet Russia in Eastern Europe.[45] France, however, remained adamantly opposed to any compromise with the Soviet government. The French had been the staunchest supporters of Pilsudski during the Polish war, and the Treaty of Riga, negotiated without the collapse of Bolshevism, had been a bitter disappointment. The French had been the largest foreign investor in Imperial Russia during the late nineteenth and early twentieth centuries, and therefore they had the most to lose when the Soviets repudiated the debts of the Tsarist and Provisional governments. Yet despite unabated French hostility toward Soviet Russia, British withdrawal from intervention meant the failure of that policy, for after World War I France increasingly looked to Britain for leadership in international affairs.

The intervention of the Allied governments in Russian affairs was unsuccessful primarily because of Bolshevik military victories during the Civil War. The Bolsheviks had acquired power rather easily in 1917, filling a political vacuum when no one else seemed willing to lead. Their real achievement was their military triumph in the Civil War. While Allied intervention floundered in part due to the disunity and poor military and political leadership of the Whites, Soviet diplomacy also proved to be superior to that of the Whites and their Allied supporters. Chicherin deserves a great deal of credit for Soviet diplomatic successes during the intervention and Civil War. By constantly presenting the Soviet government as the champion of peace, he maintained pressure on the Allies to terminate military intervention. He proclaimed his government's readiness to negotiate outstanding differences with the Western powers and thus weakened the arguments of those who favored intervention.[46]

By 1921 Soviet Russia was no longer diplomatically isolated,

3.1   Chicherin signing the Soviet-Turkish Treaty of Friendship and Recognition in Moscow, 1921

3.2 Chicherin, Radek, Litvinov, and Bratmann-Grodovskii in Berlin, 1922.

3.3 Chicherin in Genoa, 1922.

3.4 Chicherin in the train "Genoa-Rapallo," 1922.

and its western border was largely secure. The Soviet government had been able to divide the capitalist powers. Just as importantly, Chicherin's diplomatic activities embarrassed the Allies and earned his government the reputation of a proponent of peace before the European public.

The Soviet policy of exploiting the differences among the capitalist powers became especially noticeable after the Allies signed the Treaty of Versailles with Germany in 1919. The Germans bitterly resented the treaty, for it was a dictated peace. The Allies used the infamous "war guilt" clause to justify the reparations they demanded from Germany to pay for the cost of World War I. In 1918 Chicherin had not distinguished between Allied and German imperialism, arguing that the capitalist world was divided into two camps competing for the economic domination of Soviet Russia. But his attitude changed after the Paris Peace Conference and the Treaty of Versailles. He recognized that the Allies had cut off Germany from the international community and that therefore the Germans might be persuaded to reach an understanding with the Soviets.

Relations between Germany and Soviet Russia had been considerably strained during 1918, the product of the Treaty of Brest-Litovsk and German expansion into the former territory of the Russian Empire. Furthermore, the crisis was heightened when a Left SR named Blumkin assassinated the German ambassador, Count Wilhelm von Mirbach, in Moscow on 6 July. But the collapse of the Imperial German government in October and the armistice ending hostilities on the western front in November changed the international scene profoundly. These events essentially meant the repudiation of the Brest-Litovsk Treaty, which altered the attitude of the Soviet government toward Germany. Henceforth, until at least 1923, the Bolsheviks eagerly anticipated a socialist revolution in Germany. They faced a perplexing dilemma, for their desire for revolution in Germany clearly clashed with the demands of diplomacy.

Chicherin seized the initiative by striving to drive a wedge between Germany and the Allied powers. He embarked upon a systematic campaign against the Treaty of Versailles, with the explicit intention of appealing to the German government and public opinion in Germany. He claimed that the treaty was not a genuine peace, in part because the Allies had dictated it to Germany and in part because the Germans were required to pay enormous reparations.

Chicherin was especially critical of reparations, arguing that the Allies had forced Germany to mortgage its future in a futile and unjust attempt to pay for the cost of the war. More importantly, he correctly foresaw that German resentment of and attempts to undo the treaty would lead to a renewal of hostilities; thus for him Versailles was not a permanent arrangement but the prelude to a new war in Europe.[47]

In conjunction with his criticism of the Treaty of Versailles, Chicherin also attacked the League of Nations, whose charter had been written into the treaty. He was opposed to the League from its inception and remained a staunch critic of it throughout his tenure as commissar of Narkomindel. In his view the Allies established the League as a defensive union against Germany; furthermore, he held that the League was directed against Soviet Russia and designed to prevent the spread of socialism in Europe and to ensure the military and political hegemony of Britain and France.[48] In essence Chicherin articulated the attitude of his government toward the League throughout most of the 1920s. The Soviets regarded it as an organization of capitalist states formed to stave off the destruction of capitalism and the triumph of socialism and to restore the conservative nineteenth-century concert of Europe. Thus Chicherin's efforts to separate Germany from the Western Allies were intended not only to circumvent the diplomatic isolation of his government but also to seek a possible partner against the potential military threat posed by the League of Nations.

Chicherin described the League of Nations as a threat to the independence and sovereignty of individual nation states; he argued that behind a carefully elaborated facade of working to secure international peace, it would interfere in the internal affairs of countries unable to resist effectively. He was particularly concerned about the power of the League to use sanctions against states accused of aggression. Chicherin felt that the League might use its role as international arbiter as a pretext to launch an invasion against Soviet Russia.[49] For example, during the Polish-Soviet War he rejected any efforts by the League to mediate the conflict, fearing that this was a thinly veiled attempt by Britain and France to renew intervention in the Russian Civil War and overthrow the Soviet government. Chicherin preferred bilateral agreements between nations and conferences convened to discuss and resolve a specific international problem. Above all, he insisted that each nation should preserve its freedom of action.

Chicherin's criticism of the Treaty of Versailles and the League of Nations was part of his peace offensive designed to improve the position of the Soviet government in world affairs through diplomacy. By 1921 as the Civil War came to an end Lenin decided to abandon War Communism in favor of NEP. This decision involved the restoration of some market relations in the economy and a tactical retreat away from the rapid development of socialism in Soviet Russia, along with a corresponding change in Soviet foreign policy, symbolized by Chicherin's peace initiatives. "Peaceful coexistence," a concept whose origins are still debated but the essence of which Lenin clearly articulated, emerged as a principal tenet of Soviet foreign relations. This policy meant the expectation of a long period of peaceful competition between capitalism and socialism, the absence of revolutionary opportunities around the world, and stable diplomatic relations with the Western powers based largely on increased commercial and economic ties.[50]

The failure of the rapid spread of socialist revolution from Soviet Russia to Western Europe compelled the Bolsheviks to modify their expectations for the coming world transformation. By 1921 they began to realize that the Soviet state might have to coexist with the capitalist powers for a long period and that their government could not survive in an atmosphere of continual hostility and war. In addition, economic motives induced the formulation of a policy of peaceful coexistence among governments based on radically different social systems. NEP meant a concerted effort to restore the economy of Soviet Russia after the devastation of World War I and the Russian Civil War. The Soviet government desperately needed peace— a prolonged breathing space—and extensive trade with the capitalist West to accomplish this goal quickly.

Chicherin, who was primarily responsible for explaining Soviet foreign policy both in the Soviet and Western press, frequently wrote about the importance of peaceful coexistence for his government during the 1920s. Yet for him and the other Bolsheviks this policy did not mean a rejection of socialist revolution and an end to a steadfast faith in the expansion of socialism throughout the world. The goal had not changed, only the schedule by which a world socialist community would be realized. Furthermore, Chicherin emphasized that peaceful coexistence, while advocating normal diplomatic relations and the cessation of conflict between the Soviet state and the capitalist powers, did not mean the termination of competition between capitalism and socialism. During the prolonged period of peaceful coexistence, economic competition that Chicherin described as "a peaceful duel" would continue unabated; and he was supremely confident that socialism would emerge triumphant in the coming competition between the Soviet socialist state and the Western capitalist powers in their respective efforts to revitalize the economy of Europe during the twenties.[51] Therefore, for him NEP and peaceful coexistence were both products of a broad policy stressing economic reconstruction at home and peace initiatives abroad to consolidate and defend the Soviet state without abandoning the ultimate goal of the socialist transformation of society.

As chief of Narkomindel Chicherin presided over the development of a staff of professional diplomats loyal to the Soviet government. The Bolsheviks gradually realized the importance of traditional diplomacy for the defense of the revolution in Soviet Russia, and consequently Narkomindel grew in authority and prestige during the 1920s. Chicherin's diplomatic skills contributed to growth in the stature of the Commissariat. He earned a reputation among his colleagues in Europe as one of the leading diplomats of his era, for he was an able and articulate champion of Soviet foreign policy during his long tenure as head of Narkomindel. He combined an understanding of Russia's traditional interests as a great power with a firm and unswerving commitment to socialism and the defense of the new Soviet government as it struggled for survival in a hostile environment. Without giving up his vision of the socialist reconstruction of the world, he implemented a policy of peaceful coexistence in foreign affairs intended to cultivate and preserve stable relations with the Western powers. Finally, following Lenin's lead, Chicherin learned to take advantage of divisions within the capitalist camp, often successfully playing off the Western powers against each other. In this process he assigned a special role to Germany; for, like Soviet Russia, it had been excluded from the concert of Europe as a result of World War I and the Treaty of Versailles.

4

Soviet Relations with Germany

RELATIONS with Germany occupied a crucial position in Chicherin's elaboration of Soviet foreign affairs during the 1920s. His views toward Germany changed substantially during the Russian Civil War. In 1918 Imperial Germany had compelled Soviet Russia to sign the Treaty of Brest-Litovsk, which gave the Germans control of a great deal of territory of the former Russian Empire. But the treaty did not end German aggression against the Soviet government, even though the Soviets had obtained a "breathing space" by signing the dictated peace. Therefore, throughout the summer and early autumn of 1918 considerable antagonism and hostility between Imperial Germany and Soviet Russia developed.

The collapse of the Imperial German government in October and the armistice of 11 November terminating fighting on the western front fundamentally altered German-Soviet relations. Chicherin began to perceive Germany as a potential ally for Soviet Russia against Britain and France, the victors in World War I. The Treaty of Versailles, negotiated at the Paris Peace Conference of 1919, reinforced this idea. Both Germany and Soviet Russia were treated as outcasts, not invited to attend, and thus separated from the concert of Europe. Actually, Chicherin's German orientation was designed to facilitate Lenin's policy of exploiting and taking advantage of inherent contradictions and divisions among the capitalist powers, thereby seriously weakening the possibility of an united front against Bolshevism.

The Germans responded favorably to Soviet overtures. In October 1919 Germany refused to participate in the Allied blockade

against Soviet Russia and maintained a position of benevolent neutrality during the Polish-Soviet War of 1920. Moreover, Germany
and Soviet Russia began to discuss an exchange of prisoners of war
early in 1920. From these negotiations, on 19 April, the first
German-Soviet agreement since the Treaty of Brest-Litovsk was
concluded on "the mutual repatriation of prisoners of war and
interned civilians." The settlement provided for the establishment
of "welfare centers" in Berlin and Moscow by which Russian prisoners in Germany and German prisoners in Soviet Russia could return
to their respective homelands. The Treaty of 19 April defined as
Russian prisoners of war Russians who had fought either for the former Russian Empire or for the Soviet Republic, or against the Soviet
Republic; the agreement therefore claimed jurisdiction over all Russians in Germany and repudiated the legitimacy of non-Soviet
émigré organizations in Berlin.[1] By this treaty Germany came close
to extending de jure recognition to the Soviet government. The
agreement of 19 April also had important economic consequences,
for the first Soviet orders for steam engines from Germany immediately followed it.

During late 1920 and 1921 the repatriation of prisoners of war
between Germany and Soviet Russia was completed. The welfare
centers, which had virtually operated as diplomatic missions, lost
their official reason for existence, and the two governments began to
negotiate more permanent relations. The result was the German-
Soviet Treaty of 6 May 1921, which replaced the agreement on
prisoners of war and foreshadowed the Rapallo accord of 1922. The
functions of the prisoners of war welfare centers in Berlin and
Moscow were expanded to include commerce. Their trade officials
would be known as "German Representatives in Soviet Russia" and
"Representatives of the RSFSR in Germany" respectively; furthermore, the Treaty of 6 May provided for regular courier service
between Germany and Soviet Russia.[2] By this treaty the Weimar
Republic granted de facto recognition to the Soviet government.

To consolidate further its growing economic ties with the
Weimar Republic the Soviet government sent Krestinskii to Berlin
as Soviet plenipotentiary in October 1921. He remained at his post
of nine years until he became deputy commissar of foreign affairs in
July 1930. His presence in Berlin gave stability to German-Soviet
relations, for he supported Chicherin's German orientation as the
underpinning of Soviet foreign policy. Also, the Germans respected

Krestinskii's diplomatic skills and realized that his long tenure in Berlin worked to the advantage of German-Soviet relations.

Lenin's introduction of NEP in 1921 created a watershed of considerable dimensions in Soviet domestic and foreign affairs. Since early 1918 the Soviets had expressed an interest in developing trade with the capitalist West—an exchange of raw materials for capital products. These proposed economic transactions in part were based on political calculations—the desire to play the capitalist powers off against each other to weaken military intervention— but the harsh winter of 1920–1921 and the desperate need for commercial and industrial recovery that NEP symbolized added a new seriousness to Soviet economic initiatives to Western Europe. Moreover, the failure of the German Communists to take power in March 1921 by a general strike indicated to the Bolsheviks that the European socialist revolution would not occur quickly and that it was therefore necessary to plan for a long period of coexistence and of formal diplomatic relations with capitalist countries.

Besides trade, the Soviet government wanted de jure recognition from the capitalist nations. The Bolsheviks concluded that normal, stable relations with the capitalist powers would help avert a renewal of armed intervention into Soviet Russia and could promote the extension of credits from these governments to the Soviet Republic. The Bolsheviks were especially concerned about obtaining capital from the West to finance reconstruction and continue with the consolidation of socialism at home. They believed that credits and trade would enable them to achieve industrial-military autarchy as quickly as possible, for without such a development the Soviet state would continue to be vulnerable to Western military threats.

On the whole Soviet trade initiatives found a favorable response in the West. In the immediate postwar period Western Europe suffered from a problem of industrial overproduction and intense competition for export markets. Therefore, the capitalist countries were willing to sell manufactured goods in exchange for Soviet raw materials. But European governments were much more reluctant to grant de jure recognition and offer extensive credits to the Soviet Republic. They objected to socialist propaganda directed against capitalism. Yet the most important issue involved the Soviet government's repudiation of the foreign debts of the Tsarist regime and the Provisional Government.

At the outset of World War I Imperial Russia had the largest foreign debt of any country in the world. And this indebtedness increased during the war, as the Allied powers provided credits to the Russian government to finance the purchase of war materials. In 1914 the Tsarist government's foreign debt was more than 4 billion gold rubles. This indebtedness had risen to 12 billion gold rubles by 1917. Furthermore, after the November Revolution the Soviet government nationalized foreign property valued at approximately 2 billion gold rubles. In total, Western claims against the Soviet government amounted to about 14 billion gold rubles. About 80 percent of the prewar Russian state debt was owed to France, primarily to small private investors who had purchased Tsarist treasury bonds; and in nationalized property France had lost more than any other country.[3] The French, however, while vitally interested in the prewar debt, were relatively unconcerned about the war debt that had been accumulated at the expense of the Americans and the British.

The Soviet response to Allied claims for repayment of the war debt was to present an enormous bill, some 50 billion francs, for damages done by the Western powers during intervention. The Western nations eventually accepted the idea that Soviet counterclaims would offset the Russian war debt, and they concentrated their efforts on the repayment of the prewar state debt and restitution for confiscated property. The French, as might be expected, took the lead in applying diplomatic pressure for the recovery of the prewar claims.

The Bolsheviks insisted that they were under no ethical or legal obligation to pay the prewar Russian state debt, but they agreed to make some payments toward it, provided that the Western powers granted extensive credits to the Soviet Republic. The Soviets wanted large-scale credits in the postwar period, and they were willing to pay a moderate rate of extra interest—possibly 2 or 3 percent—on these credits, with the provision that this additional interest would be applicable to the prewar debt.[4] It might have been possible for the two sides to arrange a satisfactory settlement of the prewar state debt, but the Soviets flatly refused to consider restitution to the former foreign owners of nationalized properties. The French and Belgians were particularly adamant on this point. Yet the exploitation of industrial enterprises by foreign owners would have been completely incompatible with socialism and was therefore anathema to the Bolsheviks. The Soviet government eventually offered to lease enterprises on concession to former owners, but it would not consider any deviation from the socialist development of the country. The Soviet Republic obtained trade and diplomatic recognition from the West, but it did not acquire long-term credits.

In 1921 the Soviet government pressed the Weimar Republic to establish regular diplomatic relations. As revisionist powers dissatisfied with the postwar settlement, Germany and Soviet Russia were united by a common antipathy toward Anglo-French hegemony on the continent. But at this time Germany, seeking accommodation with Britain and France, refused to act quickly, fearing that de jure recognition of the Soviet government would only antagonize the two Western powers. Chicherin, who realized that it would be difficult for the Soviet government to obtain de jure recognition from the capitalist nations without a formal discussion of the claims each side made against the other, proposed to the Supreme Allied War Council in a letter dated 28 October that an international economic and financial convention be held to address these issues.[5] His suggestion found a receptive audience, for during the autumn European diplomats called for an international conference to undertake the economic reconstruction and recovery of Europe. It was apparent to European leaders that representatives from Germany and Soviet Russia should be invited to attend, since these two countries would play a significant role in the development of the European economy.

On 6 January 1922 the Supreme Allied War Council, which met for the sixteenth time in the French Mediterranean resort city of Cannes, agreed to convene an international economic and financial conference to be held in Genoa, Italy, during the first part of March. That afternoon the Supreme Council also passed six resolutions that in its estimation were to form the basis for reestablishing economic and political ties with Soviet Russia. The Cannes resolutions were elaborated on the principle that the West would provide capital and extend official recognition to Soviet Russia only after the latter had consented to honor all of its debts and obligations. On the following day the Italian government issued the Soviet Republic an official invitation. Chicherin, while in favor of the world convention, objected to its location. He feared anti-Soviet émigré organizations in Italy would harass and possibly even threaten the Soviet delegation; just as importantly, he thought that it would be difficult for the Soviet representatives to communicate effectively between Genoa and Moscow.[6] He suggested London as a more suitable site for the conference. In spite of Chicherin's reservations about the Allied invitation, the Politburo, which met to formulate the Soviet response on 17 January agreed to participate in the Genoa Conference and submitted a delegation headed by Lenin. The Politburo designated Chicherin as Lenin's first assistant with full authority to assume leadership of the delegation in case Vladimir Il'ich could not travel to Italy. Other members of the delegation included Krasin, Litvinov, A. A. Ioffe, N. N. Narimanov, Ia. E. Rudzutak, and V. V. Vorovskii. A special session of the Central Executive Committee confirmed the composition of the Soviet delegation on 27 January.

It is doubtful that Lenin ever intended to attend the Genoa Conference. His failing health would have made the long journey from Moscow to Italy extremely arduous for him. He also needed to be in Moscow for the Eleventh Congress of the party, scheduled for late March and early April. Even when the Genoa Conference was postponed until the middle of April, he did not seriously entertain the idea of traveling to Italy. But Chicherin, too, was in poor health, and the Politburo discussed the possibility of giving him a brief respite from his duties at Narkomindel prior to the conference. He refused to consider the suggestion, arguing that he was involved in intensive preparations for the convention; thus the Politburo agreed to postpone his rest and medical treatment until after the completion of the conference.[7]

In spite of Chicherin's dissatisfaction with Genoa as the location for an international convention, he welcomed the Soviet government's participation in a meeting with the capitalist powers to discuss the economic recovery of Europe. In his view the Genoa Conference represented the failure of the Allied blockade of Soviet Russia and the realization by Western leaders that reconstruction could not be completed without Soviet involvement. He understood that fundamental economic and political differences between Soviet Russia and the capitalist nations would make negotiations difficult, but he stressed that on the basis of peaceful coexistence the two opposing systems could collaborate to resolve common pressing economic problems. Yet Chicherin also warned that the Western countries should not misconstrue NEP; the Soviet government would not tolerate interference with its internal economic and political development as it strove to build socialism, and NEP must not be regarded as the beginning of a gradual transition from socialism to capitalism.[8]

The Soviet government assiduously prepared for the Genoa

Conference, attempting to ensure that its delegation would acquit itself well in diplomatic competition with the Western powers before world public opinion. Lenin actively participated in the preparations for the conference. He instructed every member of the Soviet delegation to be familiar with all the possible economic and political questions that might arise at the convention and for each of them to develop an expertise in one economic and one political issue. He also indicated that not only was a thorough knowledge of the problems under scrutiny from the Soviet perspective needed, but also the delegates must acquaint themselves with recent Western bourgeois literature on these topics. Furthermore, Lenin stressed flexibility in the Soviet approach to the conference. He informed the delegates they ought to anticipate the dissolution of the conference at any time, even before the completion of its work. In the event of such an occurrence, the Soviet representatives must be prepared to speak to a larger audience than the Western delegates assembled in Genoa; the Soviet side should aim its remarks, cogently expressed from both the socialist, liberal, and pacifist points of view, at world public opinion, especially at liberals and pacifists in the West to gain their support. Most importantly, Lenin warned that the Soviet delegation should expect to be confronted with an united opposition from the Western powers. While reminding the representatives of the general Soviet policy of exploiting antagonisms and disagreements within the capitalist camp, he further instructed them to take the offensive at Genoa and concentrate on weaknesses in the Western approach to economic and political issues, thus forcing Western diplomats on the defensive and diverting them from attacking the Soviet Republic.[9] Using these tactics Lenin hoped it would be possible to divide the opposition against Soviet Russia.

In essence Lenin elaborated two distinct programs in conjunction with Soviet policy toward the Genoa Conference. First, the Soviet government was interested in credits from and trade with the West, but it would not rescind the nationalization of the property of foreigners; second, the Soviets attempted to appeal to liberal, pacifist elements in the West by championing a broad program of disarmament and peace based on the principles of peaceful coexistence.[10] But, as Lenin acknowledged, the Soviet government did not have a specific pacifist program readily available for presentation at Genoa. Chicherin, in a letter to Lenin dated 10 March 1922, offered some suggestions for such a program, which Vladimir Il'ich, after some minor additions and modifications, approved. Therefore,

Chicherin was primarily responsible for the specifics of Soviet disarmament proposals and peace initiatives at Genoa.

Chicherin's pacifist program and appeal to world public opinion started with a declaration that at the Genoa Conference and every subsequent international congress and convention all nations should be equally represented, without distinction between victor and vanquished, powerful and weak, large and small, and capitalist and socialist.[11] He used the League of Nations as an example of an organization in which in his view the principle of political equality did not exist. He believed that his approach would be popular with the peoples of Africa and Asia in their efforts to achieve national liberation from Western imperial control. Directly criticizing the League, Chicherin also insisted that international conferences and commissions should be strictly prohibited from interfering with the internal economic and political affairs of participating countries. Just as importantly, he asked for voluntary cooperation between strong and weak nations and rejected coercion and sanctions to implement policies.[12] As an alternative to the forced submission of the minority to the majority, he advocated diplomacy and the influence of "moral authority" to convince member states that an international organization should adopt a particular economic or political position.[13] In this fashion, according to Chicherin, the small and weak nations would not have to be concerned about losing their freedom of action in international affairs to larger, more powerful countries.

Despite his distrust of the leaders of Social Democracy in Western Europe, Chicherin raised the idea of inviting working-class organizations to send delegations to international conferences and conventions; he maintained that the workers should have at least one-third of the representatives at such congresses.[14] He was optimistic that the workers would support colonies and suppressed peoples seeking independence from the imperial powers. But he failed to explain in detail the procedure by which delegates were to be selected for international conferences, especially if representation would not be organized along national lines.

One of the most interesting sections of Chicherin's 10 March letter to Lenin focused on a system of arbitration to avoid international conflict. Chicherin argued that war could be avoided if the disputants had the option of appealing to an impartial court of arbitration to resolve problems. He emphasized that in disagreements between the Soviet state and capitalist nations the international court of arbitration would have to consist of an equal number of judges from both sides; only with this arrangement would it be possible to preserve impartiality and ensure justice. Furthermore, Chicherin maintained that all countries should accept disarmament as a necessary prerequisite for the the avoidance of war.[15] This segment of his program was especially designed to elicit support from the smaller and weaker nations, for they could not compete with the military powers of Europe. He was also aware that the Soviet Republic was not yet in a position to challenge the industrial and military might of European capitalism.

Finally, according to Chicherin, European economic recovery could not occur unless the powerful, wealthy states were willing to help poor nations still in the process of building modern industries. He envisaged the transfer of technology and capital goods in exchange for raw materials, and in general he held that international congresses should be called to discuss the planned distribution of essential resources, such as coal, gold, and oil, and even of finished products.[16] Chicherin hoped that his ideas for economic reconstruction would prove attractive both to the major industrial powers and to the nonindustrialized nations.

Chicherin's letter of 10 March to Lenin became the basis for the Soviet approach to the Genoa Conference. Since Chicherin replaced Lenin as head of the Soviet delegation, the Politburo charged Georgii Vasil'evich with the task of chairing a selected committee of experts assigned to provide specific, technical information on economic and political issues for the delegates. Chicherin's commission met four times in the weeks preceding the conference. He also assembled a large library that he intended to transport to Genoa. Some of the volumes pertained to the history of international law, while others were collections of documents dealing with Russia's past—diplomatic agreements and treaties from Muscovy and Imperial Russia.[17] Chicherin wanted to use these materials as sources of reference during the negotiations at the conference.

Chicherin and the other principal members of the Soviet delegation departed from Moscow for Italy on 27 March. On the following day a second trainload of technical experts left Moscow. Chicherin and his colleagues arrived in Riga on 29 March to attend a two-day conference of diplomatic representatives from Estonia, Latvia, Poland, and Soviet Russia. The diplomats at the Riga Conference passed a resolution exhorting their respective Genoa delegates to work together and to coordinate their policies and presentations.[18] More importantly, the final accord resulted in a triumph for Moscow, as it called for de jure recognition of Soviet Russia. The Soviet delegation left Riga for Berlin on the evening of 30 March for home. Chicherin wanted to confer with the leaders of the Weimar Republic before proceeding on to Italy. He arrived in Berlin on 1 April.

Chicherin deliberately traveled to Italy by way of Berlin because he hoped to conclude an agreement with the German government before the Genoa Conference. Soviet leaders, especially Lenin, were not optimistic that Genoa would produce tangible diplomatic and political results in their favor. Chicherin shared these views and was concerned that the conference might be an occasion for the formation of a united capitalist bloc against the Soviet Republic. He had little hope of reaching a settlement with the Allies, largely because the French insisted on the restitution of nationalized properties to their former foreign owners and on the repayment of Russia's prewar debt. But Chicherin was equally alarmed by a British proposal of December 1921, later affirmed at the Cannes Conference. Lloyd George offered to organize an international syndicate with its headquarters in London consisting of members from Britain, France, and Germany to finance the economic reconstruction of Soviet Russia, thus attempting to exploit the country under colonial conditions.[19] The Soviet government needed foreign capital, but it refused to grant foreigners control over railroads, enterprises, and industries, as Lloyd George suggested. Chicherin, in particular, feared that the Western powers might use economic penetration as a means of dominating the Soviet Republic politically.[20] He had sanguine expectations about separating Germany from the Allies, since the Weimar Republic resolved to revise the Treaty of Versailles.

The Germans, too, had a number of reasons for wanting to reach accommodation with the Soviets. At the 1919 Paris Peace Conference the French, assuming that the Bolshevik regime would soon be overthrown, had been responsible for inserting in the Treaty of Versailles Article 116 according Russia (without reference to its government) the right to obtain reparations from Germany on the basis of the treaty whenever the Russian government would want to take advantage of this opportunity.[21] Article 116 meant that the Weimar Republic faced the possibility of demands for reparations from the Soviet government at a time when it could not meet its obligations under the treaty to the Allies, unless some satisfactory settlement of this issue could be reached with Soviet Russia. From the perspective of Article 116, a German agreement with the Soviets prior to the Genoa Conference would have essentially been a defensive measure, undertaken to prevent an Entente-Soviet rapprochement. Furthermore, the Germans were bitterly disappointed that the French refused to put the question of reparations on the agenda at Genoa; the German government had hoped to use the conference as a forum for discussing the rescheduling of payments and possibly even their termination altogether.

But the Germans were also compelled to take the initiative in negotiations with the Soviets. Germany's fear of reparation demands from Soviet Russia was only part of the framework for its diplomatic calculations in 1921–1922. Although the British suggestion to form an international consortium to finance industrialization in Soviet Russia included German participation, it was evident that Germany would be a junior partner in the arrangement. More importantly, the German government wished to reserve the potentially lucrative Soviet domestic market for its own industrialists and did not want to share Soviet natural resources with the other industrial powers of Europe.[22] Therefore, when Krestinskii, Krasin, and Karl Radek journeyed to Berlin for diplomatic negotiations in January 1922, the Soviet delegation was not alone in experiencing considerable pressure to reach a settlement of outstanding problems.

In the German Foreign Ministry, the chief of the Eastern Section, Baron Ago von Maltzan, favored a Soviet orientation in his country's foreign policy. Chicherin hoped that Maltzan would be able to persuade his government to follow this line. But Walter Rathenau, minister of foreign affairs, held the key to the German position, and he was unwilling to risk rupturing the Genoa Conference in advance and thus encountering the hostility of Britain and France by signing an agreement with Soviet Russia early in 1922. An astute diplomat, he resolved to keep his options open and await developments in Genoa. Therefore, the Soviet delegation failed to obtain what it wanted in Berlin—de jure recognition, mutual renunciation of claims, trade relations based on the most-favored nation principle, and acceptance of the Soviet foreign-trade monopoly, all of which were designed to thwart the international common front against Soviet Russia—and the negotiations were broken off on 17 February. Yet the Soviet mission was partially successful, for the two sides drafted a political agreement whose five points corresponded to the first five articles of the Treaty of Rapallo.[23]

Although disappointed by the results of the German-Soviet negotiations in January and February, Chicherin continued to apply pressure on the German government in the weeks before the Genoa Conference. The Allies unwittingly aided him in this endeavor, for Allied experts meeting at a convention in London from 20 to 28 March issued a memorandum affirming Soviet Russia's right to claim reparations from Germany under Article 116 of the Versailles Treaty. But the London memorandum also repeated the old demand that the Soviet Republic recognize Imperial Russia's prewar obligations and provide restitution for former foreign property holders. At the same time it became increasingly apparent that the capitalist powers could not sufficiently unite to present a common front against the Soviet Republic, something the Germans realized but were unwilling to communicate to Moscow. When Chicherin arrived in Berlin on 1 April Rathenau still faced the choice of signing a separate agreement with the Soviets and thus ending any hope of reaching a settlement with the Allies, or waiting for Genoa. Chicherin wanted to sign a "model agreement" on the basis of the draft Radek had worked out several months earlier. Once again Chicherin failed to obtain what he wanted, for Rathenau chose to delay signing the document until the conference, and complete accord on the nationalization of German properties by the Soviets and on most-favored nation treatment had not yet been achieved. But Georgii Vasil'evich did not travel to Italy with nothing to show for his efforts. The talks in Berlin demonstrated how close the two governments were to an agreement, as they had developed a draft treaty that could be used at the Genoa Conference.[24] And the Germans had consented to maintain close contact with the Soviets at Genoa. Both sides also promised to supply each other with information and to provide mutual support.

After spending four days in Berlin, Chicherin and the other members of the Soviet delegation arrived in Genoa on 6 April. The conference was scheduled to open on 10 April, the beginning of Holy Week. The Italian authorities housed the visiting dignitaries in small communities along the eastern and western Riviera not far from Genoa; for example, the Italians assigned the rambling, white marble, five-storied Hotel Imperiale, on the road between Santa Margherita and Rapallo, about thirty kilometers from Genoa, to the Soviet delegation. The entire Soviet delegation consisted of sixty-three people, including several Italians and some Soviet diplomatic personnel who worked in Italy.[25] Although the delegation resided in the Hotel Imperiale, the Italian government allocated the Soviets additional office quarters in the Hotel de Genes in Genoa itself, where they could work and meet with journalists. But even though the conference took place in Genoa, the most important negotiations occurred in the official residences on the Riviera of the delegations of the principal participating states. Thus the Villa d'Albertis, where Lloyd George lived, was often the site of significant informal and private conversations.[26]

The magnificent Palazzo San Giorgio in Genoa, reportedly the former location of one of Europe's oldest banks, was the location of the first plenary session of the conference on 10 April. Since the "Russian question" dominated the proceedings and because for the first time representatives of the Soviet government were present at an international convention, the Western delegates and journalists in attendance focused their attention on Chicherin. His opening speech, delivered first in French and then in English with only a few brief glances at some notes, created a sensation. According to Bessie Beatty, "By turning a feeble defense into a vigorous offense, by attacking instead of waiting to be attacked, Chicherin captured the conference at its inception."[27]

Chicherin elaborated on the program he had originally submitted to Lenin a month earlier, and which Vladimir Il'ich had subsequently modified.[28] Chicherin declared that the Soviet government was ready to participate in the reconstruction of the economic life of Europe. The Soviet Republic urged collaboration with capitalist nations according to the principles of peaceful coexistence between states representing different systems of property. But Chicherin further argued that economic recovery would be impossible without some means of guaranteeing international peace. Therefore, Soviet Russia was prepared to disarm on a reciprocal basis with the capitalist powers. He also proposed that a new "League of Peoples," based on political equality and participation by minorities and workers, replace the League of Nations. Compulsory measures and sanctions would not be part of the new world organization, and the participants would voluntarily accept and agree to abide by its resolutions. Finally, he called for the planned and equitable redistribution of the world's resources—raw materials, capital goods, and technology.

Chicherin's speech brought the "Russian question" to the attention of the press and public. He had succeeded in setting the tone for the conference at the outset. Even though there was some risk that by raising the issue of disarmament he might cause a rupture, after the initial plenary session the conference divided into four commissions—political, financial, economic, and transportation. Of these the political commission was the most important. Germany and Soviet Russia were invited to have representatives sit on all of them, which in effect meant that the two countries had been restored to great-power status.

While the commissions were doing their work, Chicherin was conducting interesting negotiations with the British and German delegations. Chicherin discussed the perplexing problems of debts, credits, and de jure recognition with Lloyd George at the Villa d'Albertis. Lloyd George was in a difficult position. On the one hand he was under considerable pressure to achieve a diplomatic victory at Genoa to offset waning popularity at home, and he could not disregard the prospects of increased trade with Soviet Russia. On the other hand his coalition government, dominated by the Conservatives, contained two outspoken opponents of Bolshevism—Foreign Secretary Lord Curzon and Colonial Secretary Winston Churchill—who insisted that he not compromise on the question of financial obligations to the West. Moreover, the French were unequivocally opposed to agreement with the Soviet government unless it consented to pay the prewar debt of the Tsarist regime and restitute nationalized property. Faced with this dilemma, Lloyd George tried to reach a settlement with Chicherin on the basis of the Cannes resolutions. But Lenin and the Politburo were unwilling to accept these conditions. He inundated Chicherin with messages instructing him not to make any concessions to Lloyd George, particularly on the subject of the return of nationalized property to or compensation for their former foreign owners, even if this posture meant rupturing the conference.[29]

On Good Friday, 14 April, Chicherin, Krasin, and Litvinov spent almost the entire day at the Villa d'Albertis in negotiations with the British delegation. Neither side, however, was willing to compromise. The Allies continued to insist on the full repayment of prewar debts and the restitution of private property before there could be any serious discussion of credits and official recognition. The Soviets found this offer completely unsatisfactory. With the Allies and the Soviets deadlocked, it appeared as if the conference might collapse.

At this critical juncture Chicherin turned to the German delegation in an effort to conclude the treaty on which the two sides had

been in virtual agreement several weeks earlier in Berlin. About 1:15
A.M. on Easter morning, 16 April, A. V. Sabanin, a member of the
Soviet delegation, phoned Maltzan to inform the Germans that the
Soviets would like to resume negotiations and invited the German
delegation to the Hotel Imperiale at 11:00 A.M. The members of the
German delegation assembled in Maltzan's room in their pajamas
and debated the issue. In their "pajama party" discussion the Germans decided to accept the Soviet offer, which they conveyed to the
Soviet delegation about 5:00 A.M. The Germans arrived at the Hotel
Imperiale at approximately noon, and Chicherin and Rathenau
conferred on the remaining points under dispute. Later that evening
they signed the Rapallo Treaty between Germany and Soviet Russia.[30] It was a simple document of six articles and provided for the
immediate resumption of consular and diplomatic relations, most-
favored nation treatment, the mutual repudiation of claims for war
costs and damages, Soviet Russia's renunciation of claims under
Article 116 of the Treaty of Versailles, and Germany's waiver of
claims for the nationalization of German property by the Soviet
Republic, unless the Soviet government at some future date would
make concessions on this point to another power.[31]

Rumors about secret military provisions to the Treaty of
Rapallo sprang up almost immediately after the Germans and Soviets signed the document, and historians have continued to debate
the issue. Trotskii initiated discussions with German armament
manufacturers in early 1921, using Viktor Kopp, a former
Menshevik who had extensive contacts in Central Europe, as an
intermediary. The Red Army desperately needed modern military
equipment, which Soviet industries in disrepair and lacking sophisticated technology, could not provide. As early as 7 April Kopp
reported that German industrialists, prohibited from manufactur-
ing munitions and weapons by the Treaty of Versailles, were
interested in supplying the equipment and technical expertise necessary for the production in Soviet Russia of artillery, planes, and
munitions. As the negotiations proceeded the Reichswehr became
involved. The Versailles Treaty severely limited the size of the German army and proscribed the training of military recruits. General
Hans von Seeckt, head of the Reichswehr, agreed to instruct Soviet
soldiers in exchange for the opportunity secretly to train German
military personnel in Soviet Russia.[32]

The question remains whether the military discussions had any
connection with the Rapallo diplomatic agreement, or if there were

two separate sets of negotiations occurring parallel with and independently of each other. Trotskii's role in the proceedings was crucial. His principal biographer, Issac Deutscher, contends that "The Politbureau authorized him to pursue negotiations in the strictest secrecy; and he held their threads in his hands during all these preliminaries to the Rapallo Treaty, until the moment came for the diplomats to act."[33] Deutscher's interpretation deserves scrutiny, for Germany and Soviet Russia signed a secret military agreement, referred to as a provisional trade agreement, on 29 July 1922, which was ratified only in February 1923. According to one explanation it was a secret supplement to the Treaty of Rapallo, whose essential provisions had been tentatively established in the Berlin discussions and later in talks in Italy; therefore, there exists at least a "reasonable possibility" of a military dimension to Rapallo.[34] But if this argument is true, then the military negotiations must have been conducted exclusively by Trotskii and other members of the Soviet government, for there is no available evidence to suggest that Chicherin was involved in military talks with the Germans, either in Berlin or Genoa. And most historians have rejected any military collaboration with the Rapallo Treaty, contending that it contained no secret clauses and that the Reichswehr did not expect its signature and had nothing to do with the final product.[35]

The Treaty of Rapallo was a great diplomatic and moral triumph for Chicherin and the Soviet Republic. It marked the high point of his diplomatic career and served as the cornerstone of Soviet foreign policy during his tenure as chief of Narkomindel. By signing an agreement with the Germans, the Soviets were able to prevent the formation of a common front against Bolshevism and further prolong the "breathing space" ushered in by the Treaty of Brest-Litovsk. At the Genoa Conference Chicherin demonstrated that he was able to compete successfully with the leading diplomats of Europe. Lloyd George later acknowledged that Chicherin had performed superbly, deftly exploiting weaknesses in the opposition while skillfully defending his own position.[36]

For the Soviet government the Rapallo Treaty became a model for bilateral agreements based on the principles of peaceful coexistence. Chicherin's negotiations with the Allies floundered on the issues of the payment of Russia's prewar debts and the restitution of nationalized properties. In essence, the Soviets feared that agreement with the Allies would mean the loss of political control over the economic development of Soviet Russia. Germany offered credits, recognition, and trade without the threat of political domination. Chicherin summarized the dilemma the Soviets faced in the follow fashion:

> The fundamental issue at Genoa was: Shall Russia be developed with the aid of foreign capital, without enslaving Russia, or shall foreign capital completely dominate that country? ... The issue was clearly drawn between submission to the capitalists of the world or independent development with the aid of that capital. ...[37]

In this view, therefore, Rapallo meant that Germany would assist with the economic modernization of Soviet Russia, yet the Bolsheviks would proceed with the social reform of the country.

While the Treaty of Rapallo was largely the result of Chicherin's diplomatic skills, other factors also influenced the rapprochement between Germany and Soviet Russia. The Germans played a significant role in the deliberations—a role that has not been adequately understood. They knew negotiations between the Allied and Soviet delegations had failed and therefore rushed to conclude an agreement with the Soviets on Sunday, 16 April, to demonstrate German political strength and preserve relations with Soviet Russia as Germany's domain.[38] But the Germans needed the threat of an agreement between Chicherin and Lloyd George as a pretext to justify their actions. The idea that the Allies would reach a settlement with the Soviets by offering them the possibility of collecting reparations from Germany under Article 116 of the Versailles Treaty served this purpose. Yet the Soviets had no intention of using Article 116, and Chicherin and Lloyd George did not even broach the question of reparations.[39] It would have been unthinkable for the Soviets to demand reparations from Germany on the basis of the Treaty of Versailles, since the Soviet government did not recognize it and rejected its provisions.

The Allies were the ultimate losers at the Genoa Conference. Britain was unable to reshape Europe for its own purposes and according to its own calculations. The Rapallo accord undercut Lloyd George's efforts to conclude an agreement based on German and Soviet submission to British economic and political domination. The anti-Bolsheviks in his cabinet and French intransigence on the questions of debts and nationalized properties limited his freedom of action. His smugness, underestimation of the Soviets, and reluctance to compromise contributed to his diplomatic defeat.

The Rapallo agreement should not have surprised him, for the Allies had monitored the German-Soviet talks in Berlin before the conference and were aware of the resumption of these discussions in Italy. Yet Lloyd George seemed genuinely surprised by the Rapallo Treaty, even though he had long warned the West about the possibility of German-Soviet cooperation.[40]

At Genoa Chicherin also negotiated a commercial treaty with Czechoslovakia, which was ratified in Prague on 5 June. Although the Czech government refused to extend de jure recognition to the Soviet Republic, the former agreed to terminate its relations with anti-Soviet émigré organizations in Prague. His work finished after the conference, Chicherin departed from Genoa for Berlin on 3 June; he intended to spend several months in Germany undergoing medical treatment from German physicians and in general resting from his labors in Italy. He underwent two operations, from which he had sufficiently recovered by early October to return to Moscow and resume his duties at Narkomindel.

The Treaty of Rapallo had restored consular and diplomatic relations between Germany and Soviet Russia, and Chicherin was quite interested in whom the Weimar Republic would appoint as its ambassador to Moscow. Maltzan and Rathenau indicated that Count Brockdorff-Rantzau, German minister of foreign affairs during the Paris Peace Conference, would be an ideal candidate. The Versailles Treaty was a personal humiliation for Brockdorff-Rantzau, the dignified, proud, and intensely patriotic scion of an ancient aristocratic family from Schleswig-Holstein. He had resigned when the German cabinet rejected his proposal not to sign the dictated peace. He expressed a willingness to accept the post in Moscow as long as he would be independent of the foreign minister. Determined to revise the Treaty of Versailles, he informed Berlin that he would go to Moscow only if the German government seriously intended to implement the Rapallo agreement as the cornerstone of its foreign policy. He did not want his assignment in Moscow to end in another personal Versailles.[41]

Brockdorff-Rantzau visited Chicherin at his residence in Berlin on 23 June. Chicherin was pleased and surprised by Brockdorff-Rantzau's frank discussion of German-Soviet relations, and the two men took an immediate liking to each other, which developed into an intimate friendship. Brockdorff-Rantzau used the terms "spirit of Rapallo" and "community of fate" to describe relations between Berlin and Moscow after 1922. Many of his ideas corresponded with Chicherin's, for Brockdorff-Rantzau believed that the two vanquished nations, Germany and Soviet Russia, had to cooperate with each other and coordinate foreign policy to prevent political domination by the victors in World War I. Brockdorff-Rantzau added a romantic element to the Rapallo relationship; he felt that it symbolized friendship between two states which had been cast out from the European community of nations.[42] Thus in spite of his aristocratic background and personal dislike of socialism, he maintained that Germany and Soviet Russia were bound by a common destiny that would ensure their continued great-power status and prevent Anglo-French hegemony of the continent.

Brockdorff-Rantzau was officially appointed German ambassador to the Soviet Republic on 22 September; he presented his credentials in Moscow on 6 November and served as ambassador until his death on 8 September 1928. The personal friendship between Chicherin and Brockdorff-Rantzau contributed substantially to German-Soviet relations between 1922 and 1928, and the two diplomats were able to resolve problems that otherwise might have engendered discontent and friction. In some respects, Brockdorff-Rantzau's personality and habits were similar to Chicherin's. For example, the German ambassador preferred to work at night, and he and Chicherin would often meet after midnight to examine the entire range of German-Soviet affairs and to discuss history, literature, and philosophy, which they both appreciated. They usually conversed in French, although Chicherin spoke German fluently and enjoyed sipping fine liquors and wines during the course of their discussions. Like Chicherin, Brockdorff-Rantzau was a bachelor, unburdened by family obligations, and uninterested in women; he devoted most of his time to his work, which he performed meticulously and thoroughly. Moreover, Brockdorff-Rantzau avoided large public gatherings and was not an effective public speaker. He performed brilliantly in private negotiations and wrote cogently and eloquently, but his oratorical skills were limited.[43]

Yet in spite of their similarities, Chicherin and Brockdorff-Rantzau were quite different in many ways, and it is surprising that they formed such an intimate friendship. Brockdorff-Rantzau chain-smoked, enjoyed French cognac, and ignored his health; he dressed immaculately and in a traditional fashion and was meticulous in his personal habits.[44] In this respect, his life-style was diametrically opposed to Chicherin's. More importantly, their political ideologies clashed, but they managed to reconcile these differences for the sake of German-Soviet relations. Brockdorff-Rantzau also seriously exaggerated Chicherin's political power, unable or perhaps unwilling to acknowledge that Narkomindel was ultimately not responsible for making policy decisions about Soviet foreign affairs. But nevertheless the enduring and remarkable friendship between the German ambassador and the Soviet commissar provided consistency and stability to German-Soviet relations during the 1920s.

From April 1922 to October 1923 the "spirit of Rapallo" dominated relations between Germany and the Soviet Union. During this period Chicherin was largely satisfied with Germany's efforts to fulfill its treaty obligations, and he praised the Weimar Republic for implementing Rapallo as the foundation of its foreign policy, especially when critics and opponents attempted to undermine the agreement. He described German-Soviet collaboration as a part of the "natural order" of international affairs and indicated that objective economic and political conditions fostered cooperation between the two states.[45] The Germans, too, seemed convinced that a Soviet orientation in foreign relations was in their best interests. Thus trade between the two countries grew substantially, a direct result of the Rapallo Treaty. In 1922, 32.7 percent of Soviet imports came from Germany, approximately 6 percent more than the preceding year, and 18 percent of Soviet exports went to Germany, an increase of 10 percent over 1921; from 1921 to 1923 Germany occupied first or second place as an importer of Soviet exports.[46] Increased commercial transactions were indicative of the general harmony that prevailed between the Soviet government and the Weimar Republic during the first eighteen months after the Genoa Conference.

In late 1923 and early 1924 several events occurred that altered the relationship between Germany and the Soviet Union. On 13 August 1923 Gustav Stresemann became chancellor of the Weimar Republic, a position he held until 23 November, when he moved to the Foreign Ministry. He served as minister of foreign affairs until his death in October 1929. He was not opposed to Germany's eastern orientation, but he hoped to strike a balance between the Soviet Union and the Western powers. In particular, he wanted Germany to join the League of Nations and resolved to end hostility with France over reparations and border disputes. On two occasions, in

March 1921 and January 1923, the French occupied the Ruhr Valley to coerce Germany to pay reparations. The 1923 occupation ended in failure, for the Germans responded with passive resistance, and by the summer of that year the French grudgingly started to assess their reparations claims more realistically. The 1923 occupation thus marked the beginning of postwar stabilization in Western Europe.

In addition, the German Communists made a final bid to take power in October, an abortive revolution Moscow and the Comintern supported. There had been nothing in the Treaty of Rapallo prohibiting socialist propaganda against the Weimar Republic, and the Soviets had not given up the hope of causing a revolution in Germany, but Stresemann's government considered Soviet support for the October uprising a violation of the spirit of the agreement. He became even more convinced that Germany had to stabilize its relations with the Western powers and rejoin the concert of Europe by entering the League of Nations.

Chicherin initially welcomed Stresemann's overtures to France, interpreting them as an attempt to reduce tension in Western Europe, which in turn would lead to greater stability in world affairs. But Chicherin became increasingly concerned that Stresemann intended to undo the Treaty of Rapallo and reorient German foreign policy toward the Western Allies. Chicherin reminded Stresemann that the Soviet government had been the first to protest against the 1923 Ruhr occupation and that it would be a mistake to assume that Britain and France would restore Germany to the concert of Europe as an equal partner, for the Western powers would maintain supremacy. Most importantly, Chicherin argued that Germany could best negotiate with France from a position of strength, which only the Rapallo Treaty could guarantee. In his view the accord provided considerable economic and political benefits both to Germany and the Soviet Union and therefore ought to serve as the basis for German foreign policy, regardless of other negotiations and possible diplomatic agreements the Weimar Republic might pursue in the future. And he repeated the Soviet government's commitment to comply with the terms of the treaty, for it was the cornerstone of Soviet foreign relations.[47] Thus Chicherin urged Stresemann to consider the abrogation of the Rapallo Treaty as much too high a price to pay for rapprochement with France.

Furthermore, Chicherin's criticism of the League of Nations

remained unchanged. He insisted that the League was an organization of states designed to maintain the predominance of the victorious powers in World War I; membership would deprive Germany of independence in international affairs, since Britain controlled the League Council.[48] He also warned Stresemann that entry into the League would mean that the Weimar Republic had joined a coalition hostile to the Soviet Union.[49] The possibility that Germany might apply for League membership raised the specter that once again the Soviet government would be isolated against a common capitalist front, one of Chicherin's principal concerns throughout his tenure as chief of Narkomindel. Writing in February 1924 he indicated that if the League had been structured differently, if it was a genuine "League of Peoples" based on political equality and did not employ sanctions or compulsory measures to enforce decisions, then Germany and the Soviet Union might consider joint membership in such an international organization.[50] But later in October Chicherin categorically dispelled rumors hinting that the Soviet Union might be willing to join the League as it was then constituted, providing that Germany also became a member. He called such a suggestion a "complete fabrication," although he did not rule out the possibility of sending an observer to monitor League activities.[51] His antipathy toward and distrust of the League was so great that in a letter to the League general secretary dated 30 October he declined an invitation for the Soviet Union to participate in a conference sponsored by the League to control the world trade in opium. Chicherin declared that the Soviet government had taken strong measures against the opium trade and narcotics in general, but a discussion of the problem with the capitalist countries would be fruitless, as they were unprepared to act resolutely for fear of antagonizing commercial interests that profited from the traffic in narcotics.[52] Chicherin's writings in late 1923 and 1924 were clearly intended to persuade the Weimar Republic not to join the League of Nations. He attempted to turn the Stresemann government away from a policy of reconciliation with the Western powers and to reinforce the economic and political ties between Germany and the Soviet Union.

In spite of his commitment to socialist revolution, Chicherin had been opposed to Soviet support for the communist rebellion in Germany in October 1923. He correctly foresaw that if such a policy failed, it would cause irreparable damage to relations between the Weimar Republic and the Soviet Union. But the party leaders on the whole, especially Trotskii and Radek, were still convinced that Germany was ripe for revolution. The failure of the communist coup d'etat in Germany was important for the development of Bolshevik ideology on international revolution. After 1923 as a matter of necessity the party accorded increasing significance to diplomacy over revolution in world affairs.

Relations between Germany and the Soviet Union were further strained in May 1924. On 3 May a German Communist in Berlin under police escort escaped and sought refuge in the headquarters of the Soviet Trade Delegation. The police raided the Trade Delegation building and conducted a thorough search for their escaped prisoner, taking the opportunity to examine the documents and official papers on file. The Soviet government was outraged by what it considered to be direct violation of its monopoly on foreign trade and lodged a formal protest with the Weimar Republic, claiming that the German-Soviet Commercial Treaty of 1921 extended formal diplomatic immunity to the headquarters of the Trade Delegation.[53] The Soviets demanded an official apology, the reaffirmation of the government monopoly on foreign trade, the speedy punishment of the guilty officials and police agents, and the explicit recognition of the extraterritorial status of the Trade Delegation building in Berlin.

Chicherin attempted to resolve the problem as quickly as possible. He acknowledged that on the basis of the 1921 treaty the German police had clearly violated Soviet diplomatic rights. But he also expressed the view that the incident should not be allowed to prevent further economic and political cooperation between Germany and the Soviet Union and blamed German officials in favor of a Western orientation in foreign policy for exacerbating tension between the two countries. He pointed out that the police raid had been undertaken without the authorization, or even the knowledge, of the Ministry of Foreign Affairs; and before the 3 May event the German government had always observed the extraterritoriality of the Soviet Trade Mission.[54] Therefore, the Soviets could appeal to established practice and tradition.

Chicherin proposed negotiations to mitigate the dispute. In June he dispatched Kopp to Berlin to carry on discussions with Maltzan. The Kopp-Maltzan talks resulted in a successful compromise, which Chicherin and Rantzau accepted as the framework for a settlement. The Germans granted extraterritorial immunity to one room of the headquarters of the Soviet Trade Delegation, which had a separate entrance and was partitioned from the rest of the building. Although Chicherin and Rantzau had worked out the details of the agreement by 18 July, it was not officially signed in Berlin until 29 July. Chicherin was reasonably satisfied with the accord, for it essentially gave the Soviets what they wanted without causing the Germans grave embarrassment, but he warned that in future negotiations with the Weimar Republic his government would press for diplomatic immunity for the entire headquarters of the Trade Mission.[55]

Chicherin and Rantzau were able to repair some of the damage to German-Soviet relations caused by the insurrection of the German Communists and the police raid on the Berlin headquarters of the Soviet Trade Delegation. But they were not able to generate a complete renewal of the spirit of cooperation and harmony of the immediate post-Rapallo period. Germany remained the key element in Soviet foreign-policy calculations until the end of the decade, although relations between the two states became gradually yet increasingly strained after 1923. Chicherin regretted this development, and he blamed the Weimar Republic for sacrificing the Rapallo agreement for the sake of rapprochement with the West. Yet he also considered a diplomatic settlement between France and Germany desirable.

Beginning in late 1923 and 1924 Chicherin began to articulate an idea he hoped would enable the Soviet Union to participate in a Franco-German rapprochement. He proposed that the three great continental powers—France, Germany, and the Soviet Union—form a "continental system" to counteract British imperialism and Britain's predominance in European affairs through the League Council. He regarded Britain as the most determined and obstinate foe of Bolshevism, and, if he could do little to prevent rapprochement between France and Germany, he could at least try to drive a wedge between the continental powers and the British Empire. And Chicherin thought that growing Anglo-Franco antagonism and competition, which in his view gradually emerged in the postwar period, would contribute to the realization of his plans.[56]

Chicherin continued to advocate the continental bloc until the end of the decade, periodically presenting his ideas in Berlin and Paris and thus attempting to turn the tables against the British by confronting them with a united front of continental powers. But his aspirations for this plan clouded his usually accurate and lucid appraisal of international affairs. He failed to understand the extent

to which France followed Britain's lead in foreign relations throughout the interwar years. He frequently wrote about "intensifying
Anglo-Franco antagonism" as one of the key factors in European
diplomacy, but he exaggerated the degree to which France was able
and willing to forge its foreign policy independently of Britain.[57]
Much To Chicherin's chagrin and dismay, Stresemann seemed to
want Britain to mediate a settlement between France and Germany.
Therefore, Chicherin's vision of a united continental system floundered on close diplomatic cooperation between Britain and France
and the determination of the Weimar Republic to stabilize its relations with them.

In spite of the failure of his attempts to coordinate policy with
France and Germany against Britain, Chicherin did not abandon
his efforts to improve Franco-Soviet relations, largely in order to
convince Stresemann that the Soviet government could also pursue
an independent foreign policy. Chicherin regarded France as an
increasingly important card to play against Germany, for by the
autumn of 1924 Stresemann clearly intended to seek admission to
the League of Nations. Chicherin was pleased that the government
of Edouard Herriot, after a long delay, announced France's official
recognition of the Soviet government on 28 October.[58] Krasin
became the first Soviet ambassador to France. Since he remained
commissar of foreign trade, his appointment indicated the economic importance the Soviet government attached to improved
relations with Paris.

While courting France, Chicherin devised other tactics to persuade the Weimar Republic to return to the Rapallo agreement as
the foundation of its foreign policy and prevent the diplomatic isolation of the Soviet Union. In the face of growing cooperation
between Germany and the Western powers, a subtle change
occurred in his writings in 1925, for he realized that he would probably not be able to stop the Weimar Republic from joining the League
of Nations. Unwilling to break with Germany on this issue,
Chicherin applied pressure on Stresemann to make German membership contingent upon the emasculation of Article 16 of the
League Covenant. According to Article 16, member states were obligated to support sanctions, including military operations, when the
League Council decided in favor of such action against an aggressor.
Stresemann insisted Germany would continue to abide by its treaty
responsibilities to the Soviet Union and that entry into the League
would occur only if the Council granted exemption from Article 16.

Chicherin secretly hoped that Germany and the Western Allies would reach a deadlock over sanctions, thus preventing German membership in the League.

The Soviet government expressed genuine alarm about Article 16. The Soviets were principally concerned that it might open the possibility for a renewal of foreign intervention. If Germany joined the League without exemption from Article 16, the Soviets anticipated the prospect of war with Poland; according to the Soviet view of European affairs, the Poles would be more inclined to attack the Soviet Union if they knew that France could send military support through Germany. Therefore, the Soviets were worried not only about German participation in League sanctions but also by the right of transit across Germany for foreign troops called into action by the League Council, as stipulated in Article 16. Soviet concerns were understandable yet exaggerated. Since the Treaty of Versailles had severely limited the size of the German army, the Weimar Republic was opposed to the passage of foreign troops, especially a French army, across its territory. The Germans were just an anxious about exemption from Article 16 as the Soviets.

In February 1925 the Soviet government made a final attempt to persuade Germany not to seek rapprochement with the West and petition for admission into the League of Nations. A. I. Rykov, who succeeded Lenin as chairperson of the Council of People's Commissars, discussed with Rantzau the possibility of a German-Soviet military alliance directed against Poland.[59] But the Germans rebuffed the Soviet offer. At this point the Soviets decided to change tactics and use Poland to lure Germany away from the West. Chicherin approached the Poles about the possibility of negotiating a nonaggression pact, a commercial treaty, and in general a settlement of outstanding problems since the 1921 Treaty of Riga.[60] The Polish government faced a dilemma, for it sought to maintain an independent foreign policy and did not want to be the object of a military alliance between Germany and the Soviet Union. But Chicherin's discussions with the Poles failed to produce fruitful results. The talks essentially broke down over the issue of dominance of the Baltic states, since neither Moscow nor Warsaw was willing to allow the other side supremacy in the region.

In February 1925 the Weimar Republic had rejected Rykov's offer of a military alliance primarily because Stresemann was in the process of stabilizing relations with France. He proposed a Rhineland mutual guarantee pact that Aristide Briand, who became

French minister of foreign affairs in March, accepted, with the provision that Germany become a member of the League of Nations. Stresemann further suggested that Austen Chamberlain, the foreign minister of Britain, mediate the negotiations on these issues. On 15 September invitations were issued for a diplomatic conference at the Italian-Swiss lakeside resort of Locarno to begin 5 October. Before traveling to Locarno, however, Stresemann needed to shore up German relations with the Soviet Union, in part to indicate to the Western powers that Germany had not entirely abandoned its eastern orientation. He wanted to include a preamble affirming German-Soviet friendship to a trade treaty the two countries were negotiating. Chicherin hoped to turn the preamble into a new neutrality accord by which Germany would agree not to enter the League of Nations. He had first proposed such a treaty to Rantzau in December 1924. But Stresemann was intent on traveling to Locarno to secure Germany's western frontier and thus achieve a lasting rapprochement with France. Even though talks for a German-Soviet commercial agreement continued, Stresemann refused to expand the preamble into a binding political treaty that would prevent Germany's membership in the League.

Chicherin was highly critical of the forthcoming Rhineland pact and carried on an energetic campaign in the Soviet press during the summer and autumn against the Locarno discussions and about the conditions for Germany's entrance into the League. He pressed the German government about Article 16 of the League Covenant, determined to emasculate it, even if he could not prevent Germany from seeking a place on the council in Geneva. Chicherin argued that the Locarno agreements would render Germany a "satellite or vassal" of Britain and that the British were merely exploiting the Germans in the former's competition with the French for military and political dominance of Europe.[61] In his view Britain resolved to weaken France permanently on the continent and sought closer relations with Germany to accomplish this goal. By mediating and therefore controlling negotiations between France and Germany the British government could easily emerge victorious in its rivalry with the Third Republic. Thus Chicherin interpreted the Locarno pact as an intensification of the antagonism and hostility between London and Paris and as the "final capitulation" of Germany to Britain.[62]

Furthermore, Chicherin and the Soviet government explained

the Locarno pact as the culmination in the formation of an "Anglo-American bloc" initiated by the Dawes Plan of 1924. In November 1923 when the French withdrew from the Ruhr Valley they agreed to have the reparations issue examined by two international committees. From the resulting study a plan emerged—named after an American, Charles G. Dawes, the chairperson of the committee proposing it—that attempted to reschedule reparations so that Germany could realistically pay them. The Dawes Plan went into effect during the summer of 1924. It started Germany's annual reparations payments at 250 million dollars, but they were to be gradually increased over the next five years, until they more than doubled by the end of the period. The key to the plan was a foreign loan, which was almost as much as the first reparations installment, and more than half of which American financiers provided. According to Chicherin, the Dawes Plan was an extension of American financial influence into Europe and represented the beginning of a new and even more powerful capitalist economic offensive against the Soviet state.[63] The Soviet government perceived the Locarno agreements as the political offspring of the Dawes Plan, both designed to consolidate and reinforce bourgeois, capitalist control in Europe.[64]

In addition, Chicherin warned the Weimar Republic that in spite of British assurances France had no intention of agreeing to the general demilitarization of the Rhineland; on the contrary, he argued that Paris considered demilitarization exclusively Germany's obligation, for the French were preoccupied with security and wanted to ensure that if the need arose, they could dispatch troops stationed in the Rhineland to assist Poland and Czechoslovakia.[65] More importantly, he expressed alarm over British and French insistence that Germany's admittance to the League would be contingent upon its willingness to abide by all the obligations of the League Covenant, including Article 16, without exception.[66] Chicherin argued that Briand and Chamberlain were exerting enormous pressure on Stresemann to abandon the Rapallo Treaty and make application for admission to the League Council without concern for the Soviet Union. Moreover, writing in August 1925 Chicherin commented that Stresemann had begun to waver; yet the German foreign minister insisted that he could achieve a diplomatic balance between East and West by continuing to adhere to the Rapallo Treaty while at the same time participating in the Locarno agreements and that entrance into the League would not mean joining a military coalition hostile to the Soviet state. But Chicherin experienced grave doubts that Stresemann could receive exemption from Article 16 and still gain a seat for Germany on the council. As an example, Chicherin pointed out that during the summer Stresemann ceased to demand a formal, legal statement of exemption from Article 16, an ominous warning for the Soviet government that the Weimar Republic might be seriously contemplating the abrogation of the Rapallo accord.[67]

By the autumn of 1925 Chicherin's anxiety that Germany might sign the Rhineland pact and enter the League of Nations without obtaining exemption from Article 16 was considerably heightened. Although he criticized the French for this development, in his interpretation Britain was principally responsible. He charged that the British government, promising to mediate between France and Germany, had proclaimed itself the arbiter of European affairs.[68] In his view London perceived the Locarno agreements as a means of realigning the balance of power in Europe, luring Germany away from the Soviet Union, and undermining the power of France with the intention of securing British supremacy. Britain had successfully broken up the nascent continental bloc between France and Germany initiated several years earlier. Finally, Chicherin's message for the German government was clear: by seeking rapprochement with the West and entering the League of Nations without exemption from Article 16 the Weimar Republic was joining forces with a coalition hostile toward the Soviet Union and therefore threatening to nullify the Treaty of Rapallo.[69] He appealed to Stresemann to reconsider his actions before relations between Berlin and Moscow were irreparably damaged. Yet Chicherin's writings in the last part of 1925 reveal that he entertained little hope of halting German rapprochement with the Western Allies.

Despite his uncertainty about dissuading Germany from signing the Locarno agreements, Chicherin decided to travel to Berlin in early October. He announced that his failing health and the need for rest and medical treatment were the reasons for the trip to Central Europe, as he wanted to consult with German physicians. Indeed it was true that he required relaxation and medical attention, for his labors during the year had left him weak and exhausted. More importantly, Chicherin wanted to confer with Stresemann before the latter departed for Locarno. Chicherin intended to make a final effort to persuade the Weimar Republic not to join the League, or at least to emasculate Article 16 if Germany should continue with its plans to seek admittance. Chicherin also arranged to stop in Warsaw enroute to Berlin. If Germany would not agree to reinforce the Rapallo Treaty at the expense of Poland, then once again he resolved to threaten Stresemann with the possibility of Polish-Soviet rapprochement.

Chicherin departed from Moscow for Warsaw amidst great fanfare on 25 September. The Soviet press gave extensive coverage to his trip abroad, carefully reporting the negotiations in Warsaw and Berlin. Polish and German journalists, too, displayed considerable interest in his visit, and Chicherin took advantage of the opportunity to articulate and explain his views on European affairs before the public. His abilities as a polemicist sustained him in this endeavor, for he appealed over the Polish and German governments to their respective peoples, hoping in this fashion to exert pressure on the leadership.

In Warsaw Chicherin acknowledged that Polish-Soviet relations had not been harmonious and that many issues remained unresolved since the Treaty of Riga of 1921. Yet he declared that the Soviet government was ready to discuss seriously the problems that separated the two countries and expressed optimism that relations would be substantially improved.[70] In particular, he emphasized a proposed commercial agreement and possibly a nonaggression pact to guarantee the existing Polish-Soviet border that in his view would initiate more favorable political relations.[71] Moreover, he continued his attack on Britain, claiming that the British government was determined to isolate the Soviet Union diplomatically and economically as a prelude to renewed military intervention—a "crusade" against the Soviet state.[72] But Chicherin realized that he was no closer to an agreement with the Poles than he had been in the spring of 1925, for the Soviets remained convinced that Poland sought hegemony in the Baltic with the intention of leading a coalition of Baltic states against the Soviet Union. His visit to Warsaw was an attempt to pressure Stresemann by threatening him with the prospect of Polish-Soviet rapprochement. This strategy failed, for Stresemann recognized the antagonism and hostility between Poland and the Soviet Union. There was no possibility of an understanding between the two nations as long as Poland functioned as the protector of the Baltic states.

After spending several days in Warsaw, Chicherin moved on to Berlin, where he arrived on 30 September. He spent two days with Stresemann and other government officials before the German delegation departed for Locarno. Chicherin repeated the Soviet objections to the Locarno pact and to Germany's entrance into the League of Nations. In particular, he reminded Stresemann that favorable relations with the Soviet Union depended on Germany's ability and willingness to emasculate Article 16. Chicherin also reiterated that the Soviet government did not intend to apply for admission to the League, but he acknowledged that the Soviets were interested in sending an observer to monitor League activities; he explained that this approach would enable the Soviets to preserve their freedom of action, as they refused to accept the provisions of the League Covenant.[73] Finally, Chicherin expressed optimism about a German-Soviet commercial accord, the details of which the negotiators had almost completed, and which was due to be signed soon in Moscow while talks were in progress at Locarno.[74]

Stresemann had skillfully scheduled the initialing of the commercial treaty to coincide with the signing of the Locarno pact, for he hoped to use both agreements to demonstrate a balance between East and West in German foreign policy. But even though Chicherin declared that the commercial accord meant that Germany had not abandoned the Treaty of Rapallo, he was not entirely satisfied with the document. He had failed to transform it into a binding neutrality agreement that would amplify and reinforce Rapallo. The proposed preamble, a benevolent statement of friendship, did not prevent Germany from joining the League. But Stresemann assured Chicherin that Germany would not act against the Soviet Union under the terms of Article 16 and that the German delegation in Geneva would defend and support Soviet interests before the League and world public opinion.[75]

On 2 October Stresemann left Berlin for Locarno where he spent ten days engaged in informal talks with representatives of the Western powers. The agreements that emerged from these discussions were initialed in Locarno on 16 October and signed in London on 1 December. They included a principal treaty guaranteeing the Franco-German and the Belgium-German borders, to which Britain and Italy also adhered, and a series of bilateral arbitration treaties. The Locarno Treaty meant that Germany agreed to accept a central portion of the Versailles settlement; the Weimar Republic regarded its western frontier as final, including the demilitarization of the Rhineland, and renounced aspirations for regaining Alsace-Lorraine. In return, the Western Allies were to admit Germany into the League of Nations and grant it a permanent seat on the Council, thus officially recognizing the country's great-power status and participation in the concert of Europe. But Chicherin achieved a partial victory, for Stresemann emasculated Article 16 at Locarno; all the participants in the treaty signed a note that would allow Germany to opt out of League sanctions and foreign troop transit rights.[76] Although the Locarno agreements produced a positive settlement in Western Europe, there was no solution to Germany's frontier disputes with Czechoslovakia and Poland. Thus the Locarno Treaty did nothing to alleviate tensions in Eastern Europe.

The Soviet government received the Locarno Treaty with an outburst of criticism and considerable apprehension. The German-Soviet Commercial Treaty, which Litvinov and Rantzau signed on 12 October, did little to appease and mollify the Soviets. They were pleased that the accord included a specific acceptance of the Soviet monopoly of foreign trade, but they also realized that a statement endorsing the Treaty of Rapallo as the basis of German-Soviet relations did not signify a neutrality pact. At the same time the two sides concluded a consular convention, and the Weimar Republic extended short-term credit for Soviet purchases in Germany in the amount of 106 million marks.[77] In essence, the Soviet government perceived Locarno as a victory for British diplomacy, which had sought to drive a wedge between Germany and the Soviet Union and thus isolate the Soviets in Europe.

On 17 October Chicherin departed from Berlin for Wiesbaden, where he intended to rest and receive medical attention. During his stay in Berlin he had arranged to travel to France after his trip to Wiesbaden, for he still hoped for an improvement in Franco-Soviet relations and wished to conduct negotiations with Briand. In an effort to express his good will toward the French, Chicherin removed Krasin as ambassador to France and replaced him with K. Ia. Rakovskii, who was a well known Francophile. The announcement of the switch came at the end of October. Krasin went to Britain as Soviet charge d'affaires, where Chicherin believed that his service to the Soviet government would be more useful.

Chicherin arrived in Paris on 30 November. Briand had gone to London for the signing of the Locarno Treaty, so Chicherin spent approximately ten days on the French Riviera until the foreign minister returned. Arriving in Paris on 11 December, Chicherin discussed Franco-Soviet affairs with Briand for about a week. Even though Chicherin had been optimistic about improving relations, the talks produced a deadlock.[78] France continued to insist that the

Soviet government honor prewar Tsarist debts and provide restitution to foreigners whose property had been nationalized after the
November Revolution. Furthermore, France was generally satisfied
with the Locarno agreements, which it ratified in March 1926.

Chicherin left Paris for Moscow on 17 December. Shortly
before his departure he signed a neutrality and nonaggression treaty
with the ambassador of Turkey who had traveled to Paris specifically for this purpose. The agreement subsequently became a model
for similar Soviet treaties with Germany, Lithuania, Afghanistan,
and Persia. The Soviet government devised the nonaggression and
neutrality agreements as a counterpoint to the Locarno Treaty. In
the accord with Turkey Moscow offered nonaggression and neutrality in exchange for arbitration, Locarno, and security.[79] Just as
significantly, the settlement with Turkey was directed against the
League of Nations. The Soviet-Turkish Treaty consisted of three
articles: Article 1 provided for neutrality if one party was the victim
of aggression by a third power; Article 2 stipulated that the contract-
ing sides agreed not to attack each other or to engage in hostile
economic, financial, and military agreements or associations
directed against the other party; and Article 3 indicated that the
accord would remain in effect for three years.[80]

The successful conclusion of the Soviet-Turkish Treaty gave a
new direction to Soviet foreign policy and enabled the Soviets to
claim a partial diplomatic victory after the defeat Locarno represented. Chicherin also wanted to sign a neutrality agreement with
Germany, based on the 1925 Treaty with Turkey, that would effectively undermine the Locarno Treaty. He recognized that it would
be virtually impossible to destroy rapprochement between Germany and the Western powers, but he intended to foster a greater
balance in German foreign policy and win back some of the ground
he had lost at Locarno. Events offered him the appropriate opportunity, for formal implementation of the Locarno Treaty was contingent upon Germany's admission into the League of Nations.
Pursuant to this end and in accordance with the Locarno protocol,
the League convened a special session of the assembly in March
1926, at which Germany was to be admitted to the council. But
when the German delegates arrived in Geneva on 7 March, they
were dismayed to discover that Brazil and Poland demanded simul-
taneous election to a permanent seat on the council. Ten days later,
on 17 March, the extraordinary session of the assembly adjourned
without resolving the dilemma, and Germany did not receive a seat

on the council. The German delegation returned home embarrassed and humiliated.[81] The question of Germany's membership in the League was postponed until September.

Chicherin, seizing the opportunity, pressed Stresemann to sign a nonaggression and neutrality pact. Chicherin had initially proposed such an agreement to the German foreign minister in December when he had stopped briefly in Berlin enroute to Moscow from Paris. At that time Stresemann had refused to consider an accord identical to the Soviet-Turkish Treaty, for it would have effectively barred Germany's entrance into the League. He was under pressure to return to an eastern orientation in Germany's foreign policy, but he was confident that Germany would soon take a seat on the council in Geneva. When his plans were suddenly disrupted in March, Chicherin pressed the advantage and demanded that Germany conclude a neutrality pact with the Soviet Union immediately. Stresemann reluctantly conceded, and the result was the German-Soviet Neutrality and Nonaggression Treaty of 24 April 1926, which he and Krestinskii signed in Berlin.

The Berlin Treaty was modeled after the Soviet-Turkish Treaty of 1925. The new agreement reaffirmed the Rapallo Treaty as the foundation of relations between the Soviet government and the Weimar Republic; in the event of an attack by a third power or a group of powers on one of the two countries, each side pledged neutrality; each party agreed not to participate in an economic or financial coalition or boycott against the other; the treaty was to remain in effect for five years; and Germany promised long-term credits to the Soviet government which two months later were settled at 300 million marks at an annual rate of interest of 9.4 percent.[82] Stresemann appended a note to the agreement that was just as significant as the treaty itself. He had to demonstrate to the Western powers that the Berlin Treaty did not conflict with the Locarno Treaty and Germany's intentions to enter the League of Nations. But he also needed to reassure the Soviets that the Neutrality and Nonaggression Treaty would ensure their security in the event of Germany's entrance into the League; in essence, he had to reaffirm that the Soviets had nothing to fear from Germany under the terms of Article 16. Stresemann repeated that the German government would oppose any anti-Soviet tendencies in the council and the issue of German sanctions against Soviet Russia under Article 16 could only arise if the Soviets were the aggressor; moreover, the Germans would determine responsibility for aggression.[83]

In late December 1925, after a short visit in Berlin on his way to Moscow from Paris, Chicherin had also stopped in Kovno for a day. On 23 December he offered the Lithuanian government a neutrality and nonaggression pact patterned after the Berlin Treaty. Negotiations began in January, and Chicherin was optimistic that they would be successful. Lithuania and the Soviet Union did not have a common frontier. Furthermore, Lithuania harbored hostility toward Poland because of the Polish occupation of Vilna; and relations with Germany were strained as a result of the Lithuanian control over Memel. In March Chicherin made a similar offer to Estonia, Latvia, and Finland, but they were not interested in a bilateral treaty with the Soviet Union. Yet the discussions between Lithuania and the Soviet Union were successful, and the two countries signed a Treaty of Neutrality and Nonaggression, similar to the Berlin Treaty, on 28 September. The Estonian and Latvian governments eventually compromised, as they decided to settle their frontier disputes with the Soviet state. Latvia signed such an agreement with the Soviet Union on 19 July and Estonia did so over a year later, on 18 August 1927. These conventions were substitutes for treaties of neutrality and nonaggression, and they served the interests of the Soviet government, for they reduced tension between the Soviets and the Baltic states.[84]

As a result of the Soviet-Turkish Treaty, the Berlin Treaty, and the Lithuanian-Soviet Treaty, Chicherin was able to record some diplomatic successes to counterbalance the Locarno Treaty. If for him the Locarno agreements primarily represented a British victory in the international arena, then he interpreted the Berlin pact as a defeat for Britain. He had not compelled Germany to turn away from rapprochement with the West, but he had labored diligently to restore some balance between East and West in German foreign policy. On the one hand he was successful, for even though Germany became a member of the League Council in September 1926, the Soviet government had no reason to fear that the Weimar Republic would participate in economic and military sanctions against it. Moreover, the Berlin Treaty reinforced the Treaty of Rapallo and the German-Soviet Economic Treaty of 1925, emphasizing neutrality, nonaggression, and nonparticipation in hostile economic, financial, and military coalitions and stressing bilateral, defensive agreements between nations rather than collective action, sanctions, and compulsory measures through the League. The security system the Soviets erected in response to Locarno was designed to prevent the economic and military domination of the Soviet Union. And Chicherin should receive much of the credit for executing an effective diplomatic counterattack after the Allied victory at Locarno.

On the other hand the Treaty of Berlin represented the culmination of the Rapallo era in Soviet foreign affairs only to a limited extent. The 1925–1926 economic and political agreements with Germany enabled the Soviet Union to draw its ally away from a complete Western orientation and thus prevent its own diplomatic isolation, but these treaties were not commensurate with the Rapallo accord. Stresemann was able to strike a balance between the Western powers and the Soviet state that was not part of the atmosphere of the early post-Rapallo period, when there was a clear eastern approach to German foreign policy. In this respect the Soviets felt much less confident and secure about German friendship and support in 1925–1926 than they had in 1922–1923. Ultimately the Soviets, particularly Chicherin, blamed Britain for their increasingly precarious position in European affairs. In general the Soviet government was inclined to believe that the British were chiefly responsible for a deterioration in German-Soviet relations. The crowning blow was the Locarno agreements.

5

Soviet Relations with Great Britain

ALTHOUGH Chicherin considered the Treaty of Rapallo and friendly relations with Germany the cornerstone of Soviet foreign affairs during the 1920s, he also stressed the significance of Soviet policy toward Great Britain. Germany indeed was important, even crucial, to Soviet leaders, but Britain loomed larger in the Soviet perspective of world affairs. Chicherin's extensive writings on Britain were representative of the ambivalent and mixed views Communist leaders held toward the capitalist West throughout the decade. His statements about Britain expressed consistency in foreign policy between the Soviet Union and Imperial Russia, for on this subject Soviet diplomatic and political goals coincided with the traditional national interests of the Russian state.

Chicherin has usually been described as a Germanophile and an Anglophobe. While he was certainly anti-capitalist and anti-imperialist, this evaluation needs further clarification and explanation. During emigration from 1904 to 1918, he became well acquainted with Western Europe, especially Britain, where he had been imprisoned for anti-war agitation and propaganda. Imprisonment increased his criticism and resentment of British government and society. Furthermore, Chicherin had served in the Tsarist Ministry of Foreign Affairs during a period of intense geopolitical competition between Britain and Imperial Russia, particularly in the Near East and Asia. His service in the Tsarist Foreign Ministry taught him to regard the British government as a formidable adversary. By attacking Britain he was defending Russian national interests, as the Tsarist government articulated and perceived them

113

in the late nineteenth and early twentieth centuries.[1] In 1907 a diplomatic understanding between the two powers, which culminated with the wartime coalition against Germany, engendered a resolution of some outstanding problems. But the Bolshevik Revolution and the expansion of British colonial holdings after World War I led to a renewal of antagonism and hostility between Britain and the Russian state, now controlled by the new Soviet government.

Ideological competition between capitalism and socialism exacerbated the geopolitical conflict between the two great powers. Chicherin was cosmopolitan and an internationalist, and his ideological convictions coincided with and reinforced his determination to defend the Soviet state against British imperialism in international affairs. He displayed a mixture of admiration, contempt, and fear for Britain. Even though he regarded Germany as the key to Soviet foreign policy, he was concerned about obtaining diplomatic recognition from and establishing trade with Britain, a consideration that remained a constant theme throughout his writings during the 1920s.[2] For Chicherin and the Bolsheviks, Britain was the greatest world power and the bastion of capitalism in the West.[3] They recognized the growing economic, military, and political strength of the United States, but geographic distances and American isolationism after World War I led them to focus their attention on Britain.

Chicherin felt that the United States was not yet ready to replace Britain as the political leader of the capitalist West. He asserted that "Britain represents today the cream of capitalist society, endowed with a vast horizon and vast perspectives."[4] He based his evaluation largely on the diversity, perseverance, and strength of British culture and political institutions, one of which was an expertise in diplomacy. His respect for British diplomatic practices and techniques was profound; he held that for centuries members of the gentry and aristocracy had faithfully and loyally served the British government, resulting in a sophisticated diplomacy raised to an art, unmatched anywhere in the world, and the envy of the other powers. In addition, Chicherin indicated that British agents operated skillfully in large numbers on all the continents, endowed with characteristics of courage, determination, initiative, intelligence, patriotism, and resourcefulness that would ensure success in the field.[5] Respect now turned to apprehension, since Chicherin believed that with a veritable army of dedicated and well-informed agents around the world, Britain was an especially dangerous adversary. In his view the United States could not hope to compete with Britain for leadership of the West until it, too, developed the tradition of expert diplomacy on the world stage. The industrial and military power of the United States was obvious, but Chicherin felt it would play only a limited role in world events as long as its diplomatic and political leaders were constrained by provincialism, a lack of appreciation for history, and insufficient knowledge about other continents.[6]

As a polemicist, Chicherin delivered some of his most scathing criticism against the British Empire, for among the Bolsheviks it was generally regarded as the most dangerous foe of the Soviet state. He both envied and feared the network of British naval bases around the world that had been established to protect Britain's economic and political interests.[7] Just as British imperial designs had clashed with Russian colonial ambitions in the prerevolutionary era, so, too, in the Soviet period Chicherin regarded Britain as the principal obstacle to the spread of socialist revolution abroad, especially in Asia and the Near East.[8] And although he realized that World War I had brought about a gradual but irreversible shift in the center of power from Britain to the United States and impatiently anticipated the break up and disintegration of the British Empire, he nevertheless warned that the British government posed a serious threat to Bolshevism.

Yet in spite of Chicherin's insistence that Britain was the leader of the capitalist West in opposition to the Soviet Republic, he was sincerely interested in obtaining de jure recognition from the British government. Even though he sometimes scoffed at official recognition and referred to it as merely a "technicality," it was apparent that he wanted British de jure recognition of the Soviet government. He hoped it would give the Soviets greater respectability abroad and decrease, even if only slightly, the possibility of renewed military action against Bolshevism. Furthermore, Chicherin believed that official recognition would increase the prospects for trade with and long-term credits from Britain. But he consistently demanded that relations must operate to the mutual advantage of both countries— that the Bolsheviks would not allow the British to exploit the Soviet state and milk it of its natural resources without receiving economic and financial benefits in return.[9] In this respect his views toward Britain were highly ambivalent. Although he recognized the value of stable relations with Britain, he was also extremely wary of such relations, anxious that they might lead to British economic and political domination of the Soviets.

Chicherin sometimes misconstrued relations between Britain and France in Europe after World War I, hoping for competition between the Western Allies where it did not exist. He also maintained that France followed Britain's lead in Asia and the Near East, contending the French traded their support of British policy in the East for Britain's agreement to guarantee French security against Germany.[10] He often called for France to pursue a foreign policy independent of Britain in both Europe and the East, but his writings revealed only a tentative awareness that the French were neither capable of nor willing to reject British leadership.

Chicherin believed that only the Soviet Republic could present a serious obstacle to British imperial expansion in the world. But he did not want to engage in conflict with Britain, recognizing that the Soviet government needed a long period of peace to restore the economy and complete social reforms. His distrust of the British Empire reinforced his conviction that it posed a threat to the Soviet state for the foreseeable future.

Chicherin's ambivalent views toward Britain can be better understood by examining his relations with Lloyd George, British prime minister from December 1916 to October 1922. Lloyd George personified the British Empire for Chicherin, and Georgii Vasil'evich's appreciation of the diplomatic and political skills of the British prime minister was mixed with an aversion toward and rejection of the economic and social system he represented. Chicherin understood that Lloyd George was in a difficult position at the end of World War I. Britain faced a recession and rising unemployment, and the war had disrupted its overseas markets. Lloyd George's coalition government had won an overwhelming victory in the election of December 1918, but the prime minister's popularity was slipping by the beginning of the new decade.

In foreign affairs Lloyd George had to contend with a French government determined to punish Germany for World War I. The Western Allies had emerged triumphant in the conflict, but their resources were spent and their populations exhausted and disillusioned. Furthermore, on 2 July 1918 Allied intervention in the Russian Civil War and a blockade of the Soviet state had not produced their desired result, for the Bolsheviks remained in power. At a meeting of the Supreme Allied War Council in Paris on 14 January 1920, Lloyd George proposed to terminate the blockade and resume trade with the All-Russian Union of Consumer and Cooperative Societies (Tsentrosoiuz), a nonpolitical commercial organization.

His plan was an indication that the British had abandoned any serious hopes of overthrowing the Soviet government militarily. The council approved the proposal two days later. But British Conservatives, particularly the two strongly anti-Bolshevik members of the cabinet, Curzon and Churchill, pressed Lloyd George not to seek a diplomatic agreement with the Soviet government. Yet the prospect of lucrative commercial contracts for British manufacturers induced the prime minister to compromise and at least attempt to reach an economic settlement with the Soviets.

Chicherin praised Lloyd George for taking the initiative in terminating Allied intervention in the Russian Civil War. But Chicherin questioned Lloyd George's motives, speculating that the British government's desire for peace and a willingness to negotiate outstanding problems with the Soviet Republic were merely a facade designed to mask Britain's efforts to undermine Bolshevism. According to Chicherin, Britain's support for Poland in the Polish-Soviet War of 1920, British resolve to form a *cordon sanitaire* against the Soviet state in Eastern Europe from the Baltic Sea to the Black Sea, and the expansion of British influence in Asia and the Near East provided a clear indication of British intentions and served to warn the Soviets they should not be duped or lulled into complacency by proclamations of peace.[11]

Chicherin portrayed Lloyd George as an especially difficult adversary because of his political skills. Having failed to overthrow the Soviet government militarily, Lloyd George decided to try a different approach; he hoped "to tame" the Soviets by reaching a commercial and economic agreement with them. The peaceful penetration of British investment capital into Soviet Russia and extensive trade between the two countries would eventually transform Soviet society, a tactic which became even more popular with Lloyd George after the introduction of NEP in 1921. Chicherin repeatedly warned that Lloyd George intended to take a calculated risk—to gamble that NEP would lead to the reestablishment of capitalism and bourgeois democracy in Russia before the Soviet government could consolidate its position and develop socialism on a firm foundation. According to Chicherin, British peace initiatives and economic proposals were conceived to realize the same goal as military intervention—the destruction of Bolshevism. In Chicherin's view Lloyd George held it was wiser to offer accommodation and compromise to dangerous enemies, thus ingeniously disarming them with such proposals, than to provoke a conflict and settle political differences militarily.[12]

Even before the termination of the Allied blockade of Soviet Russia Lloyd George took some cautious steps to reduce hostilities between London and Moscow. In May 1919 the British government sent a radio message to the Soviets proposing negotiations for an exchange of prisoners of war. The Soviets accepted the British offer on 10 June, and Litvinov and James O'Grady, a Labor M.P., met in Copenhagen to begin discussions of this issue on 25 November. The Soviets attached a great deal of importance to Litvinov's mission; in the absence of diplomatic relations with the West, he was virtually the only official representative of the Soviet government abroad, and he intended to extend his stay in Copenhagen as long as possible.[13] The British had not anticipated lengthy deliberations, but Litvinov remained in Copenhagen for nine months.

On 12 February 1920 Litvinov and O'Grady signed an Anglo-Soviet agreement on the exchange of prisoners of war. The actual transfer of prisoners, however, did not begin until 5 November, a delay that held up negotiations on a commercial accord between the two governments. The Soviets regarded the prisoners-of-war agreement as a diplomatic victory, since it removed a significant impediment to the establishment of normal relations between Britain and the Soviet Republic.[14] Moreover, the settlement served as a model for future agreements between the Soviet state and other Western countries regarding prisoners of war.

During the deliberations on the exchange of prisoners of war the British and Soviets were also involved in negotiations on a trade treaty. The political climate had changed considerably since Lloyd George's initial proposal to the Supreme Allied War Council in January 1920. The Soviet leadership, on learning of his offer, immediately ordered the communist takeover of Tsentrosoiuz and appointed a delegation including Krasin and Litvinov to travel to London to conduct trade talks with the British. But the British government refused to grant Litvinov a visa, since he had been expelled from Britain in 1918; thus the discussions began not in London but in Copenhagen.[15] Finally, however, Lenin agreed to dispatch the Soviet Trade Delegation to London without Litvinov. To mollify the British government, the head of the mission Krasin and his colleagues were co-opted on the board of Tsentrosoiuz, thus preserving the fiction that the British were carrying on negotiations with a non-political commercial organization "representing the Russian people" instead of with official agents of the Soviet Republic.[16] The Soviet Trade Delegation arrived in London on 26 May 1920, and the talks that became an Anglo-Soviet political confrontation commenced on 31 May.

While the Soviet Trade Mission was in London, Tsentrosoiuz created Arkos (*Vserossiiskoe kooperativnoe aktsionernoe obshchestvo*), a Soviet Trading Company operating on the basis of British laws. During the first six months of its existence Arkos purchased approximately 3 million pounds sterling of British products for the Soviet government. Yet in spite of Arkos's success, talks between the British government and the Soviet Trade Delegation proceeded slowly. They were divided into three phases—from 31 May to 7 July 1920; from 8 July to 11 September 1920; and from 12 September 1920 to 16 March 1921—of which the first produced the most fruitful results. The main issues separating the two sides—the cessation of hostile propaganda and subversion and Soviet payment of Russia's foreign debts—were discussed in a series of meetings between Krasin and Lloyd George held on 31 May, 7 June, 16 June, and 29 June.[17] These talks created a framework for an Anglo-Soviet accord.

On 30 June Krasin received a note from Lloyd George enumerating the following four conditions that had to be fulfilled before trade could begin: a resolution prohibiting interference in the internal affairs of the other side, including a statement against hostile propaganda; the immediate exchange of all remaining prisoners of war; the recognition by the Soviet government that it must compensate British citizens for goods or services for which they had not been paid, and a call for a formal peace conference to settle the issue of claims and debts between the British government and previous Russian governments; and finally, the establishment of trade facilities between the two countries. Lloyd George explained to Krasin that the British government wanted a Soviet response to the note within a week. On 2 July Krasin departed for Moscow to receive further instructions from the leaders of his government. The Politburo authorized Chicherin to dispatch a telegram to Foreign Secretary Curzon on 7 July in which the Soviet government accepted "the principles" of the British note of 30 June as the basis of an agreement between the two states.[18] Chicherin added that negotiations were to resume immediately, but the Polish-Soviet War interrupted their progress.

When Krasin returned to Moscow on 5 July, the Soviet government decided to make some personnel changes in the Trade Delegation. Kamenev proposed that he should replace Krasin as head of the mission; although Lenin had serious reservations about this idea, he reluctantly consented to nominate Kamenev as head of the Commercial Delegation and Krasin as his deputy. Kamenev and Krasin reached London on 1 August, and Kamenev's anti-capitalist propaganda quickly antagonized the anti-Communists in Parliament.[19] Fortunately for the Soviets, Kamenev departed for Moscow on 11 September, leaving Krasin once more in charge of the Trade Delegation, which mollified the ire of the British Conservatives.

The British government presented Krasin with a draft agreement on 29 November. He and Sir Robert Horne, chancellor of the exchequer, amended this initial version several times until Krasin left for Moscow for consultations with his government on 8 January. During Krasin's absence from London the Soviets increased the pressure on the British by placing an order for more than 600 locomotives valued at 72 million gold rubles with German manufacturers on 28 February.[20] Consequently, British industrialists demanded a speedy conclusion to the Anglo-Soviet commercial negotiations. On 5 March Krasin returned to London with a new draft of the trade accord rewritten in favor of the Soviets—the provision against propaganda was seriously weakened and the demand for Soviet recognition of Tsarist debts completely eliminated.[21] Eleven days later on 16 March Horne and Krasin signed the Anglo-Soviet Trade Agreement. Curzon, the foreign secretary, should logically have affixed his signature to the document for the British, but his aversion to the Soviet government was so pronounced that he refused to participate in the signing ceremony.[22] The treaty called for an exchange of representatives who would not have ambassadorial status. Krasin remained in London as head of the Soviet Trade Delegation, and Robert M. Hodgson directed Britain's Commercial Mission in Moscow.

The Trade Agreement fell short of what the Soviets ultimately wanted—de jure recognition—but Lloyd George, responding to questions in the House of Commons on 23 March, acknowledged that it meant British de facto recognition of the Soviet Republic.[23] Thus, the Commercial Treaty was a triumph for Soviet diplomacy. More importantly, following shortly after Lenin had announced to the Tenth Congress of the party the introduction of a tax in kind on agricultural produce that functioned as the basis of NEP, the Trade Agreement represented a watershed in Soviet foreign policy.[24] It marked the beginning of Soviet realization that they would have to undertake serious efforts to establish normal, stable relations with the capitalist West, even if they had to compromise revolutionary principles to do so. The Commercial Treaty signified the growing involvement of the Soviet government in traditional international relations and gave the Communist party confidence in diplomacy. The Soviets previously assumed that the November Revolution had permanently destroyed nineteenth-century diplomatic relations, but the Trade Agreement was an indication of their increasing acceptance of at least some continuity in foreign affairs between Imperial Russia and the Soviet Republic.

Even though the Commercial Agreement meant British de facto recognition of and the establishment of normal economic relations with Soviet Russia, considerable political tension between the two countries continued to exist. Their competition in part was ideological—a struggle between the leading capitalist state and the young socialist republic. Just as importantly, Britain and Soviet Russia represented conflicting geopolitical and national interests. The Communists, especially Chicherin, looked to the East—Asia and the Near East—for opportunities to spread socialist revolution. But everywhere they turned they encountered opposition from the British Empire. The ideological competition between capitalism and socialism overlapped with British and Soviet national aspirations, which rendered their relations even more complicated. The Soviets were determined to undermine British imperial rule in the East, and Britain resolved to prevent the Communist party from conducting anti-capitalist propaganda and subverting British power in the area.

The role of Turkey in this dramatic competition between Britain and the Soviet Republic was crucial. After the Paris Peace Conference the Allies signed the Treaty of Sevres with Turkey in August 1920. The treaty ratified the liberation of the Arab states, which actually became mandates of Britain and France. But when the victorious powers attempted to carve up Asia Minor among themselves, Turkish nationalists resisted. The Turks were quite conscious of their precarious international position between East and West, and they were just as apprehensive of their large neighbor to the north as of the Western Allies. Furthermore, a postwar struggle between the Greeks and the Turks created a dilemma for Lloyd George's government. He did not want to antagonize Turkey, but he was under pressure to support the Greeks because of considerable popular sympathy for Greece among the British. In the end his pro-Greek policies put Britain in a difficult position when the conflict turned against Athens, and Lloyd George found himself in an embarrassing confrontation with the Ankara government. In the autumn of 1922 Curzon attempted to settle the Greco-Turkish struggle by writing a new treaty to replace the Treaty of Sevres—a dead letter from the moment of its signature—and reassert British power in the Near East by calling for an international peace conference to deal with the "Turkish question" in Lausanne, Switzerland.

Curzon initially did not intend to invite Soviet Russia to send a delegation to the conference since it was not a belligerent. But the Soviets and the Turks demanded that the Soviet Republic be represented. The problem of the future control of the Straits, providing ingress to and egress from the Black Sea, was a legitimate issue on which to base a demand for an invitation. Curzon grudgingly consented to admit a Soviet delegation to Lausanne to participate in discussions on the administration of the Straits, and the governments of Britain, France, and Italy issued an invitation to the Soviet government on 27 October.[25] Even though the Soviets were prohibited from joining negotiations on a new treaty with Turkey, Chicherin regarded the invitation to take part in talks on the Straits as a partial diplomatic victory for his government. Yet he also continued to insist on Soviet participation in the conference on an equal basis with the other nations.

The first session of the Lausanne Conference occurred from 22 November 1922 to 4 February 1923. Lenin was actively involved in Soviet preparations for the conference, his last contribution to foreign policy before illness completely incapacitated him. Chicherin had a final interview with him in the autumn of 1922. The party selected Chicherin to lead the Soviet delegation to Lausanne. The conference witnessed one of the most dramatic and engaging diplomatic confrontations of the interwar period, for Curzon, head of the British delegation, was the only diplomat in Europe capable of matching skills with Chicherin. Lord Curzon, George Nathaniel Marquess Curzon of Kedleston, a member of the cabinet since 1915, a former viceroy of India, and foreign secretary since 1919, was quintessentially aristocratic and above all concerned about the expansion and power of the British Empire. Although he did not go to Lausanne to save capitalism from socialism but rather to champion British national interests in the Near East, he was profoundly opposed to Bolshevism. The clash between Chicherin and Curzon at Lausanne symbolized the tension between the British Empire and Imperial Russia that existed at the turn of the century, and the aristocratic breeding and manners and conflicting ideology of the two principal participants reinforced this competition.

Chicherin, who arrived in Lausanne after the conference had already begun, addressed the issue of the Straits on 4 December. He argued that the Bosphorus and Dardanelles should be open in peace and war to all commercial vessels and closed to the warships of all nations except Turkey and that the Turks should be allowed to fortify the Straits against foreign aggression. Curzon insisted on free entry for all merchants and warships in peace and to all with the exception of belligerent ships in war, and he wanted the Straits demilitarized.

During the late nineteenth century the British, trying to keep the Russian fleet from entering the Mediterranean Sea from the Black Sea, proposed strict administration of the Straits and were willing to grant Turkey considerable control over the Bosphorus and Dardanelles. In contrast, the Russians attempted to reduce Turkish power over the Straits and wanted to have free access for their warships between the Black Sea and the Mediterranean Sea. But in the postwar era the two nations reversed their previous positions. The Soviet Black Sea fleet was incapable of sailing far from its home waters, so the British did not fear Soviet penetration into the Mediterranean Sea. The Soviets, however, vividly recalled the ease with with the Allies had supplied the Whites during the Russian Civil War by sailing unchallenged through the Straits, an occurrence which the Soviet government did not want to see repeated in the event of renewed foreign intervention. Chicherin regarded this as a serious strategic problem for the Soviet state. He acknowledged that a nation with a powerful navy would understandably demand the opening of the Straits, but he pointed out the danger of such a policy for a country without a strong naval force, indicating the Soviets would feel threatened by the exposure of their southern frontier if the Lausanne Conference accepted Curzon's proposal.[26]

At the Lausanne Conference Chicherin functioned as a defender of traditional Russian geopolitical interests.[27] He also used ideology to buttress his arguments. In his view Turkish resistance to

Britain was an example of the impact of the Bolshevik Revolution on the colonial and subject peoples of Asia and the Near East, for they looked to the Soviet state for support to rise up against British imperial power and establish their own national sovereignty. Furthermore, he claimed that the British were especially concerned about the Turkish question because of the penetration of American investment capital into Turkey, which meant that the British were facing mounting commercial and economic competition from Americans in the Near East. It seemed to him that Curzon hoped to consolidate and reinforce British supremacy in the Arab world.[28] Therefore for Chicherin the Lausanne Conference was the first "diplomatic skirmish" between the East, seeking independent economic and political development on the Soviet socialist model, and the capitalist West, striving to maintain imperial control over oppressed peoples.[29]

Chicherin emphasized the role of the Soviet Republic in Turkey's ability and willingness to stand up to the Western powers. According to him, a victory for the Turks was essentially a triumph for the Soviets, as it marked a further step in the process of the disintegration of the British Empire.[30] He was also aware that his statements and writing about the Lausanne Conference would have a considerable influence in the East outside of Turkey. Thus he used the conference as a forum by which he could bring his message of socialist revolution and national liberation to the world, particularly to the peoples of Asia and the Near East. Once again he proved to be an excellent polemicist, but his strong support for Turkey's position was an embarrassment for the Turks. They were treading their way carefully between the Western powers and the Soviet state, and they had no desire to antagonize completely the former or to come under the domination of the latter.

Chicherin and Curzon had a personal meeting on 13 December, which did little to ease the tension between the two antagonists and failed to result in a settlement of outstanding problems. Their confrontation dominated the proceedings. According to Ernest Hemingway, who reported about the conference for the Western press:

> It was this daily, bitter struggle between the British Empire and the future Russian empire with Curzon, a tall, cold, icicle of a man holding the whip hand with the British fleet, and Chitcherin fighting, fighting, with arguments, historical instances, facts, statistics

and impassioned pleas and finally, seeing it was hopeless, simply
talking for history, registering his objections for future generations
to read, that made the Lausanne conference so interesting.[31]

In addition to the issue of the Straits, Chicherin and Curzon disagreed on the disposition of Mosul, technically disputed between
Turkey and Britain's protégé, Iraq. Chicherin supported the Turks,
arguing that the transfer of the oil-rich Mosul to Iraq would effectively mean granting it to Britain and also serve to cut off Turkish
trade routes to Persia.[32] On this point Curzon was victorious, for the
conference agreed to refer the dispute to the League of Nations,
which, influenced by the British, allocated Mosul to Iraq in 1926.

The Lausanne Conference approved a draft convention on the
Straits on 1 February 1923. As Chicherin himself admitted, it was
essentially a victory for the British. The convention included the
provision that no single state could dispatch to the Black Sea a naval
force larger than the largest navy of any one Black Sea nation.[33] On 4
February, at the end of the first session of the conference, Chicherin
left Lausanne for Moscow. He did not attend the second session,
which ran from 24 April to 24 July, since the issue of the Straits had
been decided during the first session. The Straits Convention was
eventually signed with the peace treaty in Lausanne on 24 July.

The Soviets refused to return to Lausanne to sign the Straits
Convention; instead, they signed the document in Istanbul but
failed to ratify it. Moscow became embroiled in a diplomatic dispute with Switzerland over the assassination of Vorovskii, Soviet
trade representative in Rome since March 1921 and a member of
the Soviet delegation to the Lausanne Conference, on 10 May 1923.
His assassin was Maurice Conradi, a Russian-born Swiss, who was
vehemently anti-Bolshevik. Chicherin had been Conradi's first tar-
get, but when Georgii Vasil'evich did not attend the second session
of the conference, Conradi decided to assassinate Vorovskii.
Conradi's trial quickly developed into a confrontation between the
Communists and the White émigrés. His acquital resulted in a diplomatic rift between the Soviet Union and Switzerland, which
became part of the reason for Soviet opposition to the League of
Nations. For Chicherin the assassination of Vorovskii was a personal loss, for the two men were friends, and Vorovskii was one of
the Soviet government's best diplomats.

The Lausanne Conference represented a diplomatic setback for
the Soviet government and for Chicherin personally. He had been

unable to prevent Curzon from asserting British supremacy in the Near East, and the Straits Convention posed a serious threat to Soviet strategic interests in the Black Sea. Even though Chicherin recognized the British victory, he refused to accept the Straits Convention as a permanent settlement, insisting that with the growth of Soviet naval power his government would seek to rescind it as soon as possible.[34] Yet in spite of Chicherin's diplomatic defeat at the conference, he was able to use it effectively to present the Soviet position on international affairs and socialist revolution to countries of the East. He successfully transformed the conference into a public forum in which he registered Soviet objections to British imperial rule and support for movements of national liberation in Asia and the Near East.

In the spring of 1923 relations between Britain and the Soviet Union, already strained by the Lausanne Conference, were exacerbated even more. The occasion was the so-called Curzon ultimatum, expressed in a note Hodgson delivered to Narkomindel on 8 May. Curzon charged the Soviet government with a long list of violations of the 1921 Commercial Treaty, including the mistreatment of British citizens and the seizure of British fighting boats off the Soviet coast; reports of continued Soviet agitation and propaganda against the British Empire in Asia, especially in India, and the Near East particularly upset him. He gave the Soviets ten days to respond and threatened to abrogate the agreement if they did not comply with his demands and terminate anti-British activities in the East. The Soviet government was genuinely alarmed at the possibility of a complete break in relations, and Narkomindel dispatched a note proposing negotiations and denying anti-British agitation and propaganda in the East. For the Soviets, Curzon's note raised the specter of renewed foreign intervention. They associated his "ultimatum" with Vorovskii's assassination and claimed that the British were leading a conspiracy of capitalist powers against the Soviet state.[35] Although the Soviet government was able to mollify the British and therefore avoid a diplomatic rupture, relations remained tense throughout the summer and autumn.

Chicherin attributed the deterioration in relations between Britain and the Soviet Union in part to Lloyd George's defeat in the British election of 15 November 1922. Conservatives succeeded Lloyd George as prime minister: first, A. Bonar Law, who was in office until May 1923 when it was discovered that he had incurable throat cancer, and second, Stanley Baldwin, who became prime

minister on 21 May. But in the election of 6 December no single
party emerged with a majority; moreover, the Conservative government was defeated in the House of Commons by seventy-two votes
on 21 January 1924. On the next day J. Ramsay MacDonald, the
leader of the Labor party, became prime minister. And on 1 February Britain extended de jure recognition to the Soviet government.
At the same time MacDonald suggested that the two governments
establish an Anglo-Soviet commission to examine outstanding economic and financial problems—the validity of existing treaties; the
chronic dilemma of claims of the citizens and governments of each
nation against the other; and agitation, propaganda, and subversion
of one government against the other. Finally, the prime minister
explained to Narkomindel that he preferred to exchange representatives at the charge d'affaires rather than the ambassadorial level.
Chicherin expressed his disappointment, but he realized that the
Labor party did not have a solid majority and that the time was not
yet propitious for the establishment of relations at the ambassadorial level.[36]

Rakovskii acknowledged Soviet approval of British recognition
on 8 February; he also indicated Moscow's willingness to negotiate
economic and financial issues with the hope of reaching political
rapprochement with Britain. The British action led to the extension
of de jure recognition by other countries in 1924. On 7 February the
Italian government of Benito Mussolini officially recognized the
Soviet Republic, and the two governments agreed to exchange
ambassadors. In addition, Austria, China, Denmark, France,
Greece, Mexico, Norway, and Sweden also granted de jure recognition to the Soviet government. Japan reached agreement with the
Soviet Union early in 1925.

Chicherin was genuinely pleased by the rush to recognize the
Soviet Union officially in 1924–1925. De jure recognition
increased the prestige of Narkomindel within the Soviet government and helped to compensate for Chicherin's diplomatic defeat at
the Lausanne Conference. The recognitions were personally reward-
ing for him as well; his reputation and stature in the party rose
appreciably during this period. It was no coincidence that the party
selected him for membership on the Central Committee in 1924
and 1925.

Rakovskii, the first Soviet charge d'affaires to Britain, and
MacDonald conducted extensive negotiations throughout the
spring and summer of 1924. As usual, the question of Russian state

debts to foreign governments and nationals posed a sticky problem. By the late summer the two men were able to reach an acceptable compromise on economic and financial issues. A new Anglo-Soviet Commercial Treaty was signed on 10 August. But the Labor government faced a difficult situation. It needed to obtain ratification of the agreement from a House of Commons in which it did not have a majority.

Chicherin wrote extensively about the Labor government and the possibility of a new economic agreement that might engender political rapprochement between Britain and the Soviet Union. He waxed eloquently on the economic and political benefits that each country would derive from a binding settlement of outstanding problems, tantalizing the British with the prospect of world peace and stable international relations. But it was apparent that he had little genuine hope of realizing these ambitions. MacDonald's acquisition of power did not change Chicherin's views of the British Empire or dispel his distrust of Britain's foreign policy toward the Soviet Union; thus even with the Labor party in power, Chicherin continued to perceive the British as the principal opponents of the Soviets around the world.[37]

Chicherin believed that the Labor government, despite professions in favor of accommodation with the Soviet Union, used rhetoric as a facade to mask its real intentions. In his view Labor was under considerable pressure from both the Conservatives and the Liberals not to achieve political rapprochement with the Soviets. He was especially critical of the Liberals, arguing that they were the real power behind MacDonald and had no interest in ratifying the new economic treaty or in achieving a political accord with the Soviet Union.[38] Furthermore, Chicherin insisted that MacDonald himself did not want to reach agreement with the Soviet government. According to Chicherin the economic treaty signed by MacDonald and Rakovskii was vaguely written and did not represent a firm and binding settlement. Chicherin charged that MacDonald was constantly seeking to revise the agreement to undermine it so that Parliament would not ratify it.[39]

For Chicherin, MacDonald's position on rapprochement with the Soviet Union became clear in discussions on the crucial issues of debts and credits. Chicherin denounced the British government for continually demanding the Soviets first pay the Russian state debts and restitute the property of foreign nationals in order to establish an atmosphere of trust between the two countries, after which London would extend credits to Moscow. He repeated the Soviet policy on the question of debts: the Soviet government would honor the Tsarist debts only on condition of Britain's consent jointly to grant extensive credits at a favorable rate of interest.[40] The Soviets adamantly refused to discuss the debts without parallel negotiations on credits. Labor's acquisition of power did not move the Soviets from their position on this issue.

Chicherin made some interesting comparisons between MacDonald and William E. Gladstone, the great nineteenth-century Liberal prime minister. According to Chicherin, during the 1880s Gladstone and the Liberals campaigned against an aggressive foreign policy and extensive colonial expansion; in contrast, the Conservatives were the champions of imperial conquest and pursued an ambitious foreign policy to extend British influence throughout the world. In Chicherin's view the British Empire grew considerably under Gladstone, in spite of the prime minister's efforts to moderate British imperial appetites. Gladstone labored under the pressure of economic and political conditions outside of his control. And just as commercial and financial circles had compelled Gladstone's Liberals to expand British overseas markets and military and political power to protect these interests, so, too, MacDonald and the Labor party would be unable to resist demands for the reassertion of British supremacy in the East.[41] Actually, Chicherin noted little change in British foreign policy—essentially aggressive, imperialist, militant, and directed against the Soviet Union—since MacDonald became prime minister.[42]

Finally, Chicherin's criticism of the Labor government was similar to his attacks on Social Democracy in Western Europe before the November Revolution. His profound distrust of the Labor government to a considerable extent stemmed from his antipathy toward Western Social Democratic parties during his years in emigration. He accused MacDonald's cabinet of leading a workers' aristocracy which, while giving lip service to socialism, was actually making common cause with the Liberals and the propertied classes in Britain. Chicherin continued to rebuke Western European Socialists for insufficient devotion to socialism, and he warned the Soviets against accepting the Labor party's declarations in favor of compromise with and conciliation toward the Soviet government.[43] Thus although he publicly advocated rapprochement with Britain, it was apparent from his speeches and writings that he was not sanguine about such a development.

The Labor party was in power until 9 October when Parliament was dissolved, and MacDonald became involved in a highly controversial election campaign. A day later, 10 October, British intelligence, without MacDonald's knowledge, acquired a document known as the "Zinov'ev letter." The Foreign Office published it on 25 October, and the letter added to the growing "Red Scare" in Britain. Zinov'ev, the head of Comintern, had allegedly written a letter to the British Communist Party in which he strongly supported seditious activities to embarrass and undermine the Labor government.[44] The publication of the letter helped cause MacDonald's defeat in the election of 29 October, for Labor was denounced as an accomplice of the Communists. The Conservatives emerged triumphant; Baldwin became prime minister, and Austen Chamberlain was made foreign secretary. After the election a great debate arose regarding the authenticity of the document. In the end the intelligence community concluded that the letter was a fake.[45]

The Conservatives were in power in Britain from 1924 to 1929, and Chicherin believed that to some extent Soviet foreign policy was easier to formulate when they controlled the government, for the Conservatives did not attempt to mask their antipathy to the Soviets with calls for compromise and conciliation. He was especially critical of Chamberlain, claiming the foreign secretary was not interested in a political agreement with the Soviet state and predicting a Commons dominated by the Conservatives would not ratify the MacDonald-Rakovskii Commercial Agreement.[46] Chicherin's apprehensions proved justified, as Chamberlain effectively thwarted any progress toward Anglo-Soviet rapprochement. On 21 November Chamberlain informed Chicherin that the new Anglo-Soviet Economic Treaty would not be ratified. The Soviet government expressed its regret over this action but also indicated that it was not surprised by the decision.

In 1924–1925 Chicherin increasingly used the term common or united front to describe British foreign policy toward the Soviet Union. In his view Chamberlain was the principal architect of this policy, in effect similar to yet different from Allied intervention at the beginning of the twenties. Chicherin's understanding of united front—a coalition of capitalist states led by Britain against the Soviet Union—was partly a reaction to the negotiations culminating with the Locarno Treaty, but the terminology also cogently expressed his perception of the ultimate goal of British foreign relations. Although his writings on this topic were contradictory, and even though he still warned about the possibility of renewed military aggression from the West, he made a distinction between intervention during the Russian Civil War and British efforts to realize a common front against the Soviet state in 1924–1925.[47]

The earlier period had been dominated by an attempt to overthrow, by supporting the White counterrevolutionaries, the Soviet government militarily. But by the middle of the decade the Soviets were in a much stronger position, largely through the consolidation of centralized government and economic reconstruction. Chicherin was clearly proud of Soviet achievements and boasted the Western powers would no longer be able to invade Soviet territory with impunity, for the military and political strength of the Soviet government had been increased substantially since the Civil War. To surmount this obstacle the Western nations had developed more subtle techniques by which to subvert the Soviet Union. According to Chicherin, the British Conservatives were responsible for organizing an economic and financial united front against the Soviet government similar to the Allied blockade from 1918 to 1920.[48] They worked to undermine the Soviet monopoly of foreign trade and hoped to achieve the economic ruin of the country. In 1924–1925, although Chicherin indicated that the Soviets did not face the same grave military threat as in the immediate postrevolutionary period, nevertheless they confronted an adversary equally dangerous, insidious, and uncompromising. And the final goal, the destruction of the Soviet state, remained unchanged.

It was Chicherin's view that just as the British had supported the Whites against the Reds during the Russian Civil War, the former were now using the states of Eastern Europe against the Soviet Union. He claimed that Chamberlain's objective was to create a vast *cordon sanitaire* stretching continuously from the Baltic Sea to the Black Sea to isolate the Soviet government diplomatically and economically and to prevent the spread of socialism abroad.[49] The Baltic states were particularly significant in this scenario. Chicherin believed they were to function as Britain's base of operations; British control over them was crucial to the erection and maintenance of the *cordon sanitaire*.[50] He repeatedly warned the Baltic states that functioning as the vanguard of an anti-Soviet coalition, they would not be able to preserve their independence; they were merely pawns

of the Western powers. The Soviet government would not indefi-
nitely tolerate manifestations of undisguised hostility on its western
border. Chicherin urged the Baltic states to cultivate friendly relations with the Soviet Union, arguing that Britain was not concerned
about their interests and would only seek to exploit them to maintain its empire. As he put it, the British regarded Estonia as the
"advance post" in the defense of India.[51]

Chicherin issued a similar reprimand and warning to Poland.
He pointed out that the international situation had changed dra-
matically since the Polish-Soviet War of 1920, largely because the
Soviets were no longer as vulnerable militarily. He also asserted that
Curzon had not stopped the Red Army in its march toward Warsaw
in August 1920, for the Poles themselves had successfully driven the
Soviets back from the city; thus Poland should not operate under the
illusion that Britain could guarantee its defense. As Chicherin
described the situation, the Polish government should not allow the
British to dominate Eastern Europe and must avoid participation in
a common front against the Soviet Union.[52]

Chicherin maintained an unrelenting criticism of Chamberlain
until the latter left office in 1929. Parliament's refusal to ratify the
Anglo-Soviet Treaty of 1925 was a disappointment to Chicherin, for
it meant the failure of his efforts to achieve rapprochement with
Britain. The British action reinforced his attitude that Britain was
the leader of the opposition to the Soviet state. Even though he was
sharply critical of the Conservatives, at least for him their behavior
was predictable. Chicherin experienced considerably more difficulty in dealing with the Labor party, given his disdain for Social
Democracy in Western Europe and his own fanatical devotion to
socialist revolution.

Furthermore, Chicherin's ambivalent attitude toward Britain
was symbolic of Soviet perceptions of the country throughout the
1920s. Germany was the cornerstone of Soviet foreign policy, but
the Communists were principally concerned about their relations
with Britain. They eagerly anticipated the disintegration of the British Empire, yet they were compelled to defend traditional Russian
geopolitical interests against British competition. Ideology overlapped with national aspirations, which led to an intensification of
Anglo-Soviet antagonism in Asia and the Near East.

The Soviets also wanted to trade with Britain and hoped that de
jure recognition might reduce the possibility of British aggression
against the Soviet Union. But the Soviet government—and

Chicherin certainly expressed this view—was extremely wary of conducting normal relations with the British. The Soviets could not forget that Britain had taken the lead in support of the Whites during the Russian Civil War. And although the Allied effort to overthrow the Soviet government militarily had failed, the Communists were convinced that the British had not abandoned that goal and were improvising strategy and tactics to meet changing circumstances. Therefore Chicherin's respect for British diplomacy bordered on anxiety and even fear, for he recognized that the vast British Empire to a great extent was the product of Britain's diplomatic successes during the nineteenth century.

Chicherin was not always victorious in his diplomatic confrontations and skirmishes with the British Foreign Office. The Lausanne Conference was one of the best examples of his diplomatic defeat. But his understanding of traditional Russian national interests coupled with his commitment to socialist revolution presented a formidable challenge to the British Empire. And he registered a number of notable successes against the British, especially in Asia and the Near East.

6

Comintern and Narkomindel and Soviet Relations with the Far East, Central Asia, and the Near East

CHICHERIN'S views of Soviet relations with countries of Asia and the Near East constitute one of the most interesting and important components of Soviet foreign affairs during the 1920s. Thoroughly European by background, heritage, and education, he, like the other Bolsheviks, eagerly anticipated the spread of socialism from Soviet Russia to Western Europe after the November Revolution. But he also firmly believed in the world revolutionary movement and possibly more than any other member of the party stressed the impact the Bolshevik Revolution could have on Asia and the Near East. Chicherin correctly foresaw that competition between capitalism and socialism would occur primarily outside of Europe in the modernizing of states of Asia and the Near East, a perspective the Bolshevik leaders only gradually came to share after the failure of socialist revolution in Europe.

Chicherin believed that World War I had irrevocably changed the course of European and world affairs. Interpreting the war as an imperialist conflict, he held that it exacerbated the competition for markets among the great powers of Europe, thus increasing their efforts to secure colonies abroad. Yet for him the war also intensified the internal contradictions and disintegration of capitalism, which provided the colonies with an opportunity to fight for their economic and political independence.[1] According to Chicherin, World War I polarized international relations between East and West and made the division between the colonial, exploited peoples of Asia and the Near East and the Western imperialists the principal moral and political issue of the modern world.[2] The November Revolution heightened the tension between East and West, for according to Chicherin antagonism between capitalism and socialism became associated with the struggle of the colonies and dependent states for national liberation from Western imperial control.

After the failure of the German revolution of 1923, the "Eastern question" began to occupy an outstanding place in Soviet foreign-policy calculations. Chicherin applauded this change in emphasis, since without abandoning the European proletariat he strongly advocated Soviet support for movements of national liberation in the East. For him rising nationalist aspirations in Asia and the Near East presented a splendid opportunity for undermining Western imperialism and eventually generating socialist revolution in Europe.[3]

Chicherin stressed the affinity and potentially close relationship between Soviet Russia and countries of the East. He described Soviet Russia as neither completely Western nor Eastern but as a complex blend of these two civilizations and reserved to it a special role in international affairs. In his view the Russian workers, although oriented toward Europe and part of the European cultural and political tradition, provided an excellent model for the colonial and dependent peoples of Asia and the Near East as they strove to industrialize and throw off foreign rule.[4] Soviet Russia, the first country to modernize on the basis of socialist revolution, would serve as a viable alternative to capitalism as the developing nations struggled to build up their own nascent industries. Socialism would enable them to compete economically and militarily with the West, overcoming in a relatively short period the vast technological gap that existed between the Western powers and the countries of Asia and the Near East.

Chicherin professed that the November Revolution signaled the end of the division of the world between exploiters and exploited. The Soviet government, staunchly in favor of national self-determination, would appeal to oppressed peoples to join a common front against Western imperialism. From this perspective, Russia was the first Asiatic country to rise up against capitalist exploitation and would function as the leader of colonies seeking independence and national sovereignty. Chicherin envisaged a unique role for Russia, one that in some respects was similar to the Muscovite Orthodox interpretation of Moscow as the "Third

Rome," the repository of true Christianity destined to lead humanity to eternal salvation by the purity of its religious belief and its
willingness to endure great suffering. Furthermore, the nineteenth-
century Slavophiles, in their debate with the Westernizers, argued
for Russia's uniqueness largely on the basis of its mission to redeem
the world through Orthodoxy. Chicherin, while certainly rejecting
the Orthodox principles of Moscow as the "Third Rome" and the
writings of the Slavophiles, nevertheless cast Soviet Russia in an
almost identical missionary role, replacing Christianity with socialism as the means of emancipation and salvation. For him Soviet
socialism was a guide or model for Asia and the Near East by which
they could achieve liberation from Western economic exploitation
and political domination.[5]

Chicherin's skill as a polemicist was evident in his writings
about the East. He presented the Soviet state as the only genuine
friend of the developing countries. For him the contrast between
Tsarist and Soviet policies toward the East was stark, in spite of continuity in foreign affairs and Soviet defense of Russia's traditional
national interests. He asserted that the Tsarist government had been
exclusively concerned about imperial exploitation and the expansion of its empire, but the Soviets promoted the independent
economic and political development of Asia and the Near East.
Therefore Soviet goals for these regions were substantially different
from those of the imperialist nations. Chicherin advocated national
liberation and self-determination, and he also stressed economic
and social advancement through industrialization, which he
charged the Western powers were determined to oppose. He
regarded Great Britain as the leading opponent of national liberation in the East, since the success of such a movement would mean
the destruction of the British Empire.[6] While renouncing offensive
military alliances and coalitions, Chicherin supported a defensive
union between Soviet Russia and the East against British imperialism, which would represent the affinity between movements of
national liberation in Asia and the Near East and the struggle of
Russian workers to establish a socialist society.[7]

Chicherin's writings on Soviet relations with the East constituted a blend of diplomacy and revolution, much more than in his
pronouncements on Soviet policy toward the West. Soviet diplomatic activities toward the colonial and developing countries had
revolutionary undertones—he regarded Soviet diplomacy in the
East as more than a mere political necessity and a regretable product

of the resilience of capitalism in the West. In Asia and the Near East Chicherin's diplomatic maneuverings acquired revolutionary importance; they were intended not only to defend the Soviet state but also to contribute directly to the destruction of Western imperialism.

During the 1920s the Bolsheviks debated the type of revolution they were preparing in the East. This problem did not occur over Western Europe, where with advanced industrialization, the Soviets advocated socialist revolution and focused exclusively on the proletariat. But with the exception of Japan, the countries of Asia and the Near East were primarily colonial and underdeveloped industrially, with a small working class. Therefore the Soviets initially called for bourgeois-democractic revolution in the Pacific and Near East, in essence preparing for an Eastern version of the Russian Revolution of 1905. They regarded the bourgeoisie as the progressive class in the East and as the leader of national liberation and self-determination. At the same time, however, the Soviets attempted to support the "rising proletariat" in the East and combine their struggle against the bourgeoisie with national liberation.[8] The desire of the Soviets to see independent countries in Asia and the Near East with strong ties to Moscow sparked a dispute over how this goal was to be achieved—either bourgeois-democratic revolution or Soviet-socialist revolution. This controversy within the party reached its height during the middle of the decade and greatly exacerbated the struggle for power between Stalin and Trotskii.

Immediately after the November Revolution the Bolsheviks were principally concerned about Japan, which they regarded as their greatest enemy in the Far East. This marked a departure from the Tsarist government's policy toward Japan. In spite of the Russo-Japanese War of 1904–1905, relations between Japan and Imperial Russia had been relatively harmonious. During the prerevolutionary era Japanese foreign policy sought to avoid conflict with Russia and preferred to reach an understanding with the Tsarist government on the basis of spheres of influence in the Far East.[9] On 3 July 1916 Japan and Imperial Russia signed a secret treaty, which was primarily a military alliance against the United States. Both the Japanese and the Russians feared American expansion in the Pacific. But the Bolshevik Revolution fundamentally altered relations between the two countries. Japan's participation in military intervention during the Russian Civil War contributed to the Soviet government's strong anti-Japanese policy from 1918 to 1923. Thus the Soviets sought rapprochement with the United States to counter Japanese influence in the Pacific.

In 1924 the Soviet government reversed its policy toward Japan, largely because the Soviets were unsuccessful in achieving rapprochement with the United States. They interpreted the Dawes Plan of that year as the beginning of the reinvolvement of the United States in European affairs and a concerted attempt by Washington to thwart proletarian revolution in Europe. In this fashion the Soviet government hoped to reach agreement with China and Japan against the United States.[10] Chicherin explained that the Soviets sought to unite with the Chinese and Japanese against growing Anglo-American financial and military power in the Far East.[11] After 1924 the Soviets frequently criticized expanding Anglo-Saxon influence in the Pacific.

The reversal of Soviet policy toward Japan resulted in the Japanese-Soviet Neutrality Treaty of 20 January 1925. It provided for Japanese de jure recognition of the Soviet government and guaranteed Soviet neutrality in case of a Japanese conflict with a third power. Chicherin attached great significance to the treaty: to him it meant the settlement of outstanding problems between the two states after Japanese intervention in the Russian Civil War and the strengthening of the Soviet position in the Pacific, principally against the United States.[12] The treaty caused considerable alarm in Britain and the United States, as it represented a substantial change in Soviet foreign policy in the Far East. But despite the 1925 Neutrality Treaty and a facade of cordial relations, there was considerable tension under the surface between Japan and the Soviet Union for the duration of the decade.

Moscow considered China even more important than Japan for Soviet foreign policy in the Far East. The Soviets hoped to develop strong ties with China largely to undermine British influence in the Pacific. In 1918 the Soviet government sponsored a program of self-denial vis-à-vis China by agreeing to return the Chinese Eastern Railway and all concessions taken from China by the "Unequal Treaties." A year later, on 25 July 1919, the Karakhan Manifesto articulated these principles by calling for support of China against foreign intervention. But later that same year the Soviets rescinded the Karakhan Manifesto, as they became increasingly stalwart defenders of Russia's traditional national interests. Yet they were determined to establish friendly relations with China and urged the Chinese to pursue independence from Western domination.

Chicherin took the lead in promoting Soviet assistance to the Chinese movement of national liberation. As early as 1918 he began an active correspondence with Dr. Sun Yat-sen, the leader of the Chinese Nationalists or Kuomintang, which continued until at least 1923. Chicherin promised that the Soviets would support the Nationalists in their efforts to rid China of foreign domination and influence; in his view the socialist revolution in Russia, the initial phase of the worldwide revolt against imperialism, would serve the Kuomintang as a model in this endeavor.[13] Furthermore, he urged Sun to follow the Bolshevik example in organizing the Kuomintang and in planning to overthrow the Peking government and consolidate power in China. According to Chicherin:

> the fundamental aim of the Kuomintang Party . . . is to build up a great powerful movement of the Chinese people and that therefore propaganda and organization on the biggest scale are its first necessities. Our example was significant: our military activities were successful because a long series of years had elapsed during which we organized and instructed our followers, building up in this way a great organized party throughout the whole land, a party capable of vanquishing all its adversaries. The whole Chinese nation must see the difference between the Koumintang, a popular organized mass party, and the military dictators of the various parts of China.[14]

Chicherin also agreed the first priority for the Kuomintang ought to be national liberation. Socialist revolution in China would be possible only after the Chinese had regained control of their own destiny from the Western powers.

The Soviet government recommended cooperation between the small Chinese Communist Party and Sun's Kuomintang. In early 1923 the Soviets dispatched Joffe to conclude an alliance between the two sides. The Communists and the Nationalists agreed to work together for the overthrow of the Peking government. In October Moscow sent Mikhail Borodin to China to serve as the principal Soviet military advisor to the Kuomintang and to implement the arrangement between the Communists and the Nationalists. Soviet military and technical experts arrived in Canton with Borodin, and Sun sent many Chinese, including Chiang Kai-shek, to study in the Soviet Union.

But while the Soviets were developing strong ties with the Chinese Nationalists, Narkomindel also was negotiating with the

Peking government to reach diplomatic agreement. Peking officially recognized the Soviet government by the Sino-Soviet Treaty
of 31 May 1924. Chicherin blamed the Western powers for China's
procrastination in extending de jure recognition and hailed the
treaty as a landmark in Chinese relations with the West, for it meant
the beginning of Chinese independence from foreign control.[15] It
was apparent that his diplomatic and revolutionary activities with
respect to China worked at cross-purposes, since he obtained de jure
recognition from the Peking government at the same time that he
supported the Kuomintang in Canton.

Chicherin acknowledged that the Soviet government was sympathetic toward the Chinese Nationalists, but he denied that it was
working to overthrow the Peking regime or even involved in internal
Chinese affairs. He declared that the Soviets respected the Chinese
right of self-determination and that the Soviet government was
unequivocably opposed to interference in the affairs of another
state. Since 1923, however, the Soviets had military advisors in Canton assisting the Nationalists in their efforts to overthrow the Peking
government. But Chicherin asserted that the Western powers, primarily Britain, were responsible for meddling in Chinese politics
and wanted to destroy the Chinese movement of national liberation.
According to him, Soviet and Western policy toward China was
starkly different: the Soviets were ultimately concerned about the
establishment of a centralized, democratic government free of foreign domination, while the British generated political chaos by
goading the local warlords to take up arms against each other, thus
preserving Western control in the absence of a centralized Chinese
authority.[16] Therefore for Chicherin Soviet policy was mainly
directed against foreign rule in China.

By the middle of the 1920s China had become an important
consideration in the power struggle between Stalin and Trotskii.
Stalin argued that China was on the verge of a bourgeois-democratic
revolution and that the Kuomintang should lead the country against
foreign imperialism. He urged the Chinese Communists to form an
alliance with the Kuomintang and instructed the former to secure
the hegemony of the proletariat over the bourgeoisie, whom the
Nationalists represented against the Western powers. Trotskii, however, repudiated collaboration with the Chinese bourgeoisie and
claimed that the time was ripe to strike for communist power in
China. In this context events in China had a considerable impact on
political developments in the Soviet Union.

In 1925 the nationalist-revolutionary movement in China seemed to advance. Sun indeed had reorganized the Kuomintang along the lines of the Soviet Communist Party; for example, Chiang had trained a new officer corps at the Whampoa Military Academy. But in March of that same year Sun died, and Chiang, the new leader of the Kuomintang, did not favor strong ties with Moscow.

In early 1926 the Politburo formed a special committee, chaired by Trotskii and including Chicherin, F. E. Dzerzhinskii, and K. E. Voroshilov, to report on Soviet Far Eastern affairs and recommend policy toward China. Since Trotskii was the chair of the committee, the Soviets were not yet aware of impending changes in Sino-Soviet relations and assumed that the committee's reports would be noncontroversial. The Politburo debated the principal report of the committee on 25 March, at the height of a crisis with the Kuomintang. Chiang purged a number of Chinese Communists from high military and political positions and even arrested some Soviet advisors in Canton. Borodin tried to patch up the rift between the Communists and the Nationalists; even though he was temporarily successful, relations between the two sides were far from cordial. The committee's report recognized the progressive development of revolutionary forces in China. Most importantly, it dealt with measures to prevent a united imperialist front against China.[17] In spite of Trotskii's objections to collaboration with the Chinese bourgeoisie, the Politburo continued to pursue Stalin's line of working through the Kuomintang to achieve a bourgeois-democratic revolution in China.

In the summer of 1926 the Nationalists marched north from Canton toward Peking. They were split into two forces: one group, including the Soviet advisors and the Chinese Communists, moved inland through Wuhan; Chiang led another contingent toward the coast, where it seems he hoped to obtain Western aid. He took Shanghai and defeated the Communists there on 11 April 1927. Shortly thereafter he established his capital at Nanking, thus breaking completely with the Wuhan group. By July Borodin and most of the other Soviet military experts returned to the Soviet Union as the Wuhan government disintegrated. In retaliation Moscow repudiated the Kuomintang and ordered the Chinese Communists to stage an insurrection against Chiang. The affair of the "Canton Commune" ended in a complete defeat for the Communists in December. By 1928 Chiang finished the task of unifying China under his leadership.

During 1926–1927 Communist reverses and Nationalist successes indicated that Trotskii's analysis of events in China was substantially correct. But Stalin did not repudiate the Kuomintang until after the Central Committee had expelled Trotskii from the party in November 1927. Trotskii's expulsion enabled Stalin to attack the Nationalists without having to acknowledge the value of the former's criticism of Soviet policy toward China. Therefore Soviet relations with China formed an integral part of the succession struggle between Stalin and Trotskii and to some extent were unrelated to internal Chinese developments, which receded into the background.[18]

While cultivating friendship with Japan and increasing Soviet influence in China, Chicherin worked assiduously to develop cordial relations with countries of Central Asia and the Near East. In his conception of world affairs the traditional clash of interests between Britain and Russia and the recently intensified competition between capitalism and socialism would ultimately be decided by Anglo-Soviet relations in Central Asia and the Near East. He realized India was the key to the British Empire, and even though he could do little to undermine British control of the Indian Ocean directly, he sought to conclude diplomatic agreements favorable to the Soviet state with Afghanistan, Persia, and Turkey. In this fashion Chicherin hoped to turn Central Asia and the Near East into Soviet spheres of influence, replacing Britain as the principal power in these regions. He regarded Afghanistan, Persia, and Turkey as a potential bulwark of defense for Soviet Russia against the Western nations.

To implement this policy Chicherin first sought official diplomatic recognition from the Afghan, Persian, and Turkish governments. On 26 February 1921 the Soviets concluded a Treaty of Friendship and Recognition with Persia; they signed a similar agreement with Afghanistan on 28 February. Approximately a month later on 16 March, the same day on which the Anglo-Soviet Commercial Treaty was signed, the Soviets concluded a Treaty of Friendship and Recognition with Turkey. These agreements asserted the Soviet position as the great anti-imperialist power of Central Asia and the Near East. Furthermore, Soviet Russia negotiated a settlement of outstanding issues for the three Caucasian Republics—Armenia, Azerbaidzhan, and Georgia—with Turkey, which meant tacit Turkish recognition of Soviet control over the Caucasus. On 13 October the Soviets reached an agreement with the

Turks that successfully regulated relations between the Caucasian Republics and Turkey.[19] Chicherin deserves much of the credit for the realization of Soviet foreign-policy goals in these negotiations, for he consistently advocated strong ties between Soviet Russia and Afghanistan, Persia, and Turkey against the British Empire. He regarded the treaties of friendship and recognition as the initial step in detaching Central Asia and the Near East from Britain.

But Chicherin was not content to stop with the treaties of friendship and recognition, since he wanted to form a defensive alliance between the Soviet Union and Afghanistan, Persia, and Turkey. The need for such an agreement became particularly urgent after the signing of the Locarno Treaty in 1925. The Soviets hoped to establish a cordon of neutral states in Central Asia and the Near East against Locarno and the League of Nations. Chicherin perceived the 1925 Soviet-Turkish Neutrality and Nonaggression Treaty as a model for similar agreements with other states. The treaty, providing for neutrality, nonaggression, and nonparticipation in hostile associations and agreements directed against the other party, effectively prevented Turkey from joining the League.[20]

Using the Soviet-Turkish Treaty as the cornerstone of a series of neutrality agreements with states in Central Asia and the Near East, Chicherin appealed to Afghanistan and Persia to sign a neutrality and nonaggression pact with the Soviet Union. His skill as a polemicist and propagandist helped him to achieve this goal. Chicherin presented the Soviet Union as the only true friend of Afghanistan and Persia as they sought to develop a modern economy and maintain political independence vis-à-vis the British. He understood that Afghanistan, in particular, was crucial to British interests in India and charged British agents with supplying Afghan tribal warlords and feudal leaders with arms through India. In his view the British worked to prevent the formation of a progressive, modern government in Afghanistan, for it would seek closer economic and political ties with the Soviet Union and therefore threaten Britain's hegemony in India. In contrast to the British, Chicherin argued that the Soviets were in favor of the progressive development of Afghan society, which included the centralization of political power. From the Soviet perspective the British supported the Afghan tribes against the central government to ensure that the country would remain politically divided and weak.[21] Chicherin urged the Afghans to avoid internal conflict and dissension so that they could concentrate their efforts and resources on resisting British imperialism.

Like Afghanistan, Persia was strategically significant to the Soviet Union, and Chicherin proposed a neutrality and nonaggression treaty with the Persian government as well. His appeal to Persia was similar to the one he had made to Afghanistan. He claimed that the British were supporting feudal, reactionary warlords and tribal leaders with funds and weapons against the progressive, modernizing Persian government. And he warned that the British were not interested in the economic welfare of Persia and that they wanted to expand their imperial influence to protect India. Once again, Chicherin argued that only cordial relations with the Soviet Union would enable the Persian government to build up nascent industries and resist effectively the gradual encroachment of the British upon its territory.[22]

In 1924 events in Afghanistan and Persia were partly responsible for Chicherin's denunciation of Britain's Labor government. For him British policy in Central Asia was the acid test of the MacDonald government. Asserting that anti-Soviet activities continued unchecked, Chicherin found substantially little difference between Labor and the Conservatives.[23] During 1925 tensions between Britain and the Soviet Union in Central Asia increased sharply, but by the following year the Soviets were able to record a number of diplomatic successes against the British in the area.

Chicherin's efforts to establish a cordon of neutral states throughout Central Asia and the Near East began to reap positive results in 1926. As a result of his mediation Persia and Turkey signed a Neutrality and Nonaggression Treaty on 22 April. Shortly thereafter on 31 August an Afghan-Soviet Treaty of Neutrality and Nonaggression was signed, which was based on the 1921 Treaty of Friendship and Recognition. Over a year later on 1 October 1927 Chicherin secured the Persian-Soviet Neutrality and Nonaggression Treaty, which once again had been built on the 1921 Friendship and Recognition Treaty. The Soviets completed their system of neutrality agreements by the Afghan-Persian Treaty of Neutrality and Nonaggression on 28 November 1927, the Afghan-Turkish Treaty of Neutrality and Nonaggression on 25 May 1928, and the Soviet-Yemen Treaty of Neutrality and Nonaggression on 1 November 1928. Finally, the 1925 Soviet-Turkish Neutrality and Nonaggression Treaty was renewed on 17 December 1929.

By these treaties of neutrality and nonaggression Narkomindel created a zone of states that served as a buffer against the prospect of renewed Western intervention and functioned as an effective counterbalance to the Locarno Treaty. The agreements appealed to the Soviets' need for security, for they were preoccupied with the possibility of attack from the Western powers throughout the 1920s. Furthermore, the neutrality and nonaggression pacts represented some of Chicherin's most successful diplomatic activity while he was commissar of foreign affairs. His work in Central Asia and the Near East combined elements of traditional Russian foreign policy with a commitment to international socialist revolution. He proved to be not only an excellent diplomat but also a skilled propagandist in appealing to Afghanistan, Persia, and Turkey to reject Western, especially British, influence.

For Chicherin Soviet policy in Central Asia, the Near East, and the Far East meant the convergence of diplomacy and revolution, for he was convinced Soviet support for national liberation in the East would ultimately lead to the spread of socialist revolution in the West. After 1923 it might not have been possible for the Soviets to challenge directly or mount a frontal assault on capitalism in Western Europe, but they could gradually yet persistently undermine Western imperialism in the East. Therefore Chicherin retained his hopes for international socialist revolution by focusing on nationalist rebellions in Asia and the Near East. To him it seemed inevitable that the peoples of the East would look for leadership and support to the Soviet state, the best example of a successful revolt of an Asiatic country against the Western imperialist powers. Unlike many of the other Communists, Chicherin's concern about the "Eastern question" was much more than the regretable yet necessary refocusing of revolutionary efforts on Central Asia, the Far East, and the Near East after the failure of socialist revolution in Western Europe. For him movements of national liberation and the destruction of colonial empires in the East offered the best opportunity for the successful expansion of socialism in the West during the middle and late 1920s.

Soviet foreign policy toward the Middle East, Central Asia, and the Far East, involving a combination of diplomacy and revolution, outlined in sharp relief the anomolous relations between Narkomindel and the Third International, or Comintern. Both of these institutions were involved in the conduct of Soviet foreign affairs, although neither one made policy decisions. The Politburo set policies for Comintern and Narkomindel, but while the latter never functioned independently of the leadership, the former managed to maintain some autonomy from 1922 when Lenin was seriously incapacitated to 1928–1929 when Stalin succeeded in consolidating his authority over the party. An understanding of the relations between Comintern and Narkomindel, and particularly of Chicherin's views of these two organizations, is necessary for an appreciation of Soviet foreign affairs during the 1920s.

Immediately after the November Revolution three Americans —Boris Reinstein, Albert Rhys Williams, and John Reed—set up the Bureau of International Revolutionary Propaganda in Moscow. It was the first organization created to facilitate the spread of socialist revolution abroad. But Narkomindel also was interested in revolutionary agitation, and it quickly assumed many of the Bureau's duties and responsibilities. For approximately a year, from early 1918 until the formation of Comintern in 1919, Narkomindel served as the principal instrument for the promotion of world revolution. This arrangement suited Chicherin, for he was a talented propagandist and believed unswervingly in the internationalization of the socialist revolution. But the party leaders increasingly realized that the Soviet government would have to conduct normal relations with the capitalist states, and assigning Narkomindel responsibility for both diplomacy and revolutionary agitation proved unsatisfactory. Furthermore, to meet the challenge of efforts to revitalize the defunct Second International in Switzerland, the Bolsheviks decided to hold an international congress of socialists in Moscow with the intention of forming a new organization dedicated to the spread of socialism throughout the world.

Trotskii drafted an invitation to found a new Communist International, which a small committee of Bolsheviks, including Chicherin, approved. The invitation was published in *Pravda* on 24 January 1919. The first, formative congress of the Communist, or Third, International (Comintern) was held in Moscow from 2 to 6 March. Thirty-five delegates with voting powers attended. Lenin, Trotskii, Zinov'ev, Chicherin, and Bukharin represented the Russian Communist Party. Even though Chicherin was commissar of Narkomindel and therefore the chief diplomat of the Soviet government, he was one of the founders of Comintern.

The formation of Comintern meant the institutionalization of revolutionary agitation and propaganda. Its task was to promote class struggle and champion socialist revolution on an international

scale. Many Bolsheviks, especially those who had engaged in journalistic and literary endeavors before the November Revolution
and who were skilled propagandists, eagerly participated in
Comintern, preferring the excitement of revolutionary upheaval to
the tedious administrative work required of them now that the party
was in power. With the creation of Comintern, Narkomindel gradually ceased to function as an organization devoted to revolutionary
agitation and increasingly operated as the agency of government
responsible for diplomacy. Therefore, Narkomindel was charged
with maintaining peace, or at least helping to deter foreign aggression against the fledgling Soviet state, and with conducting relations
with foreign governments.

At first there was no formal separation of duties and responsibilities between Comintern and Narkomindel. But it became
increasingly apparent that a formal division of functions between
the two institutions was necessary. This was especially true as con-
flicts of interest often occurred. Since both organizations were
involved with Soviet foreign affairs, the party shifted its emphasis
from one to the other depending on the leadership's appraisal of the
current international scene. The party's strategy and tactics for the
moment greatly influenced its attitude toward Comintern and
Narkomindel. The Politburo accorded priority to Comintern when
the revolutionary tide in Europe seemed to be rising, as it did immediately after the November Revolution. Conversely, diplomacy was
superior to revolution during the middle and late 1920s, for the
party was acutely aware that the time was not propitious for revolutionary upheaval in Western Europe. And the period witnessed a net
gain for diplomacy.[24]

Yet it would be a mistake to argue that Comintern and
Narkomindel were constantly in competition with each other. They
also complemented one another. Although Comintern worked to
overthrow capitalist governments and Narkomindel sought to
maintain stable relations with them, both organizations were essentially pursuing the same goal—the protection and defense of the
Soviet Union. Furthermore, Soviet diplomatic and trade missions
abroad consisted of cadres from both Narkomindel and Comintern.
It was at the personnel level that fundamental differences between
the two agencies emerged. Chicherin, for example, often did not
know what Comintern was doing, even though Soviet diplomatic
delegations contained people with few diplomatic duties. And

cadres from Comintern frequently had more authority than the diplomats from Narkomindel who were their nominal superiors. This
anomalous situation made for some awkward moments in Soviet
diplomatic missions, but Comintern officials were bound to support and uphold Soviet diplomacy when they served abroad.

Stalin's victory over the other Communist leaders in the succession struggle and the ideological triumph of "socialism in one
country" over "permanent revolution" also meant that
Narkomindel prevailed over Comintern in the conduct of Soviet
foreign affairs. The ascendancy of diplomacy over revolution in part
kept Chicherin in office during the early years of Stalinism. The failure of the 1923 German revolution was a watershed in Soviet
foreign affairs, as the government gradually introduced a more
moderate foreign policy in the second half of the twenties. In
December 1925 the Fourteenth Congress of the party articulated a
shift in emphasis in Soviet foreign relations. At a time of capitalist
consolidation "the alliance between the proletariat of the USSR . . .
and the Western European proletariat and the oppressed peoples,
must be strengthened in every way, keeping a course toward the
development and victory of international proletarian revolution";
but the Congress also stressed that "it is necessary to conduct a policy of peace, and this must be at the centre of the government's
whole foreign policy and determine all its basic moves."[25] Thus the
Congress emphasized peaceful coexistence as the foundation of
Soviet foreign policy, and although the party had not abandoned its
efforts to incite international socialist revolution, diplomacy had
clearly risen at the expense of revolutionary agitation.

The emphasis the Fourteenth Congress placed on capitalist stabilization and peaceful coexistence can be traced not only to the
abortive 1923 German revolution but also the Genoa Conference
and the Treaty of Rapallo. With the treaty the Soviets grudgingly
accepted a significantly different view of the world and a new perception of the relations between capitalism and socialism. For them
Rapallo meant the reluctant relinquishment of the hope of international revolution in exchange for a binding agreement with Germany, an important state in a divided capitalist world.[26] For several
years after Rapallo there was considerable rivalry between
Comintern and Narkomindel, which ran parallel to and was part of
the ideological struggle between socialism in one country and permanent, or international, revolution.

Chicherin accepted the ideological and political implications of the Rapallo Treaty. But it did not diminish his enthusiasm for international revolution, for which he continued to hope and work. He regarded the treaty as indispensable for the survival of the Soviet state, since it was surrounded by hostile capitalist powers. While he believed that the post-World War I era witnessed the growing internal contradictions and disintegration of the capitalist world, he acknowledged that capitalism displayed remarkable resilience. Since the international socialist revolution might not occur for a long period, Chicherin placed priority on the continued existence of the Soviet state. He emphasized diplomacy, peaceful coexistence, and Russia's traditional geopolitical interests to ensure this goal, without abandoning his commitment to world revolution. In this respect he proved to be a loyal and steadfast disciple of Lenin.

The Soviet government's decision to launch a massive industrialization campaign at the end of the twenties also contributed to the increasing significance of diplomacy in Soviet foreign affairs. The Soviets perceived that they had to embark upon large-scale industrialization to complete with the West economically and militarily. And industrialization required peace. The Soviets needed to prolong the breathing space, provided by stable relations with the capitalist powers, to focus attention on their internal economic development. Peaceful coexistence was designed to obtain credits and foreign technical specialists to assist with industrialization. The advent of acute economic difficulties in the West with the Great Depression meant that credits from the capitalist states were not forthcoming, and the Soviets were thrown back on their own resources to finance industrialization. But the failure of the West to provide credits for Soviet economic development did not diminish the importance of diplomacy in the conduct of Soviet foreign policy.

Chicherin wrote relatively little about Comintern, in part because of the difficulty in explaining and reconciling traditional diplomacy and revolutionary agitation to world public opinion. He would not compromise on the issue of revolutionary propaganda, realizing that the Bolsheviks had acquired power largely on the basis of their ability to arouse and sustain support from the masses. He recognized that agitation and propaganda were indispensable for the expansion of socialist revolution abroad. Yet he also had to deal with the diplomats of Western nations who complained about Comintern's activities, particularly in Asia and the Near East, and who stressed that diplomatic recognition of and commercial and political agreements with the Soviet government were dependent on its willingness to curtail anti-capitalist propaganda. These arguments posed a serious dilemma for Chicherin, as he understood the political necessity of conducting normal diplomatic relations with the governments of capitalist states.

Chicherin persistently separated Comintern from the Soviet government, claiming that the former was completely independent, financially, ideologically, and organizationally, from the latter. In his view Comintern was a private international organization that did not take its orders from Moscow, and the Russian Communist Party was only one of many parties that joined it. Furthermore the Soviet government, the first socialist government in the world, could certainly not prohibit Comintern's Central Executive Committee from establishing its headquarters in Moscow.[27] Therefore when foreign diplomats charged that the Soviets were responsible for Comintern activities and had to curtail its revolutionary propaganda before their governments would do business with Moscow, Chicherin responded that Comintern was not within the jurisdiction of the Soviet government. His arguments were a rationalization for the benefit of foreign critics, since he readily understood the close working relationship between Comintern, the Soviet government, and the Russian Communist Party. Comintern activities sometimes embarrassed him as commissar of Narkomindel, and he certainly had no control over the former, yet the necessity of defending it before world public opinion made his work as a diplomat considerably more difficult.

Thus Chicherin argued the Soviet government strictly adhered to a policy of noninterference in the internal affairs of other states and it had no authority over private citizens who wished to address revolutionary appeals to the proletariat and oppressed peoples of the world.[28] Speaking as private persons, and especially as members of a revolutionary political party, they could and indeed had an obligation to incite rebellion against capitalist governments. He explained that Communists holding positions in the Soviet government performed their government duties while also discharging service to the party, similar to, for example, members of the Democratic or Republican parties in the United States who conducted party affairs while maintaining government offices.[29] For Chicherin it was not important that the content of revolutionary propaganda differed markedly from the form of traditional diplomacy, since the goal in each case—the defense and promotion of the socialist revolution—was the same.

Chicherin further indicated that the principal task of a revolutionary socialist party was to champion the interests of the proletariat around the world. More specifically, this meant that Comintern would oppose and resist capitalist governments by calling for its own international political program based on class struggle and the destruction of capitalism. Yet he also acknowledged that soviet governments, before the final victory of socialism over capitalism, had to adopt different tactics than the revolutionary parties that created them in order to survive in a world still dominated by capitalist states. According to Chicherin,

> The revolutionary soviet governments themselves are in a rather different position from the revolutionary parties. As actually existing governments, they are compelled to enter into certain relations with other existing governments, and these impose obligations with which they must reckon. The Commissar of Foreign Affairs, who writes in the journal of the Third International, must remember that he is bound by the position of his government, a position which is no longer that of a revolutionary party far removed from power.[30]

By this statement Chicherin tacitly admitted the difficulty for the Communist Party in power in Russia. Its revolutionary mission was to spread socialism abroad. But given existing international circumstances that were not propitious for revolution and the resilience of capitalism, as the head of the Soviet government it also needed to carry on normal, stable relations with the capitalist governments.

In elaborating the relations between Comintern and Narkomindel and in designating specific functions to each organization, Chicherin stressed that diplomacy was necessary for the defense of the Soviet Republic. In his view diplomacy was just as significant as military power in preserving the Soviet victory in Russia. But he cautioned that the Soviet government had to be extremely wary of entering into diplomatic alliances with the capitalist states. On the one hand he emphasized that as Communists the Soviets were obliged to avoid offensive coalitions and combinations with the Western powers, for they were often directed against colonial or dependent states unable to offer effective resistance. On the other hand Chicherin also indicated that the Soviet government had a right to self-protection and therefore could join defensive alliances and coalitions to deter potential aggressors; for example, he justified the neutrality and nonaggression treaties with countries of Asia and the Near East on the basis they were strictly defensive arrangements and did not serve as a facade for imperial expansion.[31] In making this argument he described the Soviet government as part of and yet at the same time divorced from traditional great-power politics.

Chicherin's commitment to socialist revolution was unwavering and his belief in the power of agitation and propaganda undiminished, but Comintern's actions and policies sometimes exasperated him and complicated his work as a professional diplomat. The anomalous position of the Soviet government as the only socialist regime in the world compounded his difficulties, for he was responsible for establishing normal relations with governments Comintern assiduously tried to subvert. His sentiments were with Comintern, that is, with revolutionary agitation, but practical necessity dictated that he develop diplomacy for the protection of Russia's traditional geopolitical interests and the defense of the Soviet Republic in a hostile environment.

7

Chicherin and Stalin

IN spite of the treaties of neutrality and nonaggression the Soviet Union signed with neighboring states during the mid–1902s, the Soviet government was anxious about the Locarno Treaty and its ramifications for European affairs. The Soviets were especially concerned about Eastern Europe, and in 1926 they feared that the Western powers would redraw the map of the region to the detriment of the Soviet state. Articles in the Soviet press once again raised the specter of an anti-Soviet bloc, and it seemed to the Soviets that the Western nations would use an "eastern Locarno" to launch a new crusade against communism. The Soviets continued to regard Britain as the leader of a common front against the Soviet Union. Relations between Britain and the Soviet Union deteriorated largely because of financial support from Comintern and Soviet trade unions for British workers in the great General Strike of 1926. The British charged that the Soviet government was actively exporting revolution abroad and that in these circumstances it was increasingly difficult to conduct normal diplomatic relations.

Chicherin was in Western Europe during the period of heightened tension between Britain and the Soviet Union. In November 1926 he left Moscow for Germany and the French Riviera to rest and receive medical treatment for diabetes and polyneuritis. Although the Western press speculated that he was traveling abroad to engage in diplomatic negotiations, his trip was of little political significance, as his failing health necessitated prolonged medical attention. He stayed in Western Europe for about seven months, returning to the Soviet Union at the end of June 1927. During

Chicherin's absence from Moscow, Litvinov was in charge of Narkomindel, which marked the latter's increasing importance in Soviet foreign affairs. Litvinov coveted Chicherin's position and hoped to be rewarded for his support of Stalin in the leadership struggle. Chicherin did not receive regular correspondence from Litvinov concerning Narkomindel and Soviet foreign affairs. Georgii Vasil'evich kept abreast of world events by reading Western newspapers. Thus Litvinov acted independently of Chicherin in managing Narkomindel.

In the autumn of 1926 the Soviet government launched a campaign to warn the public of the danger of an imperialist war; this campaign escalated in the spring of 1927. The Soviet Union experienced a number of diplomatic setbacks, and its relations with Britain were the core of the problem. On 23 February Chamberlain sent a note of protest to Narkomindel charging the Soviet government with supporting seditious activities in Britain during the 1926 General Strike and of continuing to conduct agitation and propaganda against British interests in Asia and the Near East. Some Conservatives in the cabinet had exerted influence on Chamberlain to write the note, which was similar in style to those produced by Lord Curzon, yet at first there did not seem to be a real threat of a diplomatic break. But Litvinov called the note "stupid and fresh" and responded in the same manner, which aggravated the Conservatives and made a rupture a genuine possibility.[1] On 11 March Chicherin, who had been following events in the Western press, dispatched a letter to Stalin and Rykov warning them that the British government was prepared to break diplomatic relations with the Soviet Union and that Narkomindel should have responded to Chamberlain's note in a conciliatory fashion to mollify the moderate Conservatives in the cabinet. Furthermore, Chicherin urged the Soviet leaders not to underestimate British intentions, for he warned the anti-Soviet campaign in Britain might intensify, and Narkomindel would have to exercise considerable circumspection and restraint in choosing the correct diplomatic response.[2]

On 12 May the British police initiated a search of Arkos—the joint stock company registered as a British firm and engaged in trade with the Soviet Union—and the Soviet Trade Delegation, which occupied separate offices of the same building in London. The police raid produced a vociferous protest from the Soviet government, for the head of the Soviet Trade Delegation and his office enjoyed diplomatic immunity according to the 1921 Anglo-Soviet

Commercial Treaty. On 16 May the home secretary announced to the House of Commons that the police had been looking for a missing War Office document that was never found. The alleged stolen document was merely a pretext for the raid, and the Soviets regarded the incident as a deliberate provocation.[3] On 26 May the British government suspended diplomatic relations with the Soviet Union. The Soviets perceived the rupture of relations with Britain as the logical outcome of the Locarno Treaty and the culmination of British foreign policy. The Soviet press reported that the Western powers, led by Britain, were preparing to launch an attack against the Soviet Union.[4]

As Soviet relations with Britain rapidly deteriorated in 1927, the Soviets suffered further diplomatic setbacks around the world. On 11 April Chiang Kai-shek suppressed the Chinese Communists, which further alarmed the Soviets about their precarious international position. And on 7 June a White émigré shot Petr Voikov, the Soviet representative in Warsaw. Moscow sent a note of protest to the Polish government linking Voikov's assassination with events in China and the Arkos raid. On 9 July Warsaw replied that the assassin was emotionally unstable and not a Pole and expressed regrets about the incident. But the Polish response did not alleviate Moscow's alarm.

Finally, in the autumn of 1927 the Soviets feared the possibility of a diplomatic break with France. The French recognition of the Soviet government in October 1924 had not resolved the question of Soviet compensation for French holders of Tsarist bonds, and the Soviets in turn wanted credits. The two governments agreed to negotiate the issues, and the discussions were still dragging on in 1927. On 26 July the talks recessed when the French government insisted that the Soviets had to compensate the former French owners of nationalized property. More importantly, on 7 October Briand, the French foreign minister, demanded the recall of Rakovskii, the Soviet ambassador to France. On 9 August Rakovskii had signed a manifesto for the United Opposition in its struggle against Stalin, advocating the defense of the Soviet Union and the spread of socialist revolution abroad. His signature on the manifesto produced a diplomatic crisis. On 12 October Chicherin responded to Briand with a note challenging the French position, but nevertheless the former declared that Rakovskii would depart from Paris immediately.[5] Rakovskii's recall did not result in a diplomatic break, but the Franco-Soviet economic negotiations were not resumed, which the Soviet press interpreted as a victory for reactionary circles in Britain.[6]

Soviet diplomatic defeats and failures in 1927, particularly the Arkos raid and the break with Britain in May, created a war scare in the Soviet Union that reached its height in the summer and autumn. The rupture between London and Moscow threatened German-Soviet relations, as it forced the Weimar Republic to support one side against the other. The Soviets were concerned that Berlin might join forces with London and Warsaw. They regarded Germany as the key to Soviet security. The Soviets had based their security on Germany's neutrality and refusal to participate in an anti-Soviet coalition. The Soviet war scare of 1927 was principally the result of an erosion of confidence in Germany.[7]

The Soviet government suspected that Chamberlain would attempt to cut a deal with Stresemann when the two men attended the League Council in Geneva in mid-June. On 8 June Chicherin, whose diplomacy was based on Germany's neutrality between London and Moscow, met with Stresemann in Baden-Baden. Chicherin asked if Germany would be able to resist Western demands for troop transit rights across German territory in the event of a crisis, and Stresemann responded that the assurances the German government had given the Soviets at the time of the Locarno negotiations were still in force.[8] Chicherin was satisfied with Stresemann's answer, but the Soviet government became increasingly unwilling to base its security on Germany's neutrality. The war scare led to an appeal to Russian national pride and xenophobia, and the Stalinist leadership insisted that only economic self-sufficiency and a strong military would enable the country to survive the threat from abroad. Therefore, the war scare and the erosion of confidence in Germany became a justification for large-scale industrialization, as the Soviets assumed they would have to industrialize rapidly to compete with the West economically and militarily.

Stalin exaggerated Western intentions toward the Soviet Union in 1926–1927, and he used the war scare against his political opponents, Trotskii and Zinov'ev, accusing them of disloyalty to the party and the government at a time of national crisis. From his residence in Western Europe Chicherin realized that an attack on the Soviet Union was not imminent:

"I returned home in June, 1927, from Western Europe." . . . "Everybody in Moscow was talking war. I tried to dissuade them.

Nobody is planning to attack us, I insisted. Then a colleague
enlightened me. He said, Shh. We know that. But we need this
against Trotsky."[9]

Yet it would be a mistake to regard the war scare as a sham, as merely
an attempt by Stalin to discredit and defeat his political enemies, or
as a pretext for launching a program of massive industrialization.
There were genuine, if exaggerated, fears of Western plans toward
the Soviet state, and these fears had a considerable impact on Soviet
domestic politics and foreign relations.[10]

Even though Stalin deliberately exaggerated the war danger in
connection with his campaign against the United Opposition, he
regarded war with the West as inevitable, a product of the clash of
capitalism and socialism. He wanted to postpone war, to delay it
until the internationally isolated Soviet state could develop heavy
industry with which to fight the Western powers successfully.
Although for him war with the West involved considerable risk, it
also could promote communist revolution. As a Great Russian
nationalist and an advocate of socialism in one country, Stalin did
not reject international communist revolution. He argued that
although a socialist society could be built in Russia, the Soviet
state would not be fully secure until the communist revolution
spread abroad.[11] Thus the final victory of socialism in the Soviet
Union would not be complete until socialist encirclement replaced
capitalist encirclement, which could best be achieved by war
between the Western powers and the Soviet state. Stalin believed
that war would provide opportunities for advancing communist
revolution, much like World War I contributed to the November
Revolution. But he insisted that a new revolutionary war must be
fought on terms favorable to the Soviets, that is, Soviet industrial
power would need to be sufficiently developed to enable them to
win the conflict and spread communist revolution abroad, extending Soviet dominion in the process.

During the first half of 1927 from his residence in Western
Europe Chicherin frequently wrote the Politburo about Soviet foreign policy, especially with respect to Britain and Germany. In a
letter to Stalin and Rykov dated 18 February Chicherin sharply criticized Bukharin, whom he accused of undermining Soviet relations
with Germany. In a letter to Bukharin of 6 May Chicherin repeated
the accusation, protesting errors in Soviet foreign policy at a time of
heightened tension with Britain. And finally in a letter to Stalin and

Rykov dated 3 June Chicherin charged the Soviet leaders with disrupting relations with Germany, which he believed ought to be the foundation of Soviet foreign affairs, and asserted that the leadership's misguided actions were irrevocably damaging relations with Britain. Chicherin further announced that he could not accept such fundamental mistakes in Soviet foreign policy and would return to Moscow in order to submit his resignation.[12]

In spite of Chicherin's criticism of the Soviet leadership's management of foreign policy, Stalin and the Politburo did not accept his resignation. Stalin did not want to remove Chicherin during a period of international crisis and at the height of the domestic campaign against Trotskii and the United Opposition. Just as importantly, Chicherin's resignation would have undoubtedly signaled a marked deterioration in German-Soviet affairs, which were already strained. Stalin could not risk jeopardizing relations with Berlin immediately after the break with London, for to do so would have increased the diplomatic isolation of the Soviet Union. When Chicherin returned to Moscow in late June, he was determined to repair the damage done to Soviet foreign affairs, particularly vis-à-vis Germany.

Chicherin often found himself in disagreement with Litvinov, for the latter advocated closer ties with the Western nations and did not regard the Rapallo Treaty as the cornerstone of Soviet foreign policy. While Chicherin was in Western Europe, Litvinov attempted to reach accommodation with the West. On 12 December 1925 the League Council had decided to set up a Preparatory Commission for a General Disarmament Conference scheduled for 1932. The council invited nonmembers of the League—Germany, the Soviet Union, and the United States—to participate in this Preparatory Commission. The Soviets accepted the invitation to send representatives, but they refused to endorse Geneva as the meeting place. After the murder of Vorovskii in Switzerland in 1923, the Soviet government had broken commercial and economic relations with the Swiss, and the two countries had been unable to resolve their differences. Nevertheless, the first session of the Preparatory Commission was held in Geneva in April 1926.

Chicherin rejected Geneva as the meeting place for both the Preparatory Commission and the General Disarmament Conference. He viewed the decision to convene the commission and conference in Geneva as an indication that the League Council did not want the Soviet government to send delegates; the council deliberately selected Geneva realizing that the Soviets would refuse to send representatives to an international conference held on Swiss territory.[13] But on Litvinov's initiative, the Soviets began to negotiate with the Swiss on the settlement of their outstanding problems. On 17 April 1927 the two governments reached an agreement that resulted in Soviet participation in a World Economic Conference in Geneva in May. At the conference the Soviets made a concerted effort to improve the international image of the Soviet Union and launched a campaign to secure world recognition for the principles of peaceful coexistence between nations of different socioeconomic systems. The Western nations avoided endorsing peaceful coexistence, but they recognized the general principle of economic cooperation between capitalism and socialism.

After the World Economic Conference, the Soviet government made plans to participate in the Preparatory Commission for the General Disarmament Conference. The issue of disarmament became increasingly important for the Soviet government, as it strove to improve its international position. On 29 October Chicherin announced that the Soviet Union would have representation at the fourth session of the commission, which convened on 30 November. He had not altered his views of either the General Disarmament Conference or the League of Nations and remained opposed to Soviet participation in both organizations. But he loyally and steadfastly implemented the Soviet leadership's policies, even when they clashed with his own personal beliefs and views. Actually, by this time Chicherin had little influence over the conduct of Soviet foreign affairs, for Litvinov was clearly in the ascendancy and Soviet leaders increasingly sought to reduce tension with the West.

Chicherin understood that Soviet diplomatic setbacks in 1927 threatened the stability of German-Soviet relations. Soviet domestic affairs also contributed to an increase in tension between Berlin and Moscow. The Shakhty affair of 1928 signaled the end of NEP in culture—a soft line, a policy of accommodation, toward the bourgeois cultural and technical intelligentsia—and the beginning of the Cultural Revolution. Furthermore, the Shakhty trial was a precursor of the great show trials of the 1930s. On 7 March fifty Soviet and five German engineers and technicians employed in the Shakhty district of the Donbass were arrested. They were accused of industrial sabotage and wrecking and in Moscow were brought to public trial, which began in the Hall of Trade Unions on 18 May. Chicherin was horrified that Soviet security agents had arrested the five German engineers, for he realized that the subsequent outburst of indignation in Germany threatened to disrupt German-Soviet relations immediately after the break between London and Moscow.[14] To make matters worse, not only were the German engineers indicted as individuals, but their companies were also implicated in the wrecking activities. Four of the five engineers worked for the Allgemeine Elektritsitaets Gesellschaft, or the A.E.G., whose chairperson was Felix Deutsch. He actively supported German-Soviet commerce and economic cooperation and had negotiated a large contract for work in the Soviet Union. Deutsch informed Ambassador Rantzau that the A.E.G. would cancel its contract with the Soviets unless the German engineers were released immediately.[15] Rantzau implored Chicherin and Narkomindel to secure the release of the Germans. Two were released fourteen days after their arrest, but the other three, along with the fifty Soviets, were brought to trial.

Although the Soviet government explicitly charged only some engineers and technicians with industrial sabotage and wrecking, by implication the trial was a condemnation of the nonparty intelligentsia as a whole, not just the technical specialists.[16] Stalin despised the cultural and educated elites whom the Soviet government had inherited from the Tsarist regime, and he orchestrated the Shakhty affair. He described the bourgeois technical specialists as enemies of the Soviet state, and he believed they were engaging in counterrevolutionary activities to undermine the government; he further claimed that Western capitalists, determined to weaken the country economically as a prelude to armed intervention, used the technical intelligentsia to create crises in Soviet industry.[17] According to Stalin, the bourgeois specialists, in cooperation with the former owners of industrial enterprises now living abroad, were subverting the Soviet government's efforts to industrialize the country.

Some bourgeois specialists indeed were unenthusiastic about socialism and only half-heartedly and reluctantly offered their professional services to the Soviet government, but the Shakhty engineers and technicians were not guilty of crimes of industrial sabotage and wrecking. The affair symbolized a retreat from NEP in culture; the trial was a revolutionary gesture, and the question of the innocence or guilt of the accused receded into the background.[18] On 7 July the Supreme Court of the Soviet Union rendered a verdict:

eleven of the fifty Soviets were sentenced to death, and the others received long-term imprisonment; two Germans were acquitted, but the third German was sentenced to one year in prison. All were quickly released.

The Shakhty trial unleashed a wave of repression against the nonparty intelligentsia. Party militants advocated an official policy of rejecting accommodation toward the old intelligentsia and sought out instances of industrial sabotage and wrecking by the bourgeois specialists in their districts. The affair served to organize opposition to the nonparty intelligentsia that had been held in check since the introduction of NEP in 1921.[19] Stalin was not responsible for creating antipathy toward the old intelligentsia, but he shared this view and put himself at the head of the movement calling for a reversal of NEP in culture—a hard line of proletarianization in culture and education. He staged the Shakhty trial to demonstrate his support for the party militants and to discredit his political opponents, for the leaders of the Right Opposition—Bukharin, Rykov, and M. P. Tomskii—were defenders of the nonparty intelligentsia.[20]

Chicherin's concerns about the international ramifications of the Shakhty affair were justified. Even though the Germans brought to trial were eventually released, the affair significantly aggravated relations between Berlin and Moscow. Both Chicherin and Rantzau were pessimistic about the future of German-Soviet affairs, realizing it would be difficult to repair the damage the trial had caused. Rantzau, in particular, was upset by the proceedings; although he suffered from throat cancer, he regularly attended the trial as an expression of the German government's intense interest in the outcome. He left Moscow for Germany on 18 July, shortly after the trial was over, and died on 8 September.

The additional strain produced by the Shakhty affair was detrimental to Chicherin's already precarious health. Exhausted and quite ill, his nerves shattered, he arrived in Germany on 10 September, two days after Rantzau's death, for a long period of rest and medical treatment. Chicherin was outspokenly disappointed with the Stalinist government, and a German diplomat in Moscow, Herbert von Dirksen, reported that "Well-founded rumors which leaked through to our Embassy maintained that he wanted to stay in Germany for good, whereas the Kremlin insisted with increasing vigor that he should return.[21] R. H. Bruce Lockhart corroborated von Dirksen's account, describing Chicherin in the spring of 1929 as "a tired, nervous wreck of a man seeking to forget and to be forgotten."[22]

From his residence in Germany Chicherin continued to complain to the Politburo about what he regarded as mistakes in Soviet foreign policy. On 1 May at the traditional parade on Red Square in Moscow, War Commissar Voroshilov delivered a speech attacking the Weimar Republic. Chicherin, who read the war commissar's remarks in the German press, was furious with this public agitation against Germany on one of the most important national holidays in the Soviet Union and dispatched a letter to the Politburo in which he argued Voroshilov's speech would do irreparable harm to German-Soviet relations.[23] Curiously, however, Stalin did not remove Chicherin as commissar of Narkomindel, and the Soviet government repeatedly requested that he return to Moscow. But Chicherin was reluctant to leave Germany, and he was probably too ill to make the long journey to Moscow. Finally, in the autumn the Soviet government sent the chief of the Kremlin medical staff, Dr. L. G. Levin, to Wiesbaden to inquire into Chicherin's health and to persuade him to return to Moscow. In late November the Soviet diplomat L. M. Karakhan arrived in Germany with the intention of bringing Chicherin back to the Soviet Union. Even though Chicherin's physical condition had not improved, Karakhan arranged for a trip to the Soviet Union, and the foreign commissar arrived in Moscow on 6 January 1930, after having spent more than a year abroad.

Chicherin's failing health and Litvinov's growing importance in Narkomindel helped contribute to a gradual reorientation of Soviet foreign policy. Litvinov's diplomacy emphasized disarmament and an effort to reach reconciliation with the Western powers to avoid war until the Soviet Union was industrially prepared for it. Soviet participation in the 1927 World Economic Conference and attendance at the fourth session of the Preparatory Commission for the General Disarmament Conference represented this perspective. In 1928 Soviet leaders debated the merits of adhering to the Briand-Kellogg Pact. Its sponsors, French Foreign Minister Briand and his American counterpart, Secretary of State Frank B. Kellogg, called for a general renunciation of aggressive war. But the pact was little more than a hopeful aspiration, for there was no mechanism to enforce it. Since it offended virtually nobody, nations rushed to sign it. The Soviet government, too, expressed interest in the pact, but the Soviets were not invited to participate in the negotiations that produced it.

Litvinov urged Soviet acceptance of the Briand-Kellogg Pact, but Chicherin was adamantly opposed to it. Chicherin argued that the Western powers were not really interested in obtaining Soviet adherence, since the Soviets had been excluded from the preliminary discussions concerning the pact. Furthermore, he believed it would enforce the diplomatic isolation of the Soviet government and was part of a broad scheme of the Western nations to encircle the Soviet Union. He charged that the pact was the product of counterrevolutionary forces in the West, which would use it to mask their real intentions of preparing to attack the Soviet state. Chicherin also indicated it would be virtually worthless as a means of preserving peace unless it was accompanied by a binding, compulsory agreement on universal disarmament. In an interview with the Soviet press published on 5 August, shortly before the pact was signed in Paris, he acknowledged that the Soviet government was still interested in it provided that the Western powers would negotiate with the Soviets about it.[24] Even though he was expressing the views of the Stalinist leadership when he hinted that the Soviet government would be willing to sign the pact, he personally remained opposed to it and did not think the Western nations would negotiate with the Soviet Union. In essence, Chicherin's disapproval of the Briand-Kellogg Pact was similar to his rejection of the League of Nations; he thought that they were principally directed against the Soviet state and would allow the Western powers to dictate terms to Moscow.

After extensive debate within the Politburo the Stalinist leadership decided to sign the Briand-Kellogg Pact, although the Soviets had not been involved in its formulation. The Communists signed the pact because they were willing to agree to any device that might promote peace.[25] Fifteen powers signed the pact in Paris on 27 August; the Soviets were not invited to be among the original signatories, but they issued a note of adherence on 31 August. And the Soviet Union was the first state formally to ratify the pact. This was the significance of the Litvinov Protocol, which Estonia, Latvia, Poland, Romania, and the Soviet Union signed in Moscow on 9 February 1929, more than six months before the Briand-Kellogg Pact became international law. The Free City of Danzig, Turkey, and Persia signed the protocol on 30 April, 1 July, and 4 July, respectively. The Soviet government feared that the Western powers would delay ratification of the pact for a long period, during which they or the countries bordering on Soviet territory might "legally" be able to attack the Soviet Union. Therefore the protocol made it a working instrument and served as part of the cordon of nonaggression treaties, which the Soviets erected along their borders. The protocol united by a declaration against aggression every one of the neighboring states from Estonia to Persia.[26]

The new orientation in Soviet foreign affairs did not immediately result in Chicherin's dismissal from office after his return to the Soviet Union in January 1930. Stalin retained him as commissar of Narkomindel until 25 July, when Litvinov officially replaced him. The Soviet press announced that Chicherin's retirement was due to illness.[27] Litinov, commenting about his formal appointment as head of Narkomindel, indicated that for the past two years he had actually been in charge of the Commissariat.[28] A journalist, Louis Fischer, reported that Chicherin first learned of his dismissal from the newspapers. And A. A. Gromyko, former Soviet minister of foreign affairs, correctly pointed out that Chicherin's poor health was not the only reason for his retirement.[29] Chicherin and Stalin disliked each other, and with Stalin's rise to power Chicherin's position at Narkomindel became increasingly precarious. According to Fischer, Chicherin had worked well with Lenin and respected Bukharin, "But he had only contempt for Stalin's mind and methods, and Stalin was too sensitive to denigration not to notice it."[30]

Chicherin and Stalin had clashed in March 1921, when the party was making preparations for the Tenth Congress. Stalin, as the party's leading authority on the nationalities question, had published his theses on this issue for consideration by the Bolsheviks in advance of the congress. Chicherin normally did not engage in debate on ideology and avoided internal party politics, but on this occasion he chose to criticize Stalin's treatment of the nationalities problem. The foreign commissar published his objections to Stalin's theses in a series of articles in *Pravda*.[31]

Chicherin did not attack Stalin for his handling of the nationalities in Soviet Russia and failed to offer concrete, specific proposals to replace the general secretary's recommendations. In essence, Chicherin criticized Stalin for his theoretical analysis of national liberation and socialist revolution. Chicherin claimed that Stalin presented an outmoded and simplistic formulation of the nationalities problem by insisting that its resolution would not occur until after the destruction of capitalism and that only the Soviet government championed national self-determination. According to Chicherin, developed or mature capitalism also professed national self-determination as a means of appealing to the oppressed peoples of the world. Furthermore, Chicherin argued that Stalin mistakenly continued to depict the capitalist world as divided into competing nation-states. The foreign commissar believed that World War I witnessed the emergence of a new, more advanced stage of capitalism, a phenomenon he termed superimperialism—international, multinational economic corporations or cartels with enormous political power dominated by a small financial oligarchy. After the war, capitalism increasingly evolved into superimperialism, that is, multinational trusts began to replace the traditional national states as the principal form of capitalist organization. Chicherin also maintained that, in dialectical fashion, the expansion of superimperialism by necessity contained the seeds of its own disintegration, for to him it was not the final stage or culmination of economic development but only a temporary "process or tendency."[32] At the core of his dispute with Stalin was the idea that the latter misunderstood superimperialism; in Chicherin's view it served as a tendency that would not augment nationalist oppression but, on the contrary, would reconcile nationalist tensions by uniting the propertied elements among the various nationalities under the control of the financial oligarchy.

Chicherin's criticism of Stalin on the nationalities issue was different from most of the former's writings. The foreign commissar usually wrote crisply and precisely, aware that his message would have to appeal to a broad public unprepared to deal with the theoretical intricacies of Marxism. But the language he employed to attack Stalin was obtuse, rendering his comments almost incomprehensible to many members of the party. In essence, Chicherin warned the Bolsheviks that movements of national liberation should not be identified with socialist revolution and that capitalism showed remarkable resilience by accommodating demands for national self-determination. While the road to socialist revolution in the West certainly ran through the East, he urged the Soviets to expect a lengthy transition between nationalist upheaval and socialist revolution in Asia and the Middle East.

Stalin, in remarking about Chicherin's articles at the Tenth Congress, made short work of them, claiming that he found nothing

in them but "bookishness." Stalin charged that Chicherin underesti-
mated the contradictions among capitalist states and exaggerated
the importance of multinational corporations and cartels, failing to
recognize the internal divisions within them. Stalin insisted that
Chicherin misunderstood the antagonism and tension between the
great powers and recently established nation-states, for the latter
deeply resented the economic and military superiority of the former. Stalin's principal objection to Chicherin's articles focused on
the concept of national self-determination. The general secretary
stressed that he had not employed the term and that it was not part
of the party's program; instead, he substituted the idea that every
nationality voluntarily joining the Soviet state had the right to leave
the federation at any time and form its own government. More
importantly, Stalin stressed that this concept, as opposed to the dif-
fuse, unspecific notion of national self-determination, was genuinely revolutionary and would thus appeal to the colonial and
oppressed peoples of the East.[33]

Since Chicherin did not offer any practical alternatives to
Stalin's position, the congress voted to accept Stalin's theses as part
of the party's program. The experience disgraced and humiliated
Chicherin; at one time he had been nominated for a place on the
Nationality Commission, but after his dispute with Stalin the nomi-
nating committee dropped his name from the list. Chicherin's only
attempt to enter into debate on party ideology ended in failure, and
he made a costly political mistake by attacking Stalin. The general
secretary did not forget insults and slights, and the controversy at
the congress reinforced his antipathy toward Chicherin.

The 1921 clash between Chicherin and Stalin contributed to
but was not the principal reason for the antagonism between the two
men. Chicherin was one of the finest representatives of the
nineteenth-century Russian cultural intelligentsia, and by background, education, and temperament he was substantially different
from Stalin. And with the notable exception of Stalin, most of the
old Bolsheviks were from the ranks of the intelligentsia. Stalin was
acutely aware that many of the old Bolsheviks were culturally distinguished intellectuals who spoke several European languages and
who were knowledgeable about the history and literature of Western
civilization, qualities he himself did not possess. Along with his disdain for the old intelligentsia, Stalin was suspicious of them. In 1925
he commented that the Bolshevik intellectuals had outlived their

usefulness to the party and it was time for them to step aside so people of proletarian origins could assume positions of leadership.[34] His attacks on other Bolshevik leaders, men like Trotskii, Bukharin, Zinov'ev, and Kamenev, must be understood in light of his attitude toward the intelligentsia. The lower ranks of the party, especially those who joined it after the Civil War and who were of peasant or proletarian heritage, shared Stalin's distrust of and dislike for the intelligentsia, and he used this support to defeat his political opponents.

Yet the differences between Chicherin and Stalin did not lead the former to support Trotskii in the struggle for power within the party during the mid-1920s. Chicherin's domain was foreign affairs, and he scrupulously avoided inner party politics. Also, his dislike of Trotskii was as strong as his aversion to Stalin. After Lenin's death in 1924, Chicherin became increasingly isolated from the party leadership. During the late twenties Chicherin was probably closer to Bukharin than to the others on the Politburo, although the former was not a member of the Right Opposition.[35]

When Chicherin resided in Western Europe at the end of the 1920s, he was preoccupied with writing about Mozart, whose music he had deeply admired and appreciated since childhood. Chicherin completed the manuscript, which he called a letter or an essay, shortly before his retirement at the beginning of July 1930. According to his personal secretary, B. I. Korotkin, he did not intend it for publication. But Chicherin showed the manuscript of 236 pages to A. V. Lunacharskii, the former commissar of Narkompros, who strongly recommended its publication as the first Marxist study of Mozart. Kalinin, the chairperson of the Central Executive Committee of the Supreme Soviet, added his enthusiastic endorsement. On 29 April 1934 a decision was made to publish Chicherin's manuscript in an initial edition of 250 copies. But Stalin blocked its publication, and the manuscript did not appear until after his death, largely through the efforts of Chicherin's niece, S. N. Chicherina, a composer who lived in Leningrad.[36]

After his dismissal from office in 1930 to his death in 1936, Chicherin lived an isolated, solitary existence, as he ceased to play a role in government affairs and virtually dropped out of sight. In 1931 rumors circulated that he had become an alcoholic and was so impoverished that he was reduced to begging on the streets of Moscow.[37] The Soviet government denied these reports, but they persisted, for he had been evicted from his room at Narkomindel on

Kuznetskii Most. By the following year the Central Committee took
action to provide for his care. He occupied an apartment not far
from Spaso House, the residence of the American ambassador to the
Soviet Union. According to George F. Kennan, former ambassador
of the United States to the Soviet Union, the Spaso House
furnaceman was responsible for periodically cleaning Chicherin's
quarters. Chicherin continued to suffer from diabetes and
polyneuritis, and his nervous illness probably developed into mad-
ness. His health deteriorated dramatically in January 1936, and he
was moved to the Kremlin hospital later in the year, where he died of
a brain hemorrhage on 7 July.[38]

A memorial service was held for Chicherin in the conference
room of Narkomindel on 9 July. On Stalin's orders, Krestinskii,
then deputy foreign commissar and former ambassador to Germany, delivered a funeral oration in which he denounced
Chicherin's management of Narkomindel.[39] But former Foreign
Minister Gromyko officially rehabilitated Chicherin by an article
appearing in *Izvestiia* on 5 December 1962. Gromyko acknowledged that Stalin had distorted Chicherin's considerable contribution to Soviet diplomacy and the consolidation of the Soviet
government in Russia.[40] Thus Gromyko correctly acclaimed
Chicherin as one of the leading diplomats in Soviet history.

During the 1920s Soviet foreign affairs essentially involved the
interaction between diplomacy and revolution. When the Bolsheviks acquired power in Russia in 1917, they assumed that the
November Revolution had rendered traditional diplomatic practices unnecessary for the new socialist era. They confidently and
eagerly anticipated the spread of socialism throughout the world.
For them the destruction of capitalism would mean the elimination
of conflict among nations, for the socialist states would cooperate
with each other and coordinate policies to produce fundamental
economic and social changes. But the failure of international socialist revolution compelled the Bolsheviks to use traditional diplomacy as a means of regulating and regularizing their relations with
the capitalist powers. The party increasingly understood that, confronted with capitalist encirclement, diplomacy would be instrumental in deterring foreign aggression so that the fledgling Soviet
government would have time to consolidate its position and develop
an advanced industrial economy. Therefore, while revolution

clearly dominated during the early twenties, by the end of the decade diplomacy was in the ascendancy. Yet the Soviets did not abandon their emphasis on international revolution or their belief in the inevitable clash between capitalism and socialism. Viewed from this perspective, the establishment of normal, regular diplomatic relations with the Western powers would help maintain the defense of the Soviet state until historical circumstances were once again propitious for world revolution.

As commissar of Narkomindel from 1918 to 1930, Chicherin made an original and substantial contribution to the consolidation of the Soviet government in Russia. He was widely regarded, even among his critics, as one of the leading diplomats in Europe. Moreover, he worked indefatigably to normalize diplomatic relations with the capitalist states, thus helping to legitimize the Soviet government. Although he was not a political leader and never served on the Politburo, and even though he did not create foreign policy, Chicherin had a significant impact on the conduct of foreign affairs. He, more than any other member of the party, set the style for and contributed to the prestige of Soviet diplomacy during the twenties. His dedication to socialism and loyalty to the party were unquestioned, and he performed his duties and responsibilities with a determination and zeal virtually unmatched even among the old Bolsheviks. Chicherin the revolutionary understood the need for effective, professional diplomacy for the survival of the Soviet state in a hostile world.

Chicherin's heritage and education were also part of the reason for his diplomatic skills. His family had been active in the diplomatic service, and he himself had worked in the archives division of the Tsarist Ministry of Foreign Affairs before becoming a revolutionary. Chicherin possessed a thorough knowledge of European history and literature and a remarkably retentive memory, attributes that served him well as foreign commissar. He was a splendid representative of the nineteenth-century cultural intelligentsia.

Chicherin regarded Germany as the key to Soviet foreign policy during the 1920s, and the high point of his career was the Treaty of Rapallo, which ended the international isolation of the Soviet state and guaranteed German neutrality in the event of conflict with the capitalist West. For him Britain was the principal opponent of the Soviet government, and he supported movements of national liberation in Asia and the Middle East to undermine British imperialism. As the prospects for socialist revolution in the West diminished after 1923, Chicherin increasingly focused attention on the East. His appeals for national liberation from foreign domination and arguments in favor of socialism over capitalism for industrial development found a receptive audience among the colonial and oppressed peoples of Asia and the Middle East.

As long as Lenin was alive Chicherin played an important role in the implementation and execution of Soviet foreign policy. During the mid-1920s Chicherin was able to exercise some autonomy in the management of Narkomindel and the conduct of foreign affairs, since the party leaders were preoccupied with a struggle for political power. As Stalin emerged victorious and consolidated his position at the end of the decade, Chicherin became more isolated within the party and exerted much less influence on Soviet diplomacy. Even though Stalin did not dismiss Chicherin until 1930, at least two years earlier, by 1928, Chicherin had virtually ceased to function as commissar of Narkomindel.

Litvinov, who succeeded Chicherin at Narkomindel, represented a new orientation in Soviet foreign affairs. On the one hand Litvinov sought reconciliation with the West and emphasized collective security, symbolized by the growing Soviet acceptance of the League of Nations. On the other hand Chicherin deplored the gradual deterioration in relations with Germany; remained wary of the Western powers, fearing that they were determined to dictate terms to Moscow; and was firmly opposed to the League, preferring bilateral neutrality and nonaggression agreements with neighboring states. But his retirement in 1930 did not come from policy changes alone, for Stalin dismissed him as part of the purge of the nonparty intelligentsia during the Cultural Revolution.

Chicherin established the foundation of Soviet diplomacy during the 1920s. He oversaw the development of Narkomindel into one of the most effective and significant Commissariats of the Soviet government. Just as importantly, he set high professional standards for Soviet diplomats, thus serving as a model for others to emulate. Finally, Chicherin successfully combined the defense of traditional Russian geopolitical interests with unswerving devotion to the socialist goals of the Soviet state.

Notes

Abbreviations and their full titles in transliteration for materials in the Soviet archives are as follows:

f.	*fond*
op.	*opis'*
DP	*Department politsii*
OO	*Osobyi otdel*
d.	*delo*
t.	*tom*
ch.	*chast'*

CHAPTER 1

1. I. M. Maiskii, *Liudi. Sobytiia. Fakty*, Otdelenie istorii Akademii nauk SSSR (Moskva: Nauka, 1973), 120; and *Vospominaniia sovetskogo posla v dvukh knigakh*, Kniga pervaia: *Puteshestvie v proshloe*, Otdelenie istoricheskikh nauk Akademii nauk SSSR (Moskva: Nauka, 1964), 264–65.

2. It has not been determined whether Afanasii Chicherini was of Italian origins, or whether he was a Russian merchant trading in Italy. Most memoir accounts indicate that he was an Italian. See E. M. Chossudovsky, *Chicherin and the Evolution of Soviet Foreign Policy and Diplomacy* (Geneva: Graduate Institute of International Studies, 1973), 7, n. 3. According to Robert H. Hodgson, "Obituary: George Chicherin," *Slavonic and East European Review* 15 (Apr. 1937):698, "The form of the name before the 18th century was Chicherini." But, in contrast, one source maintains that Afanasii Chicherini's son, Ivan Avanasevich, who died as a monk in a monastery, was the first to use the form Chicherin. See *Entsiklopedicheskii slovar'*, tom 76, s.v. "Chicherini."

3. S. V. Zarnitskii and A. N. Sergeev, *Chicherin*, Zhizn' zamechatel'nykh

liudei, Seriia biografii, vypusk 8 (423) (Moskva: Molodaia gvardiia, 1966), 7.

4. Baron Alexander Meyendorff, "My Cousin, Foreign Commissar Chicherin," ed. Igor Vinogradoff, *Russian Review* 30 (Apr. 1971):174, n. 1; *Entsiklopedicheskii slovar' Russkogo bibliograficheskogo instituta Granat,* Sed'moe izdanie, tom 41, *chast'* III, s.v. "Georgii Vasil'evich Chicherin"; and Hodgson, "Obituary: George Chicherin," 698–99.

5. *Entsiklopedicheskii slovar' Russkogo bibliograficheskogo instituta Granat,* s.v. "Georgii Vasil'evich Chicherin"; I. Gorokhov, L. Zamiatin, and I. Zemskov, *G. V. Chicherin: Diplomat leninskoi shkoly,* Pod obshchei redaktsiei i s vstupitel'noi statei V. S. Semenova (Moskva: Politizdat, 1966), 9; and I. M. Khovratovich, *Georgii Vasil'evich Chicherin,* Partiinye publitsisty No. 1395 (Moskva: Mysl', 1980), 5. Even though Chicherin was born on 12 November, the priest who baptized him wrote 20 November by mistake as his birthday on the birth certificate.

6. *Entsiklopedicheskii slovar' Russkogo bibliograficheskogo instituta Granat,* s.v. "Georgii Vasil'evich Chicherin"; A. Mogilat and V. Panov, "Polpred revoliutsii," *Komsomol'skaia pravda,* 29 noibria 1983 g.; Zarnitskii and Sergeev, *Chicherin,* 9; and Gorokhov, Zamiatin, and Zemskov, *G. V. Chicherin: Diplomat leninskoi shkoly,* 12.

7. Zarnitskii and Sergeev, *Chicherin,* 9. Correspondence between Georgii Vasil'evich and his brother and sister-in-law is located in *Tsentral'nyi gosudarstvennyi istoricheskii arkhiv SSSR* (TsGIA SSSR), Leningrad, and *Tsentral'nyi gosudarstvennyi arkhiv Oktiabr'skoi revoliutsii SSSR* (TsGAOR SSSR), Moscow. In addition, Georgii Vasil'evich corresponded extensively with his aunt and uncle, Aleksandra Alekseevna Chicherina and Boris Nikolaevich Chicherin. See TsGAOR SSSR, f. 1154, op. 1, d. 157; d. 588; d. 589.

8. Hodgson, "Obituary: George Chicherin," 698–99; *Entsiklopedicheskii slovar' Russkogo bibliograficheskogo instituta Granat,* s.v. "Georgii Vasil'evich Chicherin"; N. A. Ravich, *Molodost' veka* (Moskva: Voennoe izdatel'stvo Ministerstva oborony Soiuza SSR, 1960), 301; and Gorokhov, Zamiatin, and Zemskov, *G. V. Chicherin: Diplomat leninskoi shkoly,* 11–12.

9. *Entsiklopedicheskii slovar' Russkogo bibliograficheskogo instituta Granat,* s.v. "Georgii Vasil'evich Chicherin"; and Zarnitskii and Sergeev, *Chicherin,* 11.

10. Gorokhov, Zamiatin, and Zemskov, *G. V. Chicherin: Diplomat leninskoi shkoly,* 12; and *Entsiklopedicheskii slovar' Russkogo bibliograficheskogo instituta Granat,* s.v. "Georgii Vasil'evich Chicherin."

11. *Entsiklopedicheskii slovar' Russkogo bibliograficheskogo institua Granat,* s.v. "Georgii Vasil'evich Chicherin"; George Haupt and Jean-Jacques Marie, eds., *Makers of the Russian Revolution: Biographies of Bolshevik Leaders,* trans. from the Russian by C. I. P. Ferdinand, Commentaries trans. from the French by D. M. Bellos (Ithaca: Cornell Univ. Press, 1974), 331–32; Zarnitskii and Sergeev, *Chicherin,* 14; and Gorokhov, Zamiatin, and Zemskov, *G. V. Chicherin: Diplomat leninskoi shkoly,* 13.

12. *Entsiklopedicheskii slovar' Russkogo bibliograficheskogo instituta Granat,* s.v. "Georgii Vasil'evich Chicherin"; Gorokhov, Zamiatin, and Zemskov, *G. V. Chicherin: Diplomat leninskoi shkoly,* 14; L. I. Trofimova, "Stranitsa diplomaticheskoi deiatel'nosti G. V. Chicherina," *Voprosy istorii* 2

(fevral' 1973 g.):114; and G. B. Kizel'shtein, "O rukopisi G. V. Chicherina, posviashchennoi diplomaticheskoi deiatel'nosti A. M. Gorchakova," *Novaia i noveishaia istoriia AN SSSR* 4 (1966):129.

13. Zarnitskii and Sergeev, *Chicherin*, 18–19.

14. Richard K. Debo, "George Chicherin: Soviet Russia's Second Foreign Commissar" (Ph.D. diss., University of Nebraska, 1964,) 9. Also see *Entsiklopedicheskii slovar' Russkogo bibliograficheskogo institua Granat*, s.v. "Georgii Vasil'evich Chicherin"; and Maiskii, *Puteshestvie v proshloe*, 265.

15. Haupt and Marie, eds., *Makers of the Russian Revolution*, 334. And see Maiskii, *Puteshestvie v proshloe*, 265.

16. *Entsiklopedicheskii slovar' Russkogo bibliograficheskogo instituta Granat*, s.v. "Georgii Vasil'evich Chicherin"; Zarnitskii and Sergeev, *Chicherin*, 19; and Kizel'shtein, "O rukopisi G. V. Chicherina," 129.

17. Chicherin's manuscript is located in TsGIA SSSR, Leningrad.

18. I. Kovalev, "Neizvestnaia rukopis' G. V. Chicherina," *Neva* 5 (1964) :221; and Kizel'shtein, "O rukopisi G. V. Chicherina," 129–30.

19. Kovalev, "Neizvestnaia rukopis' G. V. Chicherina," 221.

20. Kizel'shtein, "O rukopisi G. V. Chicherina," 130–31.

21. Ibid., 130.

22. Zarnitskii and Sergeev, *Chicherin*, 21.

23. Zarnitskii and Sergeev, *Chicherin*, 21; *Entsiklopedicheskii slovar' Russkogo bibliograficheskogo institua Granat*, s.v. "Georgii Vasil'evich Chicherin"; Khovratovich, *Georgii Vasil'evich Chicherin*, 8; and Gorokhov, Zamiatin, and Zemskov, *G. V. Chicherin: Diplomat leninskoi shkoly*, 16.

24. *Entsiklopedicheskii slovar' Russkogo bibliograficheskogo instituta Granat*, s.v. "Georgii Vasil'evich Chicherin"; and Gorokhov, Zamiatin, and Zemskov, *G. V. Chicherin: Diplomat leninskoi shkoly*, 16.

25. Bessie Beatty, "Chicherin," *New Republic* 30 (17 May 1922):335.

26. Debo, "George Chicherin," 5–6.

27. Hodgson, "Obituary: George Chicherin," 698–99.

28. Beatty, "Chicherin," 335.

29. Maiskii, *Liudi. Sobytiia. Fakty*, 121.

CHAPTER 2

1. TsGAOR SSSR, f. 102, DP, 00, 1907, d. 9, t. 1, 36, 38–39.

2. *Entsiklopedicheskii slovar' Russkogo bibliograficheskogo institua Granat*, s.v. "Georgii Vasil'evich Chicherin"; and Angelica Balabanoff, *My Life as a Rebel* (New York: Harper, 1938), 68.

3. After Georgii Vasil'evich refused to inherit Karaul, the estate passed to Boris Andreevich Chicherin—another nephew of Boris Nikolaevich. After the Bolsheviks acquired power in Russia, the new Soviet government nationalized Karaul. On 7 July 1918 according to order No. 3324 of the Commissariat of Enlightenment (Narkompros) the estate became a national monument under the protection of the Soviet government. In 1923 the G. V. Chicherin Children's Home was established on Karaul. See G. B. Kizel'shtein, " 'Muchitel'no

174 NOTES TO PAGES 16-24

zhazhdu vysokoi tseli.' Iz arkhiva G. V. Chicherina," *Ogonek* 48 (noiabr' 1963)
:18; and Meyendorff, "My Cousin, Foreign Commissar George Chicherin,"
175.

4. TsGAOR SSSR, f. 102, DP, 00, 1907, d. 513, 4, 11, 37–39.
5. TsGAOR SSSR, f. 102, DP, 00, 1907, d. 513, 4–5, 37–39; and TsGAOR
SSSR, f. 102, DP, 00, 1913, d. 258, 4.
6. Trofimova, "Stranitsa diplomaticheskoi deiatel'nosti G. V.
Chicherina,"114–15; *Entsiklopedicheskii slovar' Russkogo bibliograficheskogo
instituta Granat,* s.v. "Georgii Vasil'evich Chicherin"; Khovratovich, *Georgii
Vasil'evich Chicherin,* 8–9; and TsGAOR SSSR, f. 102, DP, 00, 1907, d. 513, 5.
7. Debo, "George Chicherin," 25–26.
8. *Entsiklopedicheskii slovar' Russkogo bibliograficheskogo instituta
Granat,* s.v. "Georgii Vasil'evich Chicherin."
9. Leonard B. Schapiro, *The Communist Party of the Soviet Union* (New
York: Random House, 1959), 86–89. Moreover, it should be noted that the Bolshevik Center has generated heated debate among historians. For example,
Avraham Yassour, "Lenin and Bogdanov: Protagonists in the 'Bolshevik Center'," *Studies in Soviet Thought* 22 (Feb. 1981):12, makes the following
comment about the time of its establishment: "From a formal point of view the
Bolshevik Center was probably chosen from among the Bolshevik delegates to
the new Central Committee elected at the Fifth Congress in London (May
1907), and which operated thereafter under the aegis of the enlarged editorial
board of *Proletarij.* The nucleus of this factional Center had been functioning,
however, continuously since . . . 1904. . . ."
10. Robert H. McNeal, gen. ed., *Resolutions and Decisions of the Communist Party of the Soviet Union,* 4 vols. (Toronto: Univ. of Toronto Press, 1974),
vol. 1, *The Russian Social Democratic Labour Party, 1898–October 1917,* ed.
Ralph C. Elwood, 99–100.
11. Ibid., 114–15.
12. Both Schapiro, *The Communist Party of the Soviet Union,* 104–11, and
David Shub, "Kamo: The Legendary Old Bolshevik of the Caucasus," *Russian
Review* 19 (July 1960):227, indicate that the Tiflis robbery yielded 250,000
rubles. But Bertram D. Wolfe, *Three Who Made a Revolution: A Biographical
History,* Beacon Contemporary Affairs Series (Boston: Beacon Press, 1948;
reprint ed., New York: Dell, 1964), 393–94, mentions the figure 341,000 rubles.
The most detailed study of Kamo and Bolshevik expropriations in the
Transcaucasus is by A. B. Arutiunian (Arents), *Kamo. Zhizn' i revoliutsionnaia
deiatel'nost'* (Erevan: Izdatel'stvo Erevanskogo universiteta, 1958).
13. Wolfe, *Three Who Made a Revolution,* 393–94.
14. TsGAOR SSSR, f. 102, DP, 00, 1907, d. 513, 37–39; and TsGAOR
SSSR, f. 102, DP, 00, 1908, d. 5, ch. 84, t. 2, 132–35, 143–44, 149–50, 219–25.
15. TsGAOR SSSR, f. 102, DP, 00, 1908, d. 5, ch. 84, t. 2, 143–44, 149–50,
164–66, 177–78, 219–25.
16. TsGAOR SSSR, f. 102, DP, 00, 1908, d. 58, ch. 84, t. 2, 143–44, 149–
50, 164–66, 219–25; and TsGAOR SSSR, f. 102, DP, 00, 1907, d. 513, 37–39.
17. TsGAOR SSSR, f. 102, DP, 00, 1908, d. 5, ch. 84, t. 2, 219–26.
18. Ibid., 254, 268.
19. Elwood, ed., *The Russian Social Democratic Labour Party,* 129–130.

20. TsGAOR SSSR, f. 102, DP, 00, 1907, d. 513, 37–39; and *Entsiklopedicheskii slovar' Russkogo bibliograficheskogo instituta Granat*, s.v. "Georgii Vasil'evich Chicherin."

21. TsGAOR SSSR, f. 102, DP, 00, 1907, d. 513, 13, 19–20, 29–30, 32, 37–39.

22. Schapiro, *The Communist Party of the Soviet Union*, 104–11.

23. Ibid.

24. TsGAOR SSSR, f. 102, DP, 00, 1910, d. 5, 30, 38, 95, 96–97, 99, 203–8, 212–13, 322.

25. Ibid., 95, 203–8, 234–35, 242.

26. Robert C. Williams, "Collective Immortality: The Syndicalist Origins of Proletarian Culture, 1905–1910," *Slavic Review* 39 (Sept. 1980):398–99.

27. TsGAOR SSSR, f. 102, DP, 00, 1910, d. 5, 203–8.

28. Ibid., 203–8, 234–39, 242–44, 245–50.

29. TsGAOR SSSR, f. 102, DP, 00, 1910, d. 5, 203–8, 234–39, 242–44, 245–50; and *Entsiklopedicheskii slovar' Russkogo bibliograficheskogo instituta Granat*, s.v. "Georgii Vasil'evich Chicherin."

30. Debo, "George Chicherin," 46–48.

31. TsGAOR SSSR, f. 102, DP, 00, 1910, d. 5, 72, 100–101, 120, 145–46; and TsGAOR SSSR, f. 102, DP, 00, 1911, d. 5, ch. 1, 141.

32. TsGAOR SSSR, f. 102, DP, 00, 1910, d. 5, 72, 100–101, 120, 145–46; and TsGAOR SSSR, f. 102, DP, 00, 1910, d. 5, t. 3, 283.

33. TsGAOR SSSR, f. 102, DP, 00, 1910, d. 5, 72, 100–101, 120, 145–46; and TsGAOR SSSR, f. 102, DP, 00, 1911, d. 5, ch. 1, 50, 106, 111, 124–25, 133, 148–49.

34. TsGAOR SSSR, f. 102, DP, 00, 1910, d. 5, 203–8, 234–39, 242–44, 245–50.

35. TsGAOR SSSR, f. 102, DP, 00, 1910, d. 5, 121–24, 137–39, 203–8, 234–39, 242–44, 245–50; and *Entsikolpedicheskii slovar' Russkogo bibliograficheskogo instituta Granat*, s.v. "Georgii Vasil'evich Chicherin."

36. Elwood, ed., *The Russian Social Democratic Labour Party*, 157.

37. Isaac Deutscher, *The Prophet Armed, Trotsky: 1879–1921* (London: Oxford Univ. Press, 1954), 222–23.

38. I. M. Maiskii, *Puteshestvie v proshloe. Vospominaniia o russkoi politicheskoi emigratsii v Londone 1912–1917 gg.*, Otdelenie istoricheskikh nauk Akademii nauk SSSR (Moskva: Izdatel'stvo Akademii nauk SSSR, 1960), 85; and Isabel de Palencia, *Alexandra Kollontay: Ambassadress from Russia* (New York: Longmans, Green, 1947), 54–55.

39. TsGAOR SSSR, f. 102, DP, 00, 1913, d. 258, 5, 9, 10–11, 27–40.

40. *Entsiklopedicheskii slovar' Russkogo bibliograficheskogo instituta Granat*, s.v. "Georgii Vasil'evich Chicherin."

41. Ibid.

42. Hodgson, "Obituary: George Chicherin," 700.

43. S. V. Tiutiukin, "Stranitsa biografii G. V. Chicherina (1914–1917 gg.)," *Istoricheskie zapiski AN SSSR* 79 (1966):246–47.

44. Ibid., 248–50.

45. *Entsiklopedicheskii slovar' Russkogo bibliograficheskogo instituta Granat*, s.v. "Georgii Vasil'evich Chicherin."

46. I. M. Khovratovich, "Neizvestnye psevdonimy G. Chicherina," *Zhurnalist* 6 (iiun' 1974):56; Tiutiukin, "Stranitsa biografii G. V. Chicherina

(1914–1917 gg.)," 252–53, including n. 48; and L. D. Trotskii, *My Life* (New York: Scribner's, 1930; reprint ed., Universal Library, UL-72, Grosset and Dunlap, 1960), 348.

47. Maiskii, *Liudi. Sobytiia. Fakty*, 121–22; *Puteshestvie v proshloe*, 84–85; *Vospominaniia sovetskogo posla*, 266–67; and "Diplomats of the Lenin School: Georgi Chicherin," *New Times* 44 (1 Nov. 1967):10.

48. Maiskii, "Georgi Chicherin," 10; and see Iu. B. Riurikov, ed., *Mikhail Kol'tsov, kakim on byl. Vospominaniia* (Moskva: Sovetskii pisatel', 1965), 21.

49. Hodgson, "Obituary: George Chicherin," 701; and Maiskii, *Puteshestvie v proshloe*, 87; and *Vospominaniia sovetskogo posla*, 268–69.

50. Hodgson, "Obituary: George Chicherin," 701.

51. Orn, "V 'svobodnoi' Anglii," *Nashe slovo* (Paris), No. 234, 7 noiabria 1915, 1.

52. Orn, "17 oktiabria v Londone," *Nashe slovo* (Paris), No. 245, 20 noiabria 1915, 1; "Londonskaia rabochaia konferentsiia," *Nashe slovo* (Paris), No. 7 (395), 9 ianvaria 1916, 1; "Londonskaia rabochaia konferentsiia i bor'ba protiv 'konskriptsii' (I)," *Nashe slovo* (Paris), No. 22 (409), 27 ianvaria 1916, 1; "Londonskaia rabochaia konferentsiia i bor'ba protiv 'konskriptsii' (II)," *Nashe slovo* (Paris), No. 23 (410), 28 ianvaria 1916, 1; "Londonskaia rabochaia konferentsiia i bor'ba protiv 'konskriptsii' (III)," *Nashe slovo* (Paris), No. 24 (411), 29 ianvaria 1916, 1; "Londonskaia rabochaia konferentsiia i bor'ba protiv 'konskriptsii' (IV)," No. 25 (412), 30 ianvaria 1916, 1; "Dve konferentsii. (Na osnovanii angliiskoi pechati.) (I)," *Nashe slovo* (Paris), No. 107 (493), 7 maia 1916, 1; "Dve konferentsii. (Na osnovanii angliiskoi pechati). (II)," *Nashe slovo* (Paris), No. 108 (494), 9 maia 1916, 1; "Spory o sozyve Mezhdunarodnoe Sotsialisticheskoe Biuro. (Pis'mo iz Anglii.) (I)," *Nashe slovo* (Paris), No. 51 (438), 1 marta 1916, 1; and "Spory o sozyve Mezhdunarodnoe Sotsialisticheskoe Biuro. (Pis'mo iz Anglii.) (II)," *Nashe slovo* (Paris), No. 52 (439), 2 marta 1916, 1.

53. Orn, "Londonskaia rabochaia konferentsiia," 1; "Londonskaia rabochaia konferentsiia i bor'ba protiv 'konskriptsii' (I)," 1; "Londonskaia rabochaia konferentsiia i bor'ba protiv 'konskriptsii' (II)," 1; "Londonskaia rabochaia konferentsiia i bor'ba protiv 'konskriptsii' (III)," 1; "Londonskaia rabochaia konferentsiia i bor'ba protiv 'konskriptsii' (IV)," 1; "Dve konferentsii. (Na osnovanii angliiskoi pechati.) (I)," 1; and "Dve konferentsii. (Na osnovanii angliiskoi pechati.) (II)," 1.

54. Orn, "Londonskaia rabochaia konferentsiia," 1; "Londonskaia rabochaia konferentsiia i bor'ba protiv 'konskriptsii' (I)," 1; "Londonskaia rabochaia konferentsiia i bor'ba protiv 'konskriptsii' (II)," 1; "Londonskaia rabochaia konferentsiia i bor'ba protiv 'konskriptsii' (III)," 1; "Londonskaia rabochaia konferentsiia i bor'ba protiv 'konskriptsii' (IV)," 1; "Spory o sozyve Mezhdunarodnoe Sotsialisticheskoe Biuro. (Pis'mo iz Anglii.) (I)," 1; "Spory o sozyve Mezhdunarodnoe Sotsialisticheskoe Biuro. (Pis'mo iz Anglii.) (II)," 1; and "Sotsialisty drugoi epokhi," *Nashe slovo* (Paris), No. 196 (582), 26 avgusta 1916, 2; and Londonskaia gruppa sodeistviia RSDRP, "Ob otnoshenii k sotsial-patriotam," *Nashe slovo* (Paris), No. 18 (405), 22 ianvaria 1916, 1.

55. Orn, "K arestu tov. Petrova," *Nashe slovo* (Paris), No. 6 (394), 8 ianvaria 1916, 2; and "Beseda s tov. P. M. Petrovym (I)," *Izvestiia (News)* No. 17

(281), 23 ianvaria 1918, 2; and "Beseda s tov. P. M. Petrovym (II)," *Izvestiia*, No. 18 (282), 24 ianvaria 1918, 1–2.

56. Orn, "K arestu tov. Petrova," 2; "Beseda s tov. P. M. Petrovym (I)," 2; "Beseda s tov. P. M. Petrovym (II)," 1–2; "Donos 'Justice,' 'organa Sots-Demokratii,' " *Nashe slovo* (Paris), No. 5 (393), 7 ianvaria 1916, 1; "K arestu tov. Petrova," *Nashe slovo* (Paris), No. 9 (397), 12 ianvaria 1916, 1; "Shotlandskoe rabochee dvizhenie i reaktsiia v Anglii (I)," *Nashe slovo* (Paris), No. 114 (500), 16 maia 1916, 2–3; "Shotlandskoe rabochee dvizhenie i reaktsiia v Anglii (II)," *Nashe slovo* (Paris), No. 116, 18 maia 1916, 1; "Shotlandskoe rabochee dvizhenie i reaktsiia v Anglii (III)," *Nashe slovo* (Paris), No. 118 (504), 20 maia 1916, 1–2; "Shotlandskoe rabochee dvizhenie i reaktsiia v Anglii (IV)," *Nashe slovo* (Paris), No. 131 (517), 6 iiunia 1916, 1; No. 132 (518), 7 iiunia 1916, 1; and "Shotlandskoe rabochee dvizhenie i reaktsiia v Anglii (V)," *Nashe slovo* (Paris), No. 134 (520), 9 iiunia 1916, 1; No. 135 (521), 10 iiunia 1916, 1.

57. Orn, "Donos 'Justice,' 'organa Sots-Demokratii,' " 1; "Delo tov. Petrova i dvizhenie v Shotlandii," *Nashe slovo* (Paris), No. 44 (431), 23 fevralia 1916, 1; "Shotlandskoe rabochee dvizhenie i reaktsiia v Anglii (I)," 2–3; "Shotlandskoe rabochee dvizhenie i reaktsiia v Anglii (II)," 1; "Shotlandskoe rabochee dvizhenie i reaktsiia v Anglii (III)," 1–2; "Shotlandskoe rabochee dvizhenie i reaktsiia v Anglii (IV)," No. 131 (517), 1; No. 132 (518), 1; "Shotlandskoe rabochee dvizhenie i reaktsiia v Anglii (V)," No. 134 (520), 1; No. 135 (521), 1; "Manevry protiv agitatsii za osvobozhdenie t. Maklina," *Nashe slovo* (Paris), No. 160 (546), 11 iiulia 1916, 1; and "Sotsialisty drugoi epokhi," 2.

58. TsGAOR SSSR, f. 102, DP, 00, 1916, d. 99, 110–13; Orn, "Arest tov. Bridzhes-Adams," *Nashe slovo* (Paris), No. 157 (543), 7 iiulia 1916, 1; and Maiskii, *Puteshestvie v proshloe*, 88–89; and *Vospominaniia sovetskogo posla*, 270.

59. TsGAOR SSSR, f. 102, DP, 00, 1916, d. 99, 110–13.

60. TsGAOR SSSR, f. 102, DP, 00, 1916, d. 99, 110–13, 148–53; Orn, "Otmena prava ubezhishcha," *Nashe slovo* (Paris), No. 163 (549), 14 iiulia 1916, 1; and "Arest tov. Bridzhes-Adams," 1.

61. TsGAOR SSSR, f. 102, DP, 00, 1916, d. 99, 148–53; and Orn, "Otmena prava ubezhishcha," 1.

62. TsGAOR SSSR, f. 102, DP, 00, 1916, d. 99, 148–53; and Orn, "Arest tov. Bridzhes-Adams," 1.

63. TsGAOR SSSR, f. 102, DP, 00, 1916, d. 99, 148–53.

64. TsGAOR SSSR, f. 102, DP, 00, 1916, d. 99, 148–53; and Orn, "Arest tov. Bridzhes-Adams," 1.

65. TsGAOR SSSR, f. 102, DP, 00, 1916, d. 99, 148–53; Orn, "Arest tov. Bridzhes-Adams," 1; "Otema prava ubezhishcha," 1; "Pravo ubezhishcha v Anglii," *Nachalo* (Paris), No. 48, 25 noiabria 1916, 1; and "K polozheniiu russkoi emigratsii v Anglii," *Nashe slovo* (Paris), No. 143 (529), 21 iiunia 1916, 1.

66. TsGAOR SSSR, f. 102, DP, 00, 1916, d. 99, 148–53.

67. "K polozheniiu russkoi emigratsii v Anglii," 1; "Russkie emigranty v Anglii," *Nashe slovo* (Paris), No. 155 (541), 5 iiulia 1916, 1; and Orn, "Novyi

shag angliiskogo pravitel'stva v voprose o prave ubezhishcha," *Nashe slovo* (Paris), No. 200 (586), 31 avgusta 1916, 1.

68. Orn, "Novyi shag angliiskogo pravitel'stva," 1; "Pravo ubezhishcha v Anglii," 1; and TsGAOR SSSR, f. 102, DP, 00, 1916, d. 99, 110–13, 148–53.

69. TsGAOR SSSR, f. 102, DP, 00, 1916, d. 99, 110–14.

70. Orn, "Pravo ubezhishcha v Anglii," 1.

71. Debo, "George Chicherin," 70.

72. Maiskii, *Puteshestvie v proshloe*, 280–85; and K. D. Nabokov, *The Ordeal of a Diplomat* (London and Norwich: London and Norwich Press, 1921; reprint ed., Salisbury, N.C.: Documentary Publications, 1976), 94–97.

73. Maiskii, *Puteshestvie v proshloe*, 280–85.

74. Nabokov, *The Ordeal of a Diplomat*, 94–97.

75. Ibid., 99–110; and see Maiskii, *Puteshestvie v proshloe*, 280–85.

76. Nabokov, *The Ordeal of a Diplomat*, 99–110.

77. Ibid.

78. Ibid.

79. TsGAOR SSSR, f. 9502, op. 1, 1917, d. 30, 1–2.

80. Ibid., 3–4, 5–6.

81. Sir George Buchanan, *My Mission To Russia and Other Diplomatic Memories*, 2 vols. (Boston: Little, Brown, 1923), 2:226; and George Bilainkin, *Maisky: Ten Years Ambassador* (London: George Allen and Unwin, 1944), 22–23.

82. "Trotsky Warns Entente Allies Not To Interfere," *New York Times*, 3 Dec. 1917, 1; and M. I. Trush, "Diplomat leninskoi shkoly. (K 100-letiiu so dnia rozhdeniia G. V. Chicherina)," *Mezhdunarodnaia zhizn' 11 (1972):89*.

83. "British Allowed To Leave Russia," *Times* (London), 17 Dec. 1917, 8; and Richard K. Debo, "The Making of a Bolshevik: Georgii Chicherin in England 1914–1918," *Slavic Review* 25 (Dec. 1966):661–62.

84. Maiskii, *Vospominaniia sovetskogo posla*, 172.

CHAPTER 3

1. L. D. Trotskii, *Moia zhizn'. Opyt avtobiografii*, 2 vols. (Berlin: Granit, 1930; reprint ed., N'iu-Iork: Monad Press, 1977), 2:64.

2. Trotskii, *My Life*, 348.

3. Louise Bryant, *Mirrors of Moscow* (New York: Thomas Seltzer, 1923; reprint ed., Westport, Conn.: Hyperion Press, 1973), 185; Richard K. Debo, *Revolution and Survival: The Foreign Policy of Soviet Russia, 1917–1918* (Toronto: Univ. of Toronto Press, 1979), 85–90, 148–49; and Teddy J. Uldricks, *Diplomacy and Ideology: The Origins of Soviet Foreign Relations, 1917–1930*, Sage Studies in 20th Century History, vol. 9 (Beverly Hills, California: Sage, 1979), 30–31.

4. G. V. Chicherin, "Lenin i vneshniaia politika," *Izvestiia*, No. 24 (2059), 30 ianvaria 1924, 2–3; and "Lenin i vneshniaia politika," *Voprosy istorii* 3 (mart 1957 g.):20–25.

5. V. I. Lenin, *Polnoe sobranie sochinenii*, Piatoe izdanie, Institut

marksizma-leninizma pri TsK KPSS (Moskva: Politizdat, 1928–1965), 50:111. In addition, see Chossudovsky, *Chicherin and Soviet Foreign Policy*, 10–12.

6. Adam B. Ulam, "Lenin's Last Phase," *Survey* 21 (Winter-Spring 1975):149–50.

7. Lenin, *Polnoe sobranie sochinenii*, 51:173; and see Alexandre Barmine, *Memoirs of a Soviet Diplomat: Twenty Years in the Service of the U.S.S.R.*, trans. Gerard Hopkins (London: Loval Dickson, 1938; reprint ed., Westport, Conn.: Hyperion Press, 1973), 151–52; and *One Who Survived: The Life Story of a Russian under the Soviets*, with an Introduction by Max Eastman (New York: Putnam's, 1945), 115; Maiskii, "Georgi Chicherin," 12; Mogilat and Panov, "Polpred revoliutsii," 3; Beatty, "Chicherin," 335, 337; R. H. Bruce Lockhart, *British Agent*, with an Introduction by Hugh Walpole (New York: Putnam's, 1933), 218–19; and Max Eastman, *Love and Revolution: My Journey Through An Epoch* (New York: Random House, 1964), 292.

8. Beatty, "Chicherin," 335–37, Barmine, *Memoirs of a Soviet Diplomat*, 151–53; and *One Who Survived*, 115–16; K. V. Ozols, *Memuary poslannika*, (Parizh: Dom knigi, 1938), 151–52; G. A. Solomon, *Among the Red Autocrats: My Experience in the Service of the Soviets*, trans. from the German edition, ed. and rev. by Arno C. Gaebelein (New York: Arno C. Gaebelein, 1935), 73; Maiskii, "Georgi Chicherin," 12; and *Liudi. Sobytiia. Fakty*, 128; Bryant, *Mirrors of Moscow*, 181–82; William H. Chamberlin, "Meet the Real Litvinoff," *American Mercury* 54 (Mar. 1942):279–80; and *Soviet Russia: A Living Record and a History* (Boston: Little, Brown, 1929), 102–3; Riurikov, ed., *Mikhail Kol'tsov, kakim on byl*, 18–19; Marguerite E. Harrison, *Marooned in Moscow: The Story of an American Woman Imprisoned in Russia* (New York: Doran, 1921), 53–54; Clare Sheridan, *Russian Portraits* (London: Jonathan Cape, 1921), 158—60; Walter Duranty, *I Write as I Please* (New York: Simon and Schuster, 1935), 190; Emma Goldman, *My Disillusionment in Russia* (Garden City, New York: Doubleday, Page, 1923), 51–52; Dana Wilgress, "From Siberia to Kuibyshev: Reflections on Russia, 1919–1943," *International Journal* 22 (Summer 1967):369–70; Anne O'Hare McCormick, *The Hammer and the Scythe: Commmunist Russia Enters the Second Decade* (New York: Knopf, 1929), 113–14; Arthur Ransome, *Russia in 1919* (New York: Huebsch, 1919), 56; George Lansbury, *What I Saw in Russia*, New Era Series, vol. 3 (London: Parsons, 1920), 37; and William Reswick, *I Dreamt Revolution* (Chicago: Regnery, 1952), 157–59.

9. Lockhart, *British Agent*, 218. Also see Beatty, 335, 337; Barmine *Memoirs of a Soviet Diplomat*, 151–52; and *One Who Survived*, 115–16; and William J. Oudendyk, *Ways and By-Ways in Diplomacy* (London: Davies, 1939), 291.

10. Harrison, *Marooned in Moscow*, 53–54. See also Ozols, *Memuary poslannika*, 150–51; and Maiskii, "Georgi Chicherin," 12.

11. Sheridan, *Russian Portraits*, 158–60. See also Bryant, *Mirrors of Moscow*, 182–84; and Louis Fischer, *Russia's Road from Peace to War: Soviet Foreign Relations, 1917–1941* (New York: Harper and Row, 1969), 60–61.

12. Beatty, "Chicherin," 335, 337; Eastman, *Love and Revolution*, 292; Lockhart, *British Agent*, 218–19; Oudendyk, *Ways and By-Ways in Diplomacy*, 258; Harrison, *Marooned in Moscow*, 53–54; Reswick, *I Dreamt Revolution*, 157–59; and Ernest Hemingway, *By Line: Ernest Hemingway; Selected Articles*

and Dispatches of Four Decades, ed. William White (New York: Scribner's, 1967), 62, 66–68.

13. Reswick, *I Dreamt Revolution,* 157–59; Eastman, *Love and Revolution,* 292; McCormick, *The Hammer and the Scythe,* 113–14, 117; Sheridan, *Russian Portraits,* 158–60; Ravich, *Molodost' veka,* 300–301; Haupt and Marie, eds., *Makers of the Russian Revolution,* 341; Lincoln Steffens, *The Autobiography of Lincoln Steffens* (New York: Harcourt, Brace and World, 1931), 794; and Gustav Hilger and Alfred G. Meyer, *The Incompatible Allies: A Memoir-History of German-Soviet Relations, 1918–1941* (New York: Macmillan, 1953), 7–8.

14. Sheridan, *Russian Portraits,* 158–60. Also see Reswick, *I Dreamt Revolution,* 157–59; Solomon, *Among the Red Autocrats,* 73; Mogilat and Panov, "Polpred revoliutsii," 3; and Ozols, *Memuary poslannika,* 151–53.

15. Beatty, "Chicherin," 337. Also see Reswick, *I Dreamt Revolution,* 157–59.

16. Ransome, *Russia in 1919,* 56; Sheridan, *Russian Portraits,* 158–60; Bryant, *Mirrors of Moscow,* 183–84; Barmine, *Memoirs of a Soviet Diplomat,* 151–53; and *One Who Survived,* 115–16; and Haupt and Marie, eds., *Makers of the Russian Revolution,* 341.

17. Beatty, "Chicherin," 337. Also see Chamberlin, *Soviet Russia,* 102–3; Barmine, *Memoirs of a Soviet Diplomat,* 151–53; and *One Who Survived,* 115–16; and Maiskii, "Georgi Chicherin," 12.

18. Bryant, *Mirrors of Moscow,* 192–93. See also Oudendyk, *Ways and By-Ways in Diplomacy,* 291; Harrison, *Marooned in Moscow,* 53–54; and Barmine, *Memoirs of a Soviet Diplomat,* 151–52; and *One Who Survived,* 115.

19. Chamberlin, *Soviet Russia,* 102–3. Also see Ozols, *Memuary poslannika,* 151–52; and Ravich, *Molodost' veka,* 303.

20. Beatty, "Chicherin," 337. See also Ravich, *Molodost' veka,* 303; and Eastman, *Love and Revolution,* 287.

21. Uldricks, *Diplomacy and Ideology,* 10.

22. Uldricks, *Diplomacy and Ideology,* 10, 19, 21; Maiskii, "Georgi Chicherin," 12; Ivan V. Boyeff, "The Soviet State Monopoly of Foreign Trade," in *The Soviet Union and World-Problems,* ed. Samuel N. Harper (Chicago: Univ. of Chicago Press, 1935), 229; B. Kantorovich, "Organizatsionnoe razvitie NKID," *Mezhdunarodnaia zhizn'* 15 (7 noiabria 1922):51–52; and I. Zalkind, "Iz pervykh mesiatsev Narodnogo Komissariata po Inostrannym Delam," *Mezhdunarodnaia zhizn'* 10 (1927):12, 17–18. According to L. I. Trofimova, "Pervye shagi sovetskoi diplomatii," *Novaia i noveishaia istoriia* 1 (ianvar'-fevral' 1972):79, by the autumn of 1918, approximately one year later, 340 officials worked in Narkomindel.

23. Chamberlin, "Meet the Real Litvinoff," 279–80. See also C. O. Cleveland, "Memories of Chicherin," *Commonweal* 24 (28 Aug. 1936):417; Ozols, *Memuary poslannika,* 151–53; Solomon, *Among the Red Autocrats,* 73; Barmine, *Memoirs of a Soviet Diplomat,* 217–18, and *One Who Survived,* 119–20; Uldricks, *Diplomacy and Ideology,* 30–31; and Fischer, *Russia's Road from Peace to War,* 60.

24. Theodore H. Von Laue, "Soviet Diplomacy: G. V. Chicherin, People's Commissar for Foreign Affairs, 1918–1930," in *Process and Power in Soviet Foreign Policy,* ed. Vernon V. Aspaturian (Boston: Little, Brown, 1971), 128–29. But Kantorovich, in "Organizatsionnoe razvitie NKID," 54, records a

slightly higher figure—about 600 people in the central offices out of a total of approximately 1,250 officials, including those who worked abroad.

25. Teddy J. Uldricks, "The Soviet Diplomatic Corps in the Cicerin Era," *Jahrbucher für Geschichte Osteuropas* 23 (1975):219.

26. Chicherin, "Lenin i vneshniaia politika," *Izvestiia*, 2; and *Lenin i vneshniaia politika* (Moskva: Politizdat, 1977), 4.

27. G. V. Chicherin, *Vneshniaia politika Sovetskoi Rossii za dva goda. Ocherk, sostavlennyi k dvukletnei godovshchine raboche-krest'ianskoi revoliutsii* (Moskva: Gosudarstvennoe izdatel'stvo, 1920), 4–8; *Two Years of Foreign Policy. The Relations of the Russian Socialist Federal Soviet Republic with Foreign Nations, from November 7, 1917, to November 7, 1919*, Soviet Russia Pamphlets, No. 3 (New York: The Russian Soviet Government Bureau, 1920), 6–7; and *Stat'i i rechi po voprosam mezhdunarodnoi politiki*, sostavitel' L. I. Trofimova, Biblioteka vneshnei politiki (Moskva: Sotsekgiz, 1961), 25–30, 35.

28. Ministerstvo Inostrannykh Del SSSR, *Dokumenty vneshnei politiki SSSR* (Moskva: Politizdat, 1957–77), 1:213–362.

29. Chicherin, "Lenin i vneshniaia politika," *Izvestiia*, 2; *Lenin i vneshniaia politika*, 6–7; *Stat'i i rechi po voprosam mezhdunarodnoi politiki*, 228, 321–22; and "Sem' let sovetskoi vneshnei politiki," *Izvestiia*, No. 256 (2291), 7 noiabria 1924, 1; and *Izvestiia*, No. 257 (2292), 11 noiabria 1924, 1.

30. Chicherin, *Stat'i i rechi po voprosam mezhdunarodnoi politiki*, 225; and "Versal'skii dogovor. (Beseda s tov. Chicherinym)," *Izvestiia*, No. 101 (653), 13 maia 1919, 1.

31. Chicherin, "Sem' let sovetskoi vneshnei politiki," 1; *Stat'i i rechi po voprosam mezhdunarodnoi politiki*, 127, 225–31, 259–65, 321–29; and "Za piat' let," *Mezhdunarodnaia zhizn'* 15 (7 noiabria 1922):4.

32. Chicherin, "Sem' let sovetskoi vneshnei politiki," 1; *Stat'i i rechi po voprosam mezhdunarodnoi politiki*, 127, 225–31, 259–65, 321–29; "Za piat' let," *Mezhdunarodnaia zhizn'* 15 (7 noiabria 1922):4; and Narodnogo komissara po inostrannym delam G. V. Chicherina na zasedanii fraktsii RKP VIII c"ezda sovetov," *Vestnik NKID* 1–2 (15 marta 1921):3.

33. Chicherin, *Stat'i i rechi po voprosam mezhdunarodnoi politiki*, 134, 138–40; "Rech' Chicherina na zasedanii fraktsii RKP VIII c"ezda sovetov," 10; (Pervaia sel'skokhoziaistvennaia i kustarnaia promyshlennaia vystavka SSSR) *Znachenie vystavki. Rech', proiznesennaia na mitinge 16 IX-23 g. na Leninskoi ploshchadi vystavki* (Moskva: Mospoligraf, 1923), 4–5; "Dogovor s Estoniei," *Vestnik NKID* 3 (27 fevralia 1920):2–3; *Doklad Narodnogo komissara po inostrannym delam G. V. Chicherina na zasedanii VTsIK 17-go iiunia 1920 goda. (Stenogramma)* (Moskva: Tipografiia III-go kommunisticheskogo internatsionala, 1920), 2–6; and *Voprosy vneshnei politiki. Doklady i noty t. Chicherina*, Vypusk pervyi, Seriia "Nasha diplomatiia" (Saratov: Gosudarstvennoe izdatel'stvo, saratovskoe otdelenie, 1920), 46–47; and "Tchitcherin on the Premier's Policy," *Times* (London), 12 February 1920, 16.

34. Chicherin, *Two Years of Foreign Policy*, 7; *Stat'i i rechi po voprosam mezhdunarodnoi politiki*, 134, 323–26; "Sem' let sovetskoi vneshnei politiki," 1; *Doklad Chicherina na zasedanii VTsIK 17-go iiunia 1920 goda*, 2–6; *Vneshniaia politika Sovetskoi Rossii za dva goda*, 6; and *Voprosy vneshnei politiki*, 46–47.

35. Hemingway, *By Line: Ernest Hemingway*, 66–8. See also Chicherin, *Doklad Chicherina na zasedanii VTsIK 17-go iiunia 1920 goda*, 18.

36. Chicherin, "Molodoi Gvardii," *Molodaia gvardiia* 4–5 (11–12) (iiun'-iiul' 1923):5–6.

37. Chicherin, *Znachenie vystavki*, 10; "Dogovor s Estoniei," 1–6; *Stat'i i rechi po voprosam mezhdunarodnoi politiki*, 135–43; "Rech' Chicherina na zasedanii fraktsii RKP VIII c"ezda sovetov," 10–11; and *Doklad Chicherina na zasedanii VTsIK 17-go iiunia 1920 goda*, 2–6 11, 18.

38. Ministerstvo Inostrannykh Del SSSR, *Dokumenty vneshnei politiki SSSR*, 2:242–45, 317–23, 333–54, 430–31; and Chicherin, "Dogovor s Estoniei," 1–6; and *Stat'i i rechi po voprosam mezhdunarodnoi politiki*, 135–43. Also see Lenin, *Polnoe sobranie sochinenii*, 51: 69.

39. Chicherin, "Dogovor s Estoniei," 1–6; *Stat'i i rechi po voprosam mezhdunarodnoi politiki*, 135–43, 323–24; "Sem' let sovetskoi vneshnei politiki," 1; and "Rech' Chicherina na zasedanii fraktsii RKP VIII c"ezda sovetov," 10–11; "Tchitcherin on the Premier's Policy," 16; and "Po povodu mira s Estoniei," *Pravda*, No. 25, 5 fevralia 1920, 1.

40. Ministerstvo Inostrannykh Del SSSR, *Dokumenty vneshnei politiki SSSR*, 2:190, 202–3, 364–67.

41. Ibid, 317–23, 333–54, 430–31.

42. Ibid., 3:245—58.

43. Ibid., 2:438, 482, 539–41, 569–72; and 3:28–40, 60, 86–89, 101–16, 124–29, 265–82.

44. Chicherin, *Voprosy vneshnei politiki*, 47, 54; "Rech' Chicherina na zasedanii fraktsii RKP VIII c"ezda sovetov," 10–11; "Dogovor s Estoniei," 1–6; and *Stat'i i rechi po voprosam mezhdunarodnoi politiki*, 135–43.

45. Chicherin, "Dogovor s Estoniei," 3; *Stat'i i rechi po voprosam mezhdunarodnoi politiki*, 138–39, 225–30; and *Doklad Chicherina na zasedanii VTsIK 17-go iiunia 1920 goda*, 1–6; and "Tchitcherin on the Premier's Policy," 16.

46. Chicherin, *Doklad Chicherina na zasedanii VTsIK 17-go iiunia 1920 goda*, 1–2, 18; and "Rech' Chicherina na zasedanii fraktsii RKP VIII c"ezda sovetov," 3.

47. Chicherin, "Chetyre kongressa," *Vestnik NKID* 1 (20 iiunia 1919): 9–11; and "Versal'skii dogovor. (Beseda s tov. Chicherinym)," *Izvestiia*, No. 101 (653), 13 maia 1919; 1, and *Izvestiia*, No. 102 (654), 14 maia 1919, 1.

48. Chicherin, "Chetyre kongressa," 9–11; and "Versal'skii dogovor," 1. See also A. Sabanin, "Uchastie SSSR v komissii po rozoruzheniiu," *Mezhdunarodnaia zhizn'* 11 (1927):7–15.

49. Chicherin, "Chetyre kongressa," 9–12; and *Voprosy vneshnei politiki*, 55–56.

50. Uldricks, *Diplomacy and Ideology*, 69–70; and Richard F. Rosser, *An Introduction to Soviet Foreign Policy* (Englewood Cliffs, N.J.: Prentice-Hall, 1969), 126–27.

51. Chicherin, "Rech' Chicherina na zasedanii fraktsii RKP VIII c"ezda sovetov," 3–4, 8; and *Doklad Chicherina na zasedanii VTsIK 17-go iiunia 1920 goda*, 1–2.

CHAPTER 4

1. Robert C. Williams, *Culture in Exile: Russian Emigres in Germany, 1881–1941* (Ithaca: Cornell Univ. Press, 1972), 108–9.
2. Ibid.
3. George F. Kennan, *Russia and the West under Lenin and Stalin,* Atlantic Monthly Press Book (Boston: Little, Brown, 1961), 197–200.
4. Ibid., 203–4.
5. Jane Degras, ed., *Soviet Documents on Foreign Policy,* vol. I: *1917–1924,* issued under the auspices of the Royal Institute of International Affairs (London: Oxford Univ. Press, 1951), 270–72.
6. Lenin, *Polnoe sobranie sochinenii,* 54:595.
7. Ibid., 596.
8. G. V. Chicherin, "Nota Nar. komissara po inostr. delam pravitel'stvam Antanty," *Mezhdunarodnaia zhizn'* 1 (20 marta 1922):46–48; "Sem' let sovetskoi vneshnei politiki," 1; and *Stat'i i rechi po voprosam mezhdunarodnoi politiki,* 207, 321–29; and I. M. Maiskii, "Rossiia i Genuiia," *Mezhdunarodnaia zhizn'* 3 (3 aprelia 1922):2–3, "Dva otveta," *Mezhdunarodnaia zhizn'* 6 (10 maia 1922): 1–2, and "Genuezskie plody," *Mezhdunarodnaia zhizn'* 8 (8 iiunia 1922):2.
9. Lenin, *Polnoe sobranie sochinenii,* 44:374–76, 406–8.
10. Ibid.
11. Ibid., 45:34–40. And see Chicherin, "Nota pravitel'stvam Antanty," 46–48.
12. Lenin, *Polnoe sobranie sochinenii,* 45:34–40; and Chicherin, "Nota pravitel'stvam Antanty," 46–48.
13. Lenin, *Polnoe sobranie sochinenii,* 45:34–40.
14. Ibid.
15. Ibid.
16. Ibid.
17. Gorokhov, Zamiatin, and Zemskov, *Chicherin: Diplomat leninskoi shkoly,* 75.
18. N. N. Liubimov and A. N. Erlikh, *Genuezskaia konferentsiia. Vospominaniia uchastnikov* (Moskva: Izdatel'stvo Instituta mezhdunarodnykh otnoshenii, 1963), 22–23.
19. Ministerstvo Inostrannykh Del SSSR, *Dokumenty vneshnei politiki SSSR,* 4:579–82.
20. Chicherin, "Sem let' sovetskoi vneshnei politiki," 1; and *Stat'i i rechi po voprosam mezhdunarodnoi politiki,* 321–29.
21. Kennan, *Russia and the West,* 213–14.
22. Hartmut Pogge von Strandmann, "Rapallo-Strategy in Preventive Diplomacy: New Sources and New Interpretations," in *Germany in the Age of Total War,* ed. Volker R. Berghahn and Martin Kitchen (Totowa, N.J.: Barnes and Noble, 1981), 137; and Odi, "Lokarnskaia konferentsiia," *Mezhdunarodnaia zhizn'* 4–5 (1925):17.
23. Von Strandmann, "Rapallo-Strategy in Preventive Diplomacy," 128.
24. Debo, "George Chicherin," 240.

25. Liubimov and Erlikh, *Genuezskaia konferentsiia. Vospominaniia uchastnikov,* 34.

26. J. D. Gregory, *On the Edge of Diplomacy: Rambles and Reflections, 1902–1928* (London: Hutchinson, n.d.), 195–96; and Louis Fischer, *The Soviets in World Affairs: A History of the Relations between the Soviet Union and the Rest of the World, 1917–1929,* 2 vols. (New York: Jonathan Cape and Harrison Smith, 1930; 2d ed., Princeton: Princeton Univ. Press, 1951), 335–37.

27. Beatty, "Chicherin," 337. See also Hemingway, *By Line,* 26–32; Eastman, *Love and Revolution,* 285–300; Richard W. Child, *A Diplomat Looks at Europe* (New York: Duffield, 1925), 26–53; J. Saxon Mills, *The Genoa Conference* (New York: Dutton, 1922), 62; Harry Kessler, *In the Twenties: The Diaries of Harry Kessler,* with an Introduction by Otto Friedrich, trans. Charles Kessler (New York: Holt, Rinehart and Winston, 1971), 159–80; Liubimov and Erlikh, *Genuezskaia konferentsiia. Vospominaniia unchastnikov,* 44–45; Iu. Ia. Solov'ev, *Vospominaniia diplomata 1893–1922,* Izdanie vtoroe, Biblioteka vneshnei politiki (Moskva: Sotsekgiz, 1959), 390–94; and G. A. Turkan, ed., "Doklad Ia. E. Rudzutaka o Genuezskoi konferentsii," *Istoricheskii arkhiv* 2 (mart-aprel' 1922):83–95.

28. Chicherin, *Stat'i i rechi po voprosam mezhdunarodnoi politiki,* 208–12.

29. Lenin, *Polnoe sobranie sochinenii,* 45:162–65, 171–72, 183–85, 538–39, 541–42. See also Nik. Iordanskii, "Printsipy 17-go goda," *Mezhdunardonaia zhizn'* 7 (22 maia 1922):2.

30. Liubimov and Erlikh, *Genuezskaia konferentsiia. Vospominaniia uchastnikov,* 70, 72–73.

31. Ministerstvo Inostrannykh Del SSSR, *Dokumenty vneshnei politiki SSSR,* 5:223–24; and Paul Scheffer, *Seven Years in Soviet Russia: With a Retrospect,* authorized trans. Arthur Livingston (New York: Macmillan, 1932), 223–28.

32. Isaac Deutscher, *The Prophet Unarmed: Trotsky, 1921–1929* (London: Oxford Univ. Press, 1959), 56–57.

33. Ibid.

34. Gordon H. Mueller, "Rapallo Reexamined: A New Look at Germany's Secret Military Collaboration with Russia in 1922," *Military Affairs* 40 (Oct. 1976):109, 113.

35. For example, see Kennan, *Russia and the West,* 222–23.

36. I. M. Maiskii, *Vospominaniia sovetskogo posla v dvukh knigakh,* kniga vtoraia: *Mir ili voina?,* Otdelenie istoricheskikh nauk Akademii nauk SSSR (Moskva: Nauka, 1964), 88.

37. G. V. Chicherin, "Soviet Diplomacy since the War," *Living Age* 320 (22 Mar. 1924):550. See also Chicherin, "Sem' let sovetskoi vneshnei politiki," 1; and *Stat'i i rechi po voprosam mezhdunarodnoi politiki,* 325–29.

38. Strandmann, "Rapallo-Strategy in Preventive Diplomacy," 124, 137, 142–43.

39. Fischer, *The Soviets in World Affairs,* 337–38.

40. Carole Fink, *The Genoa Conference: European Diplomacy, 1921–1922* (Chapel Hill: Univ. of North Carolina Press, 1984), 175, 305.

41. Kurt Rosenbaum, *Community of Fate: German-Soviet Diplomatic Relations, 1922–1928* (Syracuse: Syracuse Univ. Press, 1965), 30–32.

42. Hilger and Meyer, *The Incompatible Allies,* 94–5. Also see Eric Sutton,

ed., *Gustav Stresemann: His Diaries, Letters, and Papers*, vol. 3, trans. Eric Sutton (New York: Macmillan, 1940), 518; and Scheffer, *Seven Years in Soviet Russia*, 320.

43. Herbert von Dirksen, *Moscow, Tokyo, London: Twenty Years of German Foreign Policy* (Norman: Univ. of Oklahoma Press, 1952), 47–50.

44. Rosenbaum, *Community of Fate*, 30–32.

45. Byvshii Diplomat, "Germanskii kinematograf i Rossiia," *Izvestiia*, No. 262 (1701), 19 noiabria 1922, 1; and Marko Polo, "Germaniia i Liga Natsii," *Izvestiia*, No. 44 (2079), 22 fevralia 1924, 2.

46. Gerald Freund, *Unholy Alliance: Russian-German Relations from the Treaty of Brest-Litovsk to the Treaty of Berlin*, with an Introduction by J. W. Wheeler-Bennett (New York: Harcourt, Brace, 1957), 142.

47. Marko Polo, "Germaniia i Liga Natsii," 2; Ne-Diplomat, "Neskol'ko spokoinykh slov o russko-germanskom konflikte," *Izvestiia*, No. 105 (2140), 10 maia 1924, 1; Hilger and Meyer, *The Incompatible Allies*, 121–24; and Post-skript, "Zheneva," *Mezhdunarodnaia zhizn'* 4 (1926):62–63.

48. Marko Polo, "Germaniia i Liga Natsii," 2; Post-skript, "Zheneva," 62–64; and Odi, "Lokarnskaia konferentsiia," 11.

49. Marko Polo, "Germaniia i Liga Natsii," 2; Post-skript, "Zheneva," 62–64; Odi, "Lokarnskaia konferentsiia," 11; and Chicherin, *Stat'i i rechi po voprosam mezhdunarodnoi politiki*, 301–4, 369, 375–76, 388.

50. Marko Polo, "Germaniia i Liga Natsii," 2; and Sovremennye alkhimiki," *Pravda*, No. 221, 28 sentiabria 1924, 4.

51. Chicherin, *Stat'i i rechi po voprosam mezhdunarodnoi politiki*, 301–4.

52. Chicherin, "Pis'mo general'nomu sekretariu Ligi Natsii 30 oktiabria 1924 goda," *Pravda*, No. 250, 1 noiabria 1924, 2.

53. Chicherin, *Stat'i i rechi po voprosam mezhdunarodnoi politiki*, 301–4; Ne-Diplomat, "Neskol'ko spokoinykh slov o russko-germanskom konflikte," 1; and Ministerstvo Inostrannykh Del SSSR, *Dokumenty vneshnei politiki SSSR*, 7:232–39, 267–70, 346–52.

54. Chicherin, *Stat'i i rechi po voprosam mezhdunarodnoi politiki*, 301–4; and Ne-Diplomat, "Neskol'ko spokoinykh slov o russko-germanskom konflikte," 1.

55. Chicherin, *Stat'i i rechi po voprosam mezhdunarodnoi politiki*, 301–4; and Ministerstvo Inostrannykh Del SSSR, *Dokumenty vneshnei politiki SSSR*, 7:409–11.

56. G. V. Chicherin, "Vmesto predisloviia," *Mezhdunarodnaia zhizn'* 1 (1923):5, 7.

57. Chicherin, "Vmesto predisloviia," 5, 7; and *Stat'i i rechi po voprosam mezhdunarodnoi politiki*, 393–95; and "Ostrov i materik," *Izvestiia*, No. 146 (2479), 30 iiunia 1925, 1.

58. Ministerstvo Inostrannykh Del SSSR, *Dokumenty vneshnei politiki SSSR*, 7:514–17.

59. Debo, "George Chicherin," 335.

60. Ministerstvo Inostrannykh Del SSSR, *Dokumenty vneshnei politiki SSSR*, 7:399–400, 438–41, 573–74, 577.

61. Osvedomlennyi, "Germanskii otvet na frantsuzskuiu notu," *Izvestiia*, No. 176 (2509), 4 avgusta 1925, 2; "Pered novymi buriami," *Pravda*, No. 138

(3069), 20 iiunia 1925, 1; "Ostrov i materik," 1; and Chicherin, *Stat'i i rechi po voprosam mezhdunarodnoi politiki*, 393–95, 431–38.

62. "Pered novymi buriami," 1; "Ostrov i materik," 1; and Chicherin, *Stat'i i rechi po voprosam mezhdunarodnoi politiki*, 393–95, 415.

63. "Pered novymi buriami," 1; "Ostrov i materik," 1; Chicherin, *Stat'i i rechi po voprosam mezhdunarodnoi politiki*, 393–95, 415; Odi, "Lokarnskaia konferentsiia," 6; "Godovshchina plana Dauzsa," *Izvestiia*, No. 185 (2518), 15 avgusta 1925, 1; and "Rastushchie sopernichestva," *Izvestiia*, No. 170 (2503), 28 iiulia 1925, 1.

64. "Godovshchina plana Dauzsa," 1; and Odi, "Lokarnskaia konferentsiia," 6.

65. "Pered novymi buriami," 1.

66. "Pered novymi buriami," 1; Osvedomlennyi, "Germanskii otvet na frantsuzskuiu notu," 2; and Chicherin, *Stat'i i rechi po voprosam mezhdunarodnoi politiki*, 431–38.

67. Osvedomlennyi, "Germanskii otvet na frantsuzskuiu notu," 2; and Chicherin, *Stat'i i rechi po voprosam mezhdunarodnoi politiki*, 431–38.

68. Osvedomlennyi, "Germanskii otvet na frantsuzskuiu notu," 2; Chicherin, *Stat'i i rechi po voprosam mezhdunarodnoi politiki*, 431–38; "Ostrov i materik," 1; "Sovremennyi protei," *Pravda*, 129 (3060), 10 iiunia 1925, 1; Odi, "Lokarnskaia konferentsiia," 12; "Tov. Chicherin o mezhdunarodnom polozhenii," *Izvestiia*, No. 227 (2560), 4 oktiabria 1925, 1; "Besedy tov. Chicherina s inostrannymi zhurnalistami, *Izvestiia*, No. 228 (2561), 6 oktiabria 1925, 1; and "Interv'iu G. V. Chicherina po povodu Ligi Natsii," *Izvestiia*, No. 78 (2709), 6 aprelia 1926, 1.

69. "Tov. Chicherin o mezhdunarodnom polozhenii," 1; "Ostrov i materik," 1; "Vneshniaia politika v osveshchenii tov. Chicherina," *Izvestiia*, No. 293 (2626), 23 dekabria 1925, 1; "Sovremennyi protei," 1; Odi, "Lokarnskaia konferentsiia," 12; "Interv'iu G. V. Chicherina po povodu Ligi Natsii," 1; and Chicherin, *Stat'i i rechi po voprosam mezhdunarodnoi politiki*, 393–95.

70. "Tov. Chicherin o mezhdunarodnom polozhenii," 1; "Sgovoritsia li s Pol'shei," *Izvestiia*, No. 56 (2687), 9 marta 1926, 1; Ministerstvo Inostrannykh Del SSSR, *Dokumenty vneshnei politiki SSSR*, 8:552–57; Chicherin, *Stat'i i rechi po voprosam mezhdunarodnoi politiki*, 461–66, 488–89; and "Na vernom puti," *Izvestiia*, No. 206 (2539), 10 sentiabria 1925, 1.

71. Ministerstvo Inostrannykh Del SSSR, *Dokumenty vneshnei politiki SSSR*, 8:552–57; "Sgovoritsia li s Pol'shei," 1; Chicherin, *Stat'i i rechi po voprosam mezhdunarodnoi politiki*, 359–60, 461–66, 488–89; and "Na vernom puti," 1.

72. "Tov. Chicherin o mezhdunarodnom polozhenii," 1; "Interv'iu G. V. Chicherina po povodu Ligi Natsii," 1; "Ostrov i materik," 1; "Sovremennyi protei," 1; "Beseda tov. Chicherina s germanskimi zhurnalistami," *Izvestiia*, No. 238 (2571), 17 oktiabria 1925, 1; "Povsemestnaia podgotovka," *Izvestiia*, No. 171 (2504), 29 iiulia 1925, 1; Odi, "Lokarnskaia konferentsiia," 6, 12; and Chicherin, *Stat'i i rechi po voprosam mezhdunarodnoi politiki*, 369, 375–76, 393–95, 405–9, 421, 487.

73. "Interv'iu G. V. Chicherina po povodu Ligi Natsii," 1; "Beseda tov. Chicherina s germanskimi zhurnalistami," 1; "Besedy tov. Chicherina s

inostrannymi zhurnalistami," 1; "Vneshniaia politika v osveshchenii tov. Chicherina," 1; and Chicherin, *Stat'i i rechi po voprosam mezhdunarodnoi politiki*, 488–89.

74. "Tov. Chicherin o mezhdunarodnom polozhenii," 1; Ministerstvo Inostrannykh Del SSSR, *Dokumenty vneshnei politiki SSSR*, 8:558–59; and Chicherin, *Stat'i i rechi po voprosam mezhdunarodnoi politiki*, 356–57.

75. Ministerstvo Inostrannykh Del SSSR, *Dokumenty vneshnei politiki SSSR*, 8:558–59, 571–72; and Freund, *Unholy Alliance*, 233–35.

76. Fischer, *Russia's Road from Peace to War*, 158–60.

77. Fischer, *Russia's Road from Peace to War*, 157; and Chicherin, *Stat'i i rechi po voprosam mezhdunarodnoi politiki*, 356–57.

78. "Vneshniaia politika v osveshchenii tov. Chicherina," 1; "Tov. Chicherin o franko-sovetskikh otnosheniiakh," *Izvestiia*, No. 288 (2621), 17 dekabria 1925, 1; and Chicherin, *Stat'i i rechi po voprosam mezhdunarodnoi politiki*, 268, 270–71.

79. Christian Rakovsky, "The Foreign Policy of Soviet Russia," *Foreign Affairs* 4 (July 1926):581–82; John W. Wheeler-Bennett, *Disarmament and Security since Locarno, 1925–1931, Being the Political and Technical Background of the General Disarmament Conference, 1932*, with an Introduction by Sir Neill L. Malcolm, Information Series No. 7 (New York: Macmillan, 1932), 312–15; and Chicherin *Stat'i i rechi po voprosam mezhdunarodnoi politiki*, 471.

80. Ministerstvo Inostrannykh Del SSSR, *Dokumenty vneshnei politiki SSSR*, 8:739–41; and Wheeler-Bennett, *Disarmament and Security since Locarno, 1925–1931*, 315.

81. "Interv'iu G. V. Chicherina po povodu Ligi Natsii," 1; and Post-skript, "Zheneva," 64.

82. Wheeler-Bennett, *Disarmament and Security since Locarno, 1925–1931*, 318–19; Fischer, *Russia's Road from Peace to War*, 158–60; and Edward H. Carr, *A History of Soviet Russia: Socialism in One Country, 1924–1926*, 3 vols. (New York: Macmillan, 1958–1964), 3:437—39.

83. Fischer, *Russia's Road from Peace to War*, 158–60.

84. T. A. Taracouzio, *War and Peace in Soviet Diplomacy* (New York: Macmillan, 1940), 120–21. Also see, Carr, *Socialism in One Country*, 3:448–49.

CHAPTER 5

1. Hemingway, *By Line*, 66–68.

2. For example, Chicherin, *Doklad Chicherina na zasedanii VTsIK 17-go iiunia 1920 goda*, 5–6.

3. Chicherin, *Doklad Chicherina na zasedanii VTsIK 17-go iiunia 1920 goda*, 3–6; and *Stat'i i rechi po voprosam mezhdunarodnoi politiki*, 292; "Ostrov i materik," 1; Byvshii Diplomat, "Reshaiushchii moment," *Izvestiia*, No. 221 (2266), 27 sentiabria 1924, 2; and Mikhail Sharonov, "Novye etapy mirovykh antagonizmov," *Pravda*, No. 201, 5 sentiabria 1924, 2.

4. "Tchitcherin on the Premier's Policy," 16.

5. Mikhail Sharonov, "Novye etapy mirovykh antagonizmov," 2; and Chicherin, *Stat'i i rechi po voprosam mezhdunarodnoi politiki*, 292.

6. Chicherin, *Doklad Chicherina na zasedanii VTsIK 17-go iiunia 1920 goda*, 9–10.

7. "Rastushchie sopernichestva," 1.

8. Chicherin, *Doklad Chicherina na zasedanii VTsIK 17-go iiunia 1920 goda*, 3–4; and *Stat'i i rechi po voprosam mezhdunarodnoi politiki*, 292; Mikhail Sharonov, "Novye etapy mirovykh antagonizmov," 2; and "Ostrov i materik," 1.

9. Chicherin, *Doklad Chicherina na zasedanii VTsIK 17-go iiunia 1920 goda*, 5–6.

10. "Ostrov i materik," 1.

11. Byvshii Diplomat, "Lozannskaia konferentsiia startsev," *Izvestiia*, No. 101 (1838), 9 maia 1923, 1; and Chicherin, *Doklad Chicherina na zasedanii VTsIK 17-go iiunia 1920 goda*, 3–4; "Sem' let sovetskoi vneshnei politiki," 1; and *Stat'i i rechi po voprosam mezhdunarodnoi politiki*, 229, 323–26.

12. Chicherin, "Sem' let sovetskoi vneshnei politiki," 1; and *Stat'i i rechi po voprosam mezhdunarodnoi politiki*, 229, 323–26; and Byvshii Diplomat, "Lozannskaia konferentsiia," 1.

13. I. M. Maiskii, "Anglo-sovetskoe torgovoe soglashenie 1921 goda," *Voprosy istorii* 5 (mai 1957 g.):64–65.

14. Maiskii, "Anglo-sovetskoe torgovoe soglashenie 1921 goda," 62–63; and Ministerstvo Inostrannykh Del SSSR, *Dokumenty vneshnei politiki SSSR*, 2:364–67.

15. Maiskii, "Anglo-sovetskoe torgovoe soglashenie 1921 goda," 68–69.

16. Michael V. Glenny, "The Anglo-Soviet Trade Agreement, March 1921," *Journal of Contemporary History* 5 (1970):64–65.

17. G. Stepanov, "Pervoe torgovoe soglashenie," *Vneshniaia torgovlia* 2 (1967): 12–13; Glenny, "The Anglo-Soviet Trade Agreement, March 1921," 66–70; and Maiskii, "Anglo-sovetskoe torgovoe soglashenie 1921 goda," 70.

18. Richard H. Ullman, *Anglo-Soviet Relations, 1917–1921*, vol. III: *The Anglo-Soviet Accord (Princeton: Princeton Univ. Press, 1972), 399–400.

19. Glenny, "The Anglo-Soviet Trade Agreement, March 1921," 71–73.

20. Stepanov, "Pervoe torgovoe soglashenie," 13.

21. Glenny, "The Anglo-Soviet Trade Agreement, March 1921," 80–82; Ministerstvo Inostrannykh Del SSSR, *Dokumenty vneshnei politiki SSSR*, 3:607–14; and Maiskii, "Anglo-sovetskoe torgovoe soglashenie 1921 goda," 76–77.

22. Robert H. Hodgson, "Memoirs of an Official Agent: Trading with Russia, 1921–23," *History Today* 4 (Aug. 1954): 532–34.

23. Stepanov, "Pervoe torgovoe soglashenie," 13.

24. Edward H. Carr, *A History of Soviet Russia: The Bolshevik Revolution, 1917–1923*, 3 vols. (New York: Macmillan, 1951–53), 3:287–89.

25. Ministerstvo Inostrannykh Del SSSR, *Dokumenty vneshnei politiki SSSR*, 5:646–47, 650–53.

26. Chicherin, "Za piat' let," 5–6.

27. Hemingway, *By Line*, 66–68; and Viscount D'Abernon, *The Diary of an Ambassador*, vol. 3, *Dawes to Locarno, 1924–26*, with historical notes by Maurice Alfred Gerothwohl (Garden City, N.Y.: Doubleday, Doran, 1931), 201.

28. G. V. Chicherin, "Lozannskaia konferentsiia i mirovoe polozhenie,"

Mezhdunarodnaia zhizn' 2 (1923):3–4, 5–6; and Marko Polo, "Afganskii vopros v moment obrazovaniia rabochego pravitel'stva," *Izvestiia*, No. 24 (2059), 30 ianvaria 1924, 1.

29. Chicherin, "Vmesto predisloviia," 2.

30. Chicherin, "Lozannskaia konferentsiia i mirovoe polozhenie," 3–4.

31. Hemingway, *By Line*, 66–68. And see Joseph C. Grew, *Turbulent Era: A Diplomatic Record of Forty Years, 1904–1945*, 2 vols., ed. Walter Johnson, assist. Nancy Harrison Hooker (Boston: Houghton Mifflin, 1952), 1:475–585.

32. Chicherin, "Lozannskaia konferentsiia i mirovoe polozhenie," 5.

33. Chicherin, "Lozannskaia konferentsiia i mirovoe polozhenie," 4; and Carr, *The Bolshevik Revolution, 1917–1923*, 3:488–89.

34. Chicherin, "Lozannskaia konferentsiia i mirovoe polozhenie," 4.

35. Ministerstvo Inostrannykh Del SSSR, *Dokumenty vneshnei politiki SSSR*, 6:288–302, 352–53; and Alfred E. Senn, *Assassination in Switzerland: The Murder of Vatslav Vorovsky* (Madison: Univ. of Wisconsin Press, 1981), 33–34, 192–93.

36. Ministerstvo Inostrannykh Del SSSR, *Dokumenty vneshnei politiki SSSR*, 7:53–55, 98–99.

37. Byvshii Diplomat, "Pench i Dzhudi," *Izvestiia*, No. 224 (2249), 1 oktiabria 1924, 1; "Reshaiushchii moment," 2; and "Ledokhod kosnulsia i Frantsii," *Izvestiia*, No. 296 (2033), 28 dekabria 1923, 1.

38. Byvshii Diplomat, "Pench i Dzhudi," 1; and Marko Polo, "Afganskii vopros v moment obrazovaniia rabochego pravitel'stva," 1.

39. Byvshii Diplomat, "Pench i Dzhudi," 1.

40. Byvshii Diplomat, "Pench i Dzhudi," 1; and Chicherin, *Stat'i i rechi po voprosam mezhdunarodnoi politiki*, 315–16.

41. Marko Polo, "Afganskii vopros v moment obrazovaniia rabochego pravitel'stva," 1.

42. Marko Polo, "Afganskii vopros v moment obrazovaniia rabochego pravitel'stva," 1; Mikhail Sharonov, "Novye etapy mirovykh antagonizmov," 2; and Chicherin, *Stat'i i rechi po voprosam mezhdunarodnoi politiki*, 294.

43. Mikhail Sharonov, "Novye etapy mirovykh antagonizmov," 2; and Chicherin, *Stat'i i rechi po voprosam mezhdunarodoi politiki*, 294–95.

44. Great Britain, Communist Party of Great Britain, *History of the Zinoviev Letter: Facts about the Infamous Letter*, Commentary by A. McManus (London: Communist Party of Great Britain, 1925), 5–11.

45. Paul W. Blackstock, *Agents of Deceit: Frauds, Forgeries and Political Intrigue among Nations*, with an Appendix by George F. Kennan (Chicago: Quadrangle Books, 1966), 107.

46. "Sovremennyi protei," 1; and "Budem nastorozhe," *Izvestiia*, No. 151 (2484), 5 iiulia 1925, 1.

47. "Budem nastorozhe," 1; and Chicherin, *Stat'i i rechi po voprosam mezhdunarodnoi politiki*, 335–36.

48. Ibid.

49. "Budem nastorozhe," 1; Chicherin, *Stat'i i rechi po voprosam mezhdunarodnoi politiki*, 335–36; "Povsemestnaia podgotovka," 1; "Na vernom puti," 1; and Marko Polo, "Pol'sha i mirovoe polozhenie," *Izvestiia*, No. 6 (2339), 8 ianvaria 1925, 2.

50. "Povsemestnaia podgotovka," 1; and Chicherin, *Stat'i i rechi po voprosam mezhdunarodnoi politiki*, 335–36.

51. "Povsemestnaia podgotovka," 1; and Marko Polo, "Pol'sha i mirovoe polozhenie," 2.

52. Marko Polo, "Pol'sha i mirovoe polozhenie," 2; and "Na vernom puti," 1.

Chapter 6

1. Chicherin, "Lozannskaia konferentsiia i mirovoe polozhenie," 3; and "Vmesto predisloviia," 2.

2. Chicherin, "Lozannskaia konferentsiia i mirovoe polozhenie," 3; "Vmesto predisloviia," 2; "Sem' let sovetskoi vneshnei politiki," 1; and *Stat'i i rechi po voprosam mezhdunarodnoi politiki*, 327.

3. Chicherin, *Voprosy vneshnei politiki*, 20–21, 41.

4. Chicherin, *Voprosy vneshnei politiki*, 20–21, 41; "Rossiia i aziatskie narody," *Vestnik NKID* 2 (13 avgusta 1919):7; "Vmesto predisloviia," 5, 8; and "Lozannskaia konferentsiia i mirovoe polozhenie," 3.

5. Ibid.

6. Ibid.

7. Chicherin, *Voprosy vneshnei politiki*, 20–21, 41; "Rossiia i aziatskie narody," *Vestnik NKID* 2 (13 avgusta 1919):7; "Vmesto predisloviia," 5, 8; Lozannskaia konferentsiia i mirovoe polozhenie," 3; and *Stat'i i rechi po voprosam mezhdunarodnoi politiki*, 286; and Politikus, "Mir i Vostok," *Kommunisticheskaia revoliutsiia* 13 (1923): 21, 23.

8. Politikus, "Mir i Vostok," 26–28.

9. Boris Nicolaevsky, "Russia, Japan, and the Pan-Asiatic Movement to 1925," *Far Eastern Quarterly* 8 (May 1949):259.

10. Ibid., 281–84.

11. Chicherin, "Vmesto predisloviia," 7.

12. "Interv'iu tov. Chicherina o dogovore s Iaponiei," *Izvestiia*, No. 18 (2351), 22 ianvaria 1925, 1.

13. A. Voznesenskii, "Rossiia i Kitai," *Izvestiia*, No. 53 (605), 9 marta 1919, 1.

14. Chicherin quoted in Fischer, *The Soviets in World Affairs*, 635. See also Fischer, *Russia's Road from Peace to War*, 67–74.

15. Chicherin, "Soglashenie SSSR s Kitaem," *Pravda*, No. 123, 1 iiunia 1924, 1.

16. Chicherin, *Stat'i i rechi po voprosam mezhdunarodnoi politiki*, 397–99; "Interv'iu s tov. Chicherinym," *Izvestiia*, No. 118 (2481), 2 iiulia 1925, 2; "Zarvavshiesia diktatory," *Izvestiia*, No. 159 (2492), 15 iiulia 1925, 1; and "Smeshnoe ubivaet," *Izvestiia*, No. 164 (2497), 21 iiulia 1925, 1.

17. Carr, *Socialism in One Country*, 769.

18. Conrad Brandt, *Stalin's Failure in China, 1924–1927*, Russian Research Center Studies, 31 (Cambridge: Harvard Univ. Press, 1958), 79.

19. Chicherin, *Stat'i i rechi po voprosam mezhdunarodnoi politiki*, 199, 202.

20. "Beseda tov. Chicherina s predstaviteliami sovetskoi pechati," *Izvestiia*, No. 272 (2903), 24 noiabria 1926, 1. For a detailed description of the articles and protocols of the treaty see Wheeler-Bennett, *Disarmament and Security since Locarno, 1925–1931*, 315.

21. Mikhail Sharonov, "Novye etapy mirovykh antagonizmov," 2; Marko Polo, "Afganskii vopros v moment obrazovaniia rabochego pravitel'stva," 1; and "Kabul'skii voprositel'nyi znak," *Izvestiia*, No. 2 (2307), 3 ianvaria 1924, 2; and "Natsional'naia bor'ba v Afganistane," *Izvestiia*, No. 144 (2477), 27 iiunia 1925, 1.

22. Osvedomlennyi, "Angliia v Kharasane," *Izvestiia*, No. 140 (273), 23 iiunia 1925, 2.

23. Marko Polo, "Afganskii vopros v moment obrazovaniia rabochego pravitel'stva," 1.

24. Von Laue, "Soviet Diplomacy: G. V. Chicherin," 120–21.

25. Robert H. McNeal, gen. ed., *Resolutions and Decisions of the Communist Party of the Soviet Union, 1898–1964*, vol. 2. *The Early Soviet Period: 1917–1929*, ed. Richard Gregor, 258–59.

26. Edward H. Carr, *German-Soviet Relations between the Two World Wars, 1919–1939* (Baltimore: John Hopkins Univ. Press, 1951), 69–70.

27. Chicherin, *Stat'i i rechi po voprosam mezhdunarodnoi politiki*, 478; and "Iuz i SSSR. Interv'iu s tov. Chicherinym," *Izvestiia*, No. 220 (2255), 26 sentiabria 1924, 2.

28. Chicherin, "Mezhdunarodnaia politika dvykh internatsionala," *Kommunisticheskii internatsional* 6 (oktiabr' 1919):819–20, 825.

29. "Iuz i SSSR. Interv'iu s tov. Chicherniym," 2.

30. Chicherin, "Mezhdunarodnaia politika dvykh internatsionala," 825–26.

31. Ibid., 819–20, 825–26.

CHAPTER 7

1. Debo, "George Chicherin," 366–67.

2. A. Gromyko, "Diplomat leninskoi shkoly. K 90-letiiu so dnia rozhdeniia G. V. Chicherina," *Izvestiia*, No. 288 (14142), 5 dekabria 1962, 2.

3. Robert D. Warth, "The Arcos Raid and the Anglo-Soviet 'Cold War' of the 1920's," *World Affairs Quarterly* 29 (July 1958):116.

4. "Po londonskoi ukaze," *Pravda*, No. 225 (3757), 2 oktiabria 1927, 1; Post-skript, "Uroki praktiki," *Mezhdunarodnaia zhizn'* 8 (1927):59–60; R. Valerin, "Ot razryva do vosstanovleniia anglo-sovetskikh otnoshenii," *Mezhdunarodnaia zhizn'* 11 (1929):49–50; and I. Taigin, "Anglo-sovetskii razryv," *Mezhdunarodnaia zhizn'* 7 (1927):11.

5. Alfred E. Senn, "The Rakovsky Affair: A Crisis in Franco-Soviet Relations, 1927," *Slavic and East-European Studies* 10, 3–4 (1965/66 Fall-Winter):113–15.

6. "Po londonskoi ukaze," 1.

7. Harvey L. Dyck, "German-Soviet Relations and the Anglo-Soviet Break, 1927," *Slavic Review* 25 (March 1966):79–80.

8. Harvey L. Dyck, *Weimar Germany and Soviet Russia, 1926–1933: A Study in Diplomatic Instability*, Studies of the Russian Institute, Columbia Univ. (New York: Columbia Univ. Press, 1966) 87–89.

9. Chicherin quoted in Fischer, *Russia's Road from Peace to War*, 172.

10. John P. Sontag, "The Soviet War Scare of 1926–27," *Russian Review* 34 (Jan. 1975):66–67.

11. Robert C. Tucker, "The Emergence of Stalin's Foreign Policy," *Slavic Review* 36 (Dec. 1977):569–70.

12. Gromyko, "Diplomat leninskoi shkoly. K 90-letiiu so dnia rozhdeniia G. V. Chicherina," 2.

13. "Interv'iu G. V. Chicherina po povodu Ligi Natsii," 1. See also Sabanin, "Uchastie SSSR v komissii po razoruzheniiu," 14.

14. Fischer, *Russia's Road from Peace to War*, 183. And see Hilger and Meyer, *The Incompatible Allies*, 217–20.

15. Fischer, *Russia's Road from Peace to War*, 183–85.

16. A. V. Lunacharskii, "Problema kul'turnoi revoliutsii," *Nauchnyi rabotnik* 5–6 (mai-iiun' 1928):25; and Lunacharskii quoted in P. N. Sakulin, "Kul'turnaia revoliutsiia i ee metody," *Nauchnyi rabotnik* 5–6 (mai-iiun' 1928):44.

17. I. V. Stalin, *Sochineniia*, 13 tomov, Institut Marksa-Engel'sa-Lenina pri TsK VKP (b) (Moskva: Politizdat, 1946–51), 11:53–57.

18. Eugene Lyons, *Assignment in Utopia* (New York: Harcourt, Brace, 1937), 120.

19. Timothy E. O'Connor, *The Politics of Soviet Culture: Anatolii Lunacharskii*, Studies in the Fine Arts: The Avant-Garde, No. 42 (Ann Arbor: UMI Research Press, 1983), 90.

20. Sheila Fitzpatrick, *Education and Social Mobility in the Soviet Union, 1921–1934*, Studies of the Russian Institute, Columbia University, Soviet and East European Studies Series (Cambridge: Cambridge Univ. Press, 1979), 119; Nicholas Lampert, *The Technical Intelligentsia and the Soviet State: A Study of Soviet Managers and Technicians, 1917–1928*, Studies in Soviet History and Society (New York: Holmes and Meier, 1979), 44–45; and Stephen F. Cohen, *Bukharin and the Bolshevik Revolution: A Political Biography, 1888–1938* (New York: Knopf, 1973), 233, 237–38.

21. Von Dirksen, *Moscow, Tokyo, London*, 80.

22. R. H. Bruce Lockhart, *Retreat from Glory* (New York: Putnam's, 1934), 335–36. See also Cleveland, "Memories of Chicherin," 417.

23. Scheffer, *Seven Years in Soviet Russia*, 329.

24. Chicherin, *Stat'i i rechi po voprosam mezhdunarodnoi politiki*, 497, 499–500.

25. Fischer, *The Soviets in World Affairs*, 775.

26. Taracouzio, *War and Peace in Soviet Diplomacy*, 122–23.

27. "Zadachi vneshnei politiki sovetskoi vlasti," *Izvestiia*, No. 204 (4051), 26 iiulia 1930, 1.

28. "Beseda Narodnogo komissara po inostrannym delam tov. M. M. Litvinova s inostrannymi korrespondentami," *Izvestiia*, No. 204 (4051), 26 iiulia 1930, 1.

29. Fischer, *Russia's Road from Peace to War*, 201; and Gromyko, "Diplomat leninskoi shkoly. K 90-letiiu so dnia rozhdeniia G. V. Chicherina," 2.

30. Fischer, *Russia's Road from Peace to War*, 201. See also Fischer, *The Soviets in World Affairs*, xvi; and Kennan, *Russia and the West under Lenin and Stalin*, 231–32.

31. G. V. Chicherin, "Protiv tezisov tov. Stalina," *Pravda*, No. 50, 6 marta 1921, 2; No. 51, 8 marta 1921, 2; and No. 52, 9 marta 1921, 2.

32. Ibid.

33. Stalin, *Sochineniia*, 5:41–43.

34. This comment came from a 1925 letter to Arkadi Maslow cited in Ruth Fisher, *Stalin and German Communism: A Study in the Origins of the State Party*, with a Preface by Sidney B. Fay (Cambridge: Harvard Univ. Press, 1948), 436.

35. Kennan, *Russia and the West under Lenin and Stalin*, 231–32.

36. E. F. Bronfin, Vstupitel'naia stat'ia, *Motsart. Issledovatel'skii etiud*, by G. V. Chicherin, Izdanie vtoroe, Obshchaia redaktsiia, kommentarii i perevod inostrannogo teksta E. F. Bronfin (Leningrad: Muzyka, 1971), 22, 24–25.

37. "Denies Tchitcherin Begs: Soviet Says Ex-Minister, Reported Arrested, Is Still at Home," *New York Times*, 31 Dec. 1931, 10; Cleveland, "Memories of Chicherin," 417; and Fischer, *Russia's Road from Peace to War*, 201.

38. George F. Kennan, *Memoirs, 1925–1950*, Atlantic Monthly Press Book (Boston: Little, Brown, 1967), nn. 63 and 64; and "Vchera skonchalsia G. V. Chicherin," *Izvestiia*, No. 157 (6014), 8 iiulia 1936, 4.

39. Fischer, *Russia's Road from Peace to War*, 201. And see "Pokhorony G. V. Chicherina," *Izvestiia*, No. 159 (6016), 10 iiulia 1936, 2.

40. Gromyko, "Diplomat leninskoi shkoly. K 90-letiiu so dnia rozhdeniia G. V. Chicherina," 2.

Selected Bibliography

PRIMARY SOURCES

ARCHIVAL COLLECTIONS

Tsentral'nyi Gosudarstvennyi Arkhiv Oktiabr'skoi Revoliutsii SSSR
   (TsGAOR SSSR), Moscow
Tsentral'nyi Gosudarstvennyi Istoricheskii Arkhiv SSSR (TsGIA
   SSSR), Leningrad

NEWSPAPERS

Delo Naroda

Izvestiia

Komsomol'skaia pravda

Nachalo (Paris)

Nashe slovo (Paris)

New York Times

Pravda

Times (London)

ARTICLES AND BOOKS

A. G. "Pervye neudachi Lokarnskikh soglashenii." *Mezhdunarodnaia zhizn'* 4 (1926):37–46.

Adler, Friedrich. *"The Anglo-Russian Report": A Criticism of the Report of the British Trades Union Delegation to Russia from the Point of View of International Socialism.* London: P. S. King and Son, 1925.

Andreev, A. *Sryv Anglo-russkogo komiteta i nashi zadachi. Doklad na sobranii Moskovskogo aktiva zheleznodorozhnikov.* Moskva: Gosudarstvennoe izdatel'stvo, 1927.

Aralov, S. I. "On Lenin's Instructions." *International Affairs* 4 (Apr. 1960):10–15.

———. "In the Turkey of Ataturk (Reminiscences of an Ambassador)." *International Affairs* 8 (Aug. 1960):81–87; 10 (Oct. 1960):97–103; 11 (Nov. 1960):96–102.

———. *Vospominaniia sovetskogo diplomata 1922–1923.* Moskva: Izdatel'stvo Instituta mezhdunarodnykh otnoshenii, 1960.

Balabanoff, Angelica. *Impressions of Lenin.* Translated by Isottsa Cesari. Ann Arbor: Univ. of Michigan Press, 1964.

———. *My Life as a Rebel.* New York: Harper, 1938.

Barmine, Alexandre. *Memoirs of a Soviet Diplomat: Twenty Years in the Service of the U.S.S.R.* Translated by Gerard Hopkins. London: Lovat Dickson, 1938; reprint ed., Westport, Conn.: Hyperion Press, 1973.

———. *One Who Survived: The Life Story of a Russian under the Soviets.* With an Introduction by Max Eastman. New York: Putnam's, 1945.

Beatty, Bessie. "Chicherin." *New Republic* 30 (17 May 1922):335–38.

Berezhkov, V. M. *Gody diplomaticheskoi sluzhby.* Moskva: Mezhdunarodnye otnosheniia, 1972.

Besedovskii, G. Z. *Na putiakh k termidoru (Iz vospominanii b. sovetsk. diplomata).* Parizh: Mishen', 1930.

Bilainkin, George. *Maisky: Ten Years Ambassador.* London: George Allen and Unwin, 1944.

Bonch-Bruevich, V. D. *Izbrannye sochineniia v trekh tomakh.* Tom 1: *O religii, religioznom sektantstve i tserkvi.* Institut istorii Akademii nauk SSSR. Moskva: Izdatel'stvo Akademii nauk SSSR, 1959.

———. *Izbrannye sochineniia v trekh tomakh.* Tom 2: *Stat'i, vospominaniia, pis'ma 1895–1914 gg.* Institut istorii Akademii nauk SSSR. Moskva: Izdatel'stvo Akademii nauk SSSR, 1961.

———. *Izbrannye sochineniia v trekh tomakh.* Tom 3: *Vospominaniia o V. I. Lenine 1917–1924 gg.* Institut istorii Akademii nauk SSSR. Moskva: Izdatel'stvo Akademii nauk SSSR, 1963.

_____. *Na boevykh postakh Fevral'skoi i Oktiabr'skoi Revoliutsii.* Izdanie vtoroe. Moskva: Federatsiia, 1931.

_____. *Vospominaniia o Lenine.* Izdanie vtoroe, dopolnennoe. Moskva: Nauka, 1969.

Boulter, V. M., comp. *Survey of International Affairs, 1925: Supplement; Chronology of International Events and Treaties, 1st January, 1920–31st December, 1925.* Published under the auspices of the Royal Institute of International Affairs. London: Oxford Univ. Press, 1928.

Bryant, Louise. *Mirrors of Moscow.* New York: Thomas Seltzer, 1923; reprint ed., Westport, Conn.: Hyperion Press, 1973.

_____. *Six Red Months in Moscow: An Observer's Account of Russia Before and During the Proletarian Dictatorship.* New York: Doran, 1918.

Buchanan, Sir George. *My Mission To Russia and Other Diplomatic Memories.* 2 vols. Boston: Little, Brown, 1923.

Bunyan, James, comp. *Intervention, Civil War, and Communism in Russia: Documents and Materials, April–December 1918.* Baltimore: Johns Hopkins Univ. Press, 1936.

Bunyan, James, and Harold H. Fisher, comps. *The Bolshevik Revolution, 1917–1918: Documents and Materials.* Hoover War Library Publications, No. 3. Stanford: Stanford Univ. Press, 1934.

Chicherin, G. V. "Chetyre kongressa." *Vestnik NKID* 1 (20 iiunia 1919):1–12.

_____. "Dogovor s Estoniei." *Vestnik NKID* 3 (27 fevral' 1920):1–6.

_____. *Doklad Narodnogo komissara po inostrannym delam G. V. Chicherina na zasedanii VTsIK 17-go iiunia 1920 goda. (Stenogramma).* Moskva: Tipografiia III-go kommunisticheskogo internatsionala, 1920.

_____. *Iz istorii internatsionala molodezhi. Ocherki.* Izdanie tret'e. Moskva: Molodaia gvardiia, 1925.

_____. "Lenin i vneshniaia politika." *Voprosy istorii* 3 (mart 1957 g.):20–25.

_____. *Lenin i vneshniaia politika.* Moskva: Politizdat, 1977.

_____. "Lozannskaia konferentsiia i mirovoe polozhenie." *Mezhdunarodnaia zhizn'* 2 (1923):3–6.

_____. "Mezhdunarodnaia politika dvukh internatsionala." *Kommunisticheskii internatsional* 6 (oktiabr' 1919 g.):817–28.

_____. "Molodoi gvardii." *Molodaia gvardiia* 4–5 (11–12) (iiun'-iiul' 1923): 5–7.

_____. *Motsart. Issledovatel'skii etiud.* Izdanie vtoroe. Obshchaia redaktsiia, vstupitel'naia stat'ia, kommentarii i perevod inostrannogo teksta E. F. Bronfin. Leningrad: Muzyka, 1971.

———. "Nota Nar. komissara po inostr. delam pravitel'stvam Antanty." *Mezhdunarodnaia zhizn'* 1 (20 marta 1922):46–48.

———. *Ocherk iz istorii iunosheskogo internatsionala.* S predisloviem O. Skara. Moskva: Gosudarstvennoe izdatel'stvo, 1920.

———. "Rech' Narodnogo komissara po inostrannym delam G. V. Chicherina na zasedanii fraktsii RKP VIII c"ezda sovetov." *Vestnik NKID* 1–2 (15 marta 1921):3–12.

———. "Rossiia i aziatskie narody." *Vestnik NKID* 2 (13 avgusta 1919):1–7.

———. "Soviet Diplomacy since the War." *Living Age* 320 (22 Mar. 1924):548–51.

———. *Stat'i i rechi po voprosam mezhdunarodnoi politiki.* Sostavitel' L. I. Trofimova. Biblioteka vneshnei politiki. Moskva: Sotsekgiz, 1961.

———. *Two Years of Foreign Policy: The Relations of the Russian Socialist Federal Soviet Republic with Foreign Nations, from November 7, 1917, to November 7, 1919.* Soviet Russia Pamphlets, No. 3. New York: Russian Soviet Government Bureau, 1920.

———. "Vmesto predisloviia." *Mezhdunarodnaia zhizn'* 1 (1923):3–8.

———. *Vneshniaia politika Sovetskoi Rossii za dva goda. Ocherk, sostavlennyi k dvukletnei godovshchine raboche-krest'ianskoi revoliutsii.* Moskva: Gosudarstvennoe izdatel'stvo, 1920.

———. *Voprosy vneshnei politiki. Doklady i noty t. Chicherina.* Vypusk pervyi. Seriia "Nasha diplomatiia." Saratov: Gosudarstvennoe izdatel'stvo, saratovskoe otdelenie, 1920.

———. "Za piat' let." *Mezhdunarodnaia zhizn'* 15 (7 noiabria 1922):3–6.

———. (Pervaia sel'skokhoziaistvennaia i kustarnaia promyshlennaia vystavka SSSR) *Znachenie vystavki. Rech', proiznesennaia na mitinge 16 IX-23 g. na Leninskoi ploshchadi vystavki.* Moskva: Mospoligraf, 1923.

Child, Richard W. *A Diplomat Looks at Europe.* New York: Duffield, 1925.

Clemens, Walter C., Jr., comp. *Soviet Disarmament Policy, 1917–1963: An Annotated Bibliography of Soviet and Western Sources.* With an Introduction by Walter C. Clemens, Jr. Hoover Institution Bibliographical Series 22. Stanford: Hoover Institution on War, Revolution, and Peace, Stanford Univ., 1965.

Cleveland, C. O. "Memories of Chicherin." *Commonweal* 24 (28 Aug. 1936):417–18.

Cumming, C. K., and Walter W. Pettit, comps. and eds. *Russian-American Relations, March, 1917–March, 1920: Documents and Papers.* Under the Direction of John A. Ryan, J. Henry Scattergood, and William A. White. At the Request of the League of Free Nations Association. New York: Harcourt, Brace, and Howe, 1920.

D'Abernon, Viscount. *The Diary of an Ambassador.* Vol. 1. *Versailles to Rapallo, 1920–1922.* With historical notes by Maurice Alfred Gerothwohl. Garden City, N.Y.: Doubleday, Doran, 1929.

_____. *The Diary of an Ambassador.* Vol. 2. *Rapallo to Dawes, 1922–1924.* With historical notes by Maurice Alfred Gerothwohl. Garden City, N.Y.: Doubleday, Doran, 1930.

_____. *The Diary of an Ambassador.* Vol. 3. *Dawes to Locarno, 1924–1926.* With historical notes by Maurice Alfred Gerothwohl. Garden City, N.Y.: Doubleday, Doran, 1931.

Degras, Jane, ed. *The Communist International, 1919–1943: Documents.* Vol. 1. *1919–1922.* Issued under the auspices of the Royal Institute of International Affairs. London: Oxford Univ. Press, 1956.

_____. *The Communist International, 1919–1943: Documents.* Vol. 2. *1923–1928.* Issued under the auspices of the Royal Institute of International Affairs. London: Oxford Univ. Press, 1960.

_____. *Soviet Documents on Foreign Policy.* Vol. 1. *1917–1924.* Issued under the auspices of the Royal Institute of International Affairs. London: Oxford Univ. Press, 1951.

_____. *Soviet Documents on Foreign Policy.* Vol. 2. *1925–1932.* Issued under the auspices of the Royal Institute of International Affairs. London: Oxford Univ. Press, 1952.

De Robien, Louis. *The Diary of a Diplomat in Russia, 1917–1918.* Translated from the French by Camilla Sykes. New York: Praeger, 1970.

Duranty, Walter. *I Write as I Please.* New York: Simon and Schuster, 1935.

Durdenevskii, V. N. "Liga Natsii i mezhdunarodnaia torgovlia oruzhiem." *Mezhdunarodnaia zhizn'* 8 (1929):38–54.

Eastman, Max. *Great Companions: Critical Memoirs of Some Famous Friends.* New York: Farrar, Straus, and Cudahy, 1959.

_____. *Heroes I Have Known: Twelve Who Lived Great Lives.* New York: Simon and Schuster, 1942.

_____. *Love and Revolution: My Journey Through an Epoch.* New York: Random House, 1964.

Egor'ev, V. "Pered novoi sessiei Komissii razoruzheniia." *Mezhdunarodnaia zhizn'* 2 (1929):13–25.

Eudin, Xenia J., and Robert M. Slusser, eds. *Soviet Foreign Policy, 1928–1934: Documents and Materials.* 2 vols. Hoover Institution Publications. University Park: Pennsylvania State Univ. Press, 1966–1967.

Fischer, Louis. *Men and Politics: An Autobiography.* New York: Duell, Sloan and Pearce, 1941; reprint ed., Westport, Conn.: Greenwood Press, 1970.

Francis, David R. *Russia from the American Embassy, April 1916– November 1918.* New York: Scribner's, 1921.

Gerv'e, O. "Desiat' let politiki Ligi Natsii." *Mezhdunarodnaia zhizn'* 1 (1930):72–85.

_____. "Desiatyi god razoruzheniia Ligi Natsii." *Mezhdunarodnaia zhizn'* 11 (1929):84–97.

_____. "Konets Komissii razoruzheniia." *Mezhdunarodnaia zhizn'* 12 (1930):54–65.

_____. "Odinnadtsatyi god Ligi Natsii." *Mezhdunarodnaia zhizn'* 11 (1930):70–85.

_____. "Nachalo kontsa Komissii razoruzheniia." *Mezhdunarodnaia zhizn'* 7 (1929):33–51.

_____. "Za ili protiv razoruzheniia." *Mezhdunarodnaia zhizn'* 6 (1929):20–33.

Goldman, Emma. *My Disillusionment in Russia.* Garden City, N.Y.: Doubleday, Page, 1923.

Goode, William T. *Bolshevism at Work.* New York: Harcourt, Brace and Howe, 1920.

Great Britain. Communist Party of Great Britain. *History of the Zinoviev Letter: Facts about the Infamous Letter.* Commentary by A. McManus. London: Communist Party of Great Britain, 1925.

Gregory, J. D. *On the Edge of Diplomacy: Rambles and Reflections, 1902–1928.* London: Hutchinson, n.d.

Grew, Joseph C. *Turbulent Era: A Diplomatic Record of Forty Years, 1904–1945.* 2 vols. Edited by Walter Johnson. Assisted by Nancy Harrison Hooker. Boston: Houghton Mifflin, 1952.

Harper, Paul V., and Ronald Thompson, eds. *The Russia I Believe In: The Memoirs of Samuel N. Harper, 1902–1941.* Chicago: Univ. of Chicago Press, 1945.

Harper, Samuel N. *Making Bolsheviks.* Chicago: Univ. of Chicago Press, 1931.

_____, ed. *The Soviet Union and World-Problems.* Chicago: Univ. of Chicago Press, 1935.

Harrison, Marguerite E. *Marooned in Moscow: The Story of an American Woman Imprisoned in Russia.* New York: Doran, 1921.

Hemingway, Ernest. *By Line: Ernest Hemingway; Selected Articles and Dispatches of Four Decades.* Edited by William White. New York: Scribner's, 1967.

Hilger, Gustav, and Alfred G. Meyer. *The Incompatible Allies: A Memoir-History of German-Soviet Relations, 1918–1941.* New York: Macmillan, 1953.

Hodgson, Robert H. "Memoirs of an Official Agent: Trading with Russia, 1921–23." *History Today* 4 (Aug. 1954):522–28.
_____. "Obituary: George Chicherin." *Slavonic and East European Review* 15 (Apr. 1937):698–703.
Iglov, S. M. "Mezhdunarodnaia ekonomicheskaia konferentsiia." *Mezhdunarodnaia zhizn'* 5 (1927):3–11.
Ioffe, A. "Pered Genuei." *Vestnik NKID* 4–5 (aprel'-mai 1922):3–6.
_____. "Politika razbitogo koryta." *Mezhdunarodnaia zhizn'* 10 (1927):21–31.
Iordanskii, N. "Printsipy 17-go goda." *Mezhdunarodnaia zhizn'* 7 (22 maia 1922):1–4.
Kontarovich, B. "Organizatsionnoe razvitie NKID." *Mezhdunarodnaia zhizn'* 15 (7 noiabria 1922):51–55.
Kazanin, M. I. *China in the Twenties.* Translated from the Russian by Hilda Kazanina. Institute of Oriental Studies, USSR. Academy of Sciences. Moscow: Nauka, 1973.
_____. *Zapiski sekretaria missii. Stranichka istorii pervykh let sovetskoi diplomatii.* Moskva: Izdatel'stvo vostochnoi literatury, 1962.
Kennan, George F. *Memoirs, 1925–1950.* Atlantic Monthly Press Book. Boston: Little, Brown, 1967.
Kennedy, Aubrey L. *Old Diplomacy and New, 1876–1922: From Salisbury to Lloyd-George.* With an Introduction by Sir Valentine Chirol. London: John Murray, 1922.
Kessler, Harry. *In the Twenties: The Diaries of Harry Kessler.* With an Introduction by Otto Friedrich. Translated by Charles Kessler. New York: Holt, Rinehart and Winston, 1971.
Kiselev, K. V. *Zapiski sovetskogo diplomata.* Moskva: Politizdat, 1974.
Kliuchnikov, Iu. V. "Liga Natsii kak 'orudie ekonomicheskogo mira'." *Mezhdunarodnaia zhizn'* 7 (1927):31–46.
Kliuchnikov, Iu. V., and A. V. Sabanin. *Mezhdunarodnaia politika noveishego vremeni v dogovorakh, notakh i deklaratsiiakh.* Chast' 2. *Ot imperialisticheskoi voiny do sniatiia blokady s Sovetskoi Rossii.* Moskva: Izdanie Litizdata NKID, 1926.
_____. *Mezhdunarodnaia politika noveishego vremeni v dogovorakh, notakh i deklaratsiiakh.* Chast' 3. *Ot sniatiia blokady s Sovetskoi Rossii do desiatiletiia Oktiabr'skoi revoliutsii.* Moskva: Izdanie Litizdata NKID, 1928.
Kornev, N. "Krizis Rapallo?" *Mezhdunarodnaia zhizn'* 3 (1930):4–18.
_____. "O krizise Rapallo." *Mezhdunarodnaia zhizn'* 7–8 (1930):75–77.
Krasin, L. B. ("Nikitich"). *Gody podpol'ia. Sbornik vospominanii, statei i dokumentov.* Sostavlen Kruzhkom druzei Krasina pod redaktsiei M. N. Liadova i S. M. Pozner. ISPART TsK VKP (b). Moskva: Gosudarstvennoe izdatel'stvo, 1928.

Kulik, I. Iu. *Zapiski konsula.* Perevod s ukrainskogo L. Rakhlinoi. Moskva: Sovetskii pisatel', 1964.

Lansbury, George. *What I Saw in Russia.* New Era Series, vol. 3. London: Parsons, 1920.

Lenin, V. I. *Polnoe sobranie sochinenii.* Piatoe izdanie. Institut marksizma-leninizma pri TsK KPSS. Moskva: Politizdat, 1928–1965.

Litvinov, M. M. *Vneshniaia politika SSSR. Rechi i zaiavleniia 1927–1935.* Moskva: Sotsekgiz, 1935.

Litvinova, A. "Vstrechi i razluki (Iz vospominanii o M. M. Litvinove)." Perevela s angliiskogo T. Litvinova. *Novyi mir* 7 (iiul' 1966 g.):235–50.

Liubimov, N. N. "Lenin i Genuia-Rapallo." *Vneshniaia torgovlia* 4 (1967):4–6.

Liubimov, N. N., and A. N. Erlikh. *Genuezskaia konferentsiia. Vospomianiia uchastnikov.* Moskva: Izdatel'stvo Instituta mezhdunarodnykh otnoshenii, 1963.

———. "The 1922 Genoa Conference." *International Affairs* 6; 8; 9; 10 (June; Aug.; Sept.; Oct. 1963):65–70; 97–103; 78–83; 71–78.

Lloyd George, David. *The Truth about Reparations and War-Debts.* Garden City, N.Y.: Doubleday, Doran, 1932.

Lockhart, R. H. Bruce. *British Agent.* With an Introduction by Hugh Walpole. New York: Putnam's, 1933.

———. *The Diaries of Sir Robert Bruce Lockhart.* 2 vols. Vol. 1. *1915–1938.* Edited by Kenneth Young. London: Macmillan, 1973.

———. *Retreat from Glory.* New York: Putnam's, 1934.

———. *The Two Revolutions: An Eye-witness Study of Russia in 1917.* With a Foreword and Postscript "The Achievements of the Russian Revolution" by John Keep. A Background Book. Chester Springs, Penn.: Dufour Editions, 1967.

Lunacharskii, A. V. "Problema kul'turnoi revoliutsii." *Nauchnyi rabotnik* 5–6 (mai-iiun' 1928):14–25.

———. *Stat'i i rechi po voprosam mezhdunarodnoi politiki.* Sostavitel' i s predisloviem L. A. Istomina. Moskva: Sotsekgiz, 1959.

Lyons, Eugene. *Assignment in Utopia.* New York: Harcourt Brace, 1937.

Maiskii, I. M. "Anglo-sovetskoe torgovoe soglashenie 1921 goda." *Voprosy istorii* 5 (mai 1957 g.):60–77.

———. *B. Shou i drugie. Vospominaniia.* Moskva: Iskusstvo, 1967.

———. "Diplomats of the Lenin School: Alexander Kollontay. *New Times* 4 (31 Jan. 1968):20–22.

———. "Diplomats of the Lenin School: Ambassador Krasin." *New Times* 3 (24 Jan. 1968):23–27.

———. "Diplomats of the Lenin School: Georgi Chicherin." *New Times* 44 (1 Nov. 1967):10–13.

_____. "Dva otveta." *Mezhdunarodnaia zhizn'* 6 (10 maia 1922):1–4.

_____. "Genuezskie plody." *Mezhdunarodnaia zhizn'* 8 (8 iiunia 1922):1–3.

_____. "Iz londonskikh vospominanii (1925–1927)." *Novyi mir* 4 (aprel' 1968 g.):195–216; 5 (mai 1968 g.):153–67.

_____. *Journey into the Past*. Translated from the Russian by Frederick Holt. London: Hutchinson, 1962.

_____. *Liudi. Sobytiia. Fakty*. Otdelenie istorii Akademii nauk SSSR. Moskva: Nauka, 1973.

_____. *Puteshestvie v proshloe. Vospominaniia o russkoi politicheskoi emigratsii v Londone 1912–1917 gg*. Otedelenie istoricheskikh nauk Akademii nauk SSSR. Moskva: Izdatel'stvo Akademii nauk SSSR, 1960.

_____. "Rossiia i Genuia." *Mezhdunarodnaia zhizn'* 3 (3 aprelia 1922):1–3.

_____. *Vospominaniia sovetskogo posla v dvukh knigakh*. Kniga pervaia: *Puteshestvie v proshloe*. Otdelenie istoricheskikh nauk Akademii nauk SSSR. Moskva: Nauka, 1964.

_____. *Vospominaniia sovetskogo posla v dvukh knigakh*. Kniga vtoraia: *Mir ili voina?* Otdelenie istoricheskikh nauk Akademii nauk SSSR. Moskva: Nauka, 1964.

McCormick, Anne O'Hare. *The Hammer and the Scythe: Communist Russia Enters the Second Decade*. New York: Knopf, 1929.

McNeal, Robert H., gen. ed. *Resolutions and Decisions of the Communist Party of the Soviet Union, 1898–1964*. 4 vols. Toronto: Univ. of Toronto Press, 1974.

Makeev, Nicholas, and Valentine O'Hara. *Russia*. Introduction by the Right Honorable H. A. L. Fisher. New York: Scribner's, 1925.

Meyendorff, Baron Alexander. "My Cousin, Foreign Commissar Chicherin." Edited by Igor Vinogradoff. *Russian Review* 30 (Apr. 1971):173–78.

Mikhailovich, I. "Pan-Evropa." *Mezhdunarodnaia zhizn'* 4 (1930):64–74.

_____. "Sokrashchenie ili 'regulirovanie' vooruzhenii." *Mezhdunarodnaia zhizn'* 4 (1929):3–9.

Mills, J. Saxon. *The Genoa Conference*. New York: Dutton, 1922.

Ministerstvo Inostrannykh Del SSSR. *Dokumenty vneshnei politiki SSSR*. 21 tom. Moskva: Politizdat, 1957–1977.

Nabliudatel'. "Itogi Londonskoi konferentsii." *Mezhdunarodnaia zhizn'* 5 (1930):3–13.

Nabokov, K. D. *The Ordeal of a Diplomat*. London and Norwich: London and Norwich Press, 1921; reprint ed., Salisbury, N.C.: Documentary Publications, 1976.

Odi. "Lokarnskaia konferentsiia. *Mezhdunarodnaia zhizn'* 4–5 (1925):3–22.

Oudendyk, William J. *Ways and By-Ways in Diplomacy.* London: Davies, 1939.

Ozols, K. V. *Memuary poslannika.* Parizh: Dom knigi, 1938.

Pal'gunov, N. G. *Tridtsat' let. (Vospominaniia zhurnalista i diplomata).* Moskva: Politizdat, 1964.

Politikus. "Mir i Vostok." *Kommunisticheskaia revoliutsiia* 13 (1923):19–28.

Post-skript. "Uroki praktiki." *Mezhdunarodnaia zhizn'* 8 (1927):55–60.

———. "Vokrug noty." *Mezhdunarodnaia zhizn'* 3 (1927):50–55.

———. "Zheneva." *Mezhdunarodnaia zhizn'* 4 (1926):62–65.

Radek, Karl. *Portraits and Pamphlets.* With an Introduction by A. J. Cummings and Notes by Alec Brown. London: n.p., 1935; reprint ed., Freeport, N.Y.: Books for Libraries Press, 1966.

———. "Russia at Geneva." *Living Age* 340 (July 1931):438–43.

———. *Vneshniaia politika Sovetskoi Rossii.* Moskva i Petrograd: Gosudarstvennoe izdatel'stvo, 1923.

Rakovskii, Christian. "The Foreign Policy of Soviet Russia." *Foreign Affairs* 4 (July 1926):574–84.

Ransome, Arthur. *Russia in 1919.* New York: Huebsch, 1919.

Ravich, N. A. *Molodost' veka.* Moskva: Voennoe izdatel'stvo Ministerstva oborony Soiuza SSR, 1960.

Reswick, William. *I Dreamt Revolution.* Chicago: Regnery, 1952.

Riurikov, Iu. B., ed. *Mikhail Kol'tsov, kakim on byl. Vospominaniia.* Moskva: Sovetskii pisatel', 1965.

Rosen, Baron. *Forty Years of Diplomacy.* 2 vols. London: George Allen and Unwin, 1922.

Rotshteina, F. A. *Mirovaia politika v 1924 godu. Sbornik statei.* Kabinet mezhdunarodnoi politiki Kommunisticheskoi akademii. Moskva: Izdatel'stvo Kommunisticheskoi akademii, 1925.

Sabanin, A. "Lozannskii mir na praktike mezhdunarodnoi deistvitel'nosti." *Mezhdunarodnaia zhizn'* 10 (1927):47–56.

———. "Rabota Ligi Natsii po razoruzheniiu." *Mezhdunarodnaia zhizn'* 5 (1927):12–26.

———. "Uchastie SSSR v Komissii po razoruzheniiu." *Mezhdunarodnaia zhizn'* 11 (1927):7–16.

Sakulin, P. N. "Kul'turnaia revoliutsiia i ee metody." *Nauchnyi rabotnik* 5–6 (mai–iiun' 1928):42–46.

Scheffer, Paul. *Seven Years in Soviet Russia: With a Retrospect.* Authorized translation by Arthur Livingston. New York: Macmillan, 1932.

Serge, Victor. *From Lenin to Stalin.* 2d ed. Translated by Ralph

Manheim. New York: Monad Press; Distributed by Pathfinder Press, 1973.

————. "Litvinov." *Esprit* 81 (June 1939):419–27.

————. *Memoirs of a Revolutionary, 1901–1941.* Translated and edited by Peter Sedgwick. London: Oxford Univ. Press, 1963.

————. *Year One of the Russian Revolution.* Translated and edited by Peter Sedgwick. Photographic research by Celestine Dars. Chicago: Holt, Rinehart and Winston, 1972.

Serge, Victor, and N. S. Trotskaia. *The Life and Death of Leon Trotsky.* Translated by Arnold J. Pomerans. New York: Basic Books, 1975.

Schapiro, Leonard, ed. *Soviet Treaty Series: A Collection of Bilateral Treaties, Agreements and Conventions, etc., Concluded between the Soviet Union and Foreign Powers.* Vol. 1. *1917–1928.* Washington, D.C.: Georgetown Univ. Press, 1950.

Sheridan, Claire. *Russian Portraits.* London: Jonathan Cape, 1921.

Shtein, B. E. "Balans idei razoruzheniia." *Mezhdunarodnaia zhizn'* 3 (1926):3–12.

————. *"Russkii vopros" v 1920–1921 gg.* Moskva: Politizdat, 1958.

Shumiatskii, B. Z. *Na postu sovetskoi diplomatii.* Izdanie vtoroe. Pod redaktsiei i s predisloviem L. I. Miroshnikova. Institut narodov Azii Akademii nauk SSSR. Moskva: Izdatel'stvo vostochnoi literatury, 1960.

Solomon, G. A. *Among the Red Autocrats: My Experience in the Service of the Soviets.* Translated from the German edition. Edited and revised by Arno C. Gaebelein. New York: Arno C. Gaebelein, 1935.

————. *Sredi krasnykh vozhdei. Lichno perezhitoe i vedennoe na sovetskoi sluzhbe.* 2 toma. Iz dokumentov partii Volia naroda. Parizh: Mishen', 1930.

Solov'ev, Iu. Ia. *Dvadtsat' piat' let moei diplomaticheskoi sluzhby (1893–1918).* S predisloviem F. Rotshteina. Moskva: Gosudarstvennoe izdatel'stvo, 1928.

————. *Vospominaniia diplomata 1893–1922.* Izdanie vtoroe. Biblioteka vneshnei politiki. Moskva: Sotsekgiz, 1959.

Stalin, I. V. *Sochineniia.* 13 tomov. Institut Marksa-Engel'sa-Lenina pri TsK VKP (b). Moskva: Politizdat, 1946–1951.

Steffans, Lincoln. *The Autobiography of Lincoln Steffans.* New York: Harcourt, Brace and World, 1931.

Stoklitskii, A. "Genuezskaia konferentsiia." *Molodaia gvardiia* 3 (iiun' 1922):206–12.

Sutton, Eric, ed. *Gustav Stresemann: His Diaries, Letters, and Papers.* Vol. 3. Translated by Eric Sutton. New York: Macmillan, 1940.

Taigin, I. "Anglo-sovetskii razryv." *Mezhdunarodnaia zhizn'* 7 (1927):3–13.

Tanin, M. "Anglo-sovetskii razryv i problema edinogo imperialistskogo fronta." *Bol'shevik* 11–12 (1927):59–68.

──────. *10 let vneshnei politiki SSSR (1917–1927)*. Moskva: Gosudarstvennoe izdatel'stvo, 1927.

Thorne, Will. *My Life's Battles*. With a Foreword by the Right Honorable J. R. Clynes. London: George Newnes, n.d.

Tillett, Ben. *Memories and Reflections*. With a Foreword by the Right Honorable Philip Snowden. London: John Long, 1931.

Triska, Jan F., ed. *Constitutions of the Communist Party-States*. Hoover Institution Publications, 70. Stanford: Hoover Institution on War, Revolution, and Peace, Stanford Univ., 1968.

Trotskii, L. D. *Leon Trotsky on China*. Introduction by Peng Shu-tse. Edited by Les Evans and Russell Block. New York: Published by Monad Press for the Anchor Foundation; Distributed by Pathfinder Press, 1976.

──────. *Moia zhizn'. Opyt avtobiografii*. 2 vols. Berlin: Granat, 1930; reprint ed., N'iu-Iork: Monad Press, 1977.

──────. *My Life*. New York: Scribner's, 1930; reprint ed., Universal Library, UL-72, Grosset and Dunlap, 1960.

──────. *Problems of the Chinese Revolution*. 2d ed. With Appendices by Zinoviev, Vuyovitch, Nassunov and Others. Translated with an Introduction by Max Shachtman. New York: Pioneer, 1932; reprint ed., Paragon Book Gallery, 1962.

──────. *Stalin: An Appraisal of the Man and His Influence*. Edited and translated by Charles Malamuth. New York: Harper, 1941.

──────. *The Third International After Lenin*. 2d ed. Translated by John G. Wright. New York: Pioneer, 1957.

──────. *Whither England?* New York: International, 1925.

Turkan, G. A., ed. "Doklad Ia. E. Rudzutaka o Genuezskoi konferentsii." *Istoricheskii arkhiv* 2 (mart–aprel' 1962):80–95.

U.S. Senate. Committee on Foreign Relations. *The Bullitt Mission to Russia: Testimony before the Committee on Foreign Relations, United States Senate, of William C. Bullitt*. New York: Huebsch, 1919.

USSR. "Anglichane na severe." S predisloviem I. Mintsa. *Krasnyi arkhiv* 19 (1926):39–52.

──────. *Entsiklopedicheskii slovar' Russkogo bibliograficheskogo instituta Granat*. Sed'moe izdanie. S. V. "Georgii Vasil'evich Chicherin."

──────. "K istorii frantsuzskoi interventsii na iuge Rossii." S predisloviem D. Kina. *Krasnyi arkhiv* 19 (1926):3–38.

──────. "Pamiati A. A. Ioffe." *Mezhdunarodnaia zhizn'* 11 (1927):5–6.

Vaks, B., comp. *Ot Oktiabria go Genui. Mezhdunarodnye otnosheniia RSFSR. Spravochnik*. Moskva: Izdanie Narodnogo Komissariata po Inostrannym Delam, 1922.

Vol'skii, N. V. [Nikolai Valentinov]. *Encounters with Lenin*. Translated by Paul Rosta and Brian Pearce. Foreword by Leonard Schapiro. London: Oxford Univ. Press, 1968.

———. "Non-Party Specialists and the Coming of the NEP." Edited by Gregory Guroff. Translated by Randall W. Magee. *Russian Review* 30 (Apr. 1971):154–63.

———. *Novaia ekonomicheskaia politika i krizis partii posle smerti Lenina. Gody raboty v VSNKh vo vremia NEP. Vospominaniia*. Pod redaktsiei Ia. Bunina i V. Butenko. S predisloviem Bertrama Vol'fa. Hoover Institution Foreign Language Publications. Stanford: Hoover Institution Press, Stanford Univ., 1971.

Von Dirksen, Herbert. *Moscow, Tokyo, London: Twenty Years of German Foreign Policy*. Norman: Univ. of Oklahoma Press, 1952.

Vorovskii, V. V. *Stat'i i materiali po voprosam vneshnei politiki*. Sostavitel N. F. Piiashev. Biblioteka vneshnei politiki. Moskva: Sotsekgiz, 1959.

Vsegov, E. "Vashington i Londonskaia konferentsiia." *Mezhdunarodnaia zhizn'* 3 (1930):19–29.

Wells, Herbert G. *Russia in the Shadows*. New York: Doran, 1921.

Wheeler-Bennett, John W., ed. *Documents on International Affairs, 1928*. With an Introduction by Sir Neill L. Malcolm. London: Oxford Univ. Press, 1929.

———. *Documents on International Affairs, 1929*. With an Introduction by Sir George MacDonogh. London: Oxford Univ. Press, 1930.

———. *Documents on International Affairs, 1930*. With an Introduction by Sir Frederic G. Kenyon. London: Oxford Univ. Press, 1931.

Wilgress, Dana. "From Siberia to Kuibyshev: Reflections on Russia, 1919–1943." *International Journal* 22 (Summer 1967):364–75.

Williams, Albert R. *Journey into Revolution: Petrograd, 1917–1918*. Edited by Lucita Williams. Foreword by Josephine Herbst. Chicago: Quadrangle Books, 1969.

Wilson, Hugh R. *Diplomat Between Wars*. New York: Longmans, Green, 1941.

Woodward, E. L., and Rohan Butler, eds. *Documents on British Foreign Policy, 1919–1939*. 1st Ser., vol. 3. London: His Majesty's Stationery Office, 1949.

Zalkind, I. "Iz pervykh mesiatsev Narodnogo Komissariata po Inostrannym Delam." *Mezhdunarodnaia zhizn'* 15 (7 noiabria 1922):55–61.

———. "NKID v semnadtsatom godu." *Mezhdunarodnaia zhizn'* 10 (1927):12–20.

SECONDARY SOURCES

ARTICLES AND BOOKS

Adamec, Ludwig W. *Afghanistan, 1900–1923: A Diplomatic History.* Published under the auspices of the Near Eastern Center, University of California, Los Angeles. Berkeley and Los Angeles: Univ. of California Press, 1967.

Airapetian, M. E., and G. A. Deborin. *Etapy vneshnei politiki SSSR.* Moskva: Sotsekgiz, 1961.

Airapetian, M. E., and P. Kabanov. *Leninskie printsipy vneshnei politiki.* Moskva: Politizdat, 1957.

Akhtamzian, A. A. "Genuezskaia konferentsiia i Rapall'skii dogovor." *Voprosy istorii* 5 (mai 1972 g.):42–63.

———. "O Brest-Litovskikh peregovorakh 1918 goda." *Voprosy istorii* 11 (noiabr' 1966 g.):32–46.

———. *Ot Bresta do Kilia. Proval antisovetskoi politiki germanskogo imperializma v 1918 godu.* Institut mezhdunarodnykh otnoshenii. Moskva: Izdatel'stvo IMO, 1963.

———. "Profili Rapall'skoi diplomatii." *Voprosy istorii* 2 (fevral' 1974 g.):100–124.

———. *Rapall'skaia politika. Sovetsko-germanskie diplomaticheskie otnosheniia v 1922–1932 godakh.* Moskva: Mezhdunarodnye otnosheniia, 1974.

Angress, Werner T. *Stillborn Revolution: The Communist Bid for Power in Germany, 1921–1923.* Princeton: Princeton Univ. Press, 1963.

Arutiunian, A. B. (Arents). *Kamo. Zhizn' i revoliutsionnaia deiatel'nost'.* Erevan: Izdatel'stvo Erevanskogo universiteta, 1958.

Ascher, Abraham. *Pavel Axelrod and the Development of Menshevism.* Russian Research Center Studies, 70. Hoover Institution Publications, 115. Cambridge: Harvard Univ. Press, 1972.

Aspaturian, Vernon V., ed. *Process and Power in Soviet Foreign Policy.* Boston: Little, Brown, 1971.

———. *The Union Republics in Soviet Diplomacy: A Study of Soviet Federalism in the Service of Soviet Foreign Policy.* Publications de l'Institut Universitaire de Hautes Etudes Internationales, No. 36. Geneva: Librairie E. Droz, 1960.

Bakhov, A. S. *Na zare sovetskoi diplomatii. Organy sovetskoi diplomatii v 1917–1922 gg.* Moskva: Mezhdunarodnye otnosheniia, 1966.

Ballestram, Karl G. "Lenin and Bogdanov." *Studies in Soviet Thought* 9 (Dec. 1969):283–310.

Baron, Samuel H. *Plekhanov: The Father of Russian Marxism.* Stanford: Stanford Univ. Press, 1963.

Bassekhes, N. "Ischeznuvshie sovetskie diplomaty." *Russkie zapiski* 19 (iiul' 1939):121–38.

Beloff, Max. *The Foreign Policy of Soviet Russia, 1919–1941.* Vol. 1. *1929–1936.* Issued under the auspices of the Royal Institute of International Affairs. London: Oxford Univ. Press, 1947.

Berghahn, Volker R., and Martin Kitchen, eds. *Germany in the Age of Total War.* Totowa, N.H.: Barnes and Noble, 1981.

Biggart, John. " 'Anti-Leninist Bolshevism': The *Forward* Group of the RSDRP." *Canadian Slavonic Papers* 23 (June 1981):134–53.

Blackstock, Paul W. *Agents of Deceit: Frauds, Forgeries and Political Intrigue among Nations.* With an Appendix by George F. Kennan. Chicago: Quadrangle Books, 1966.

_____. " 'Books for Idiots': False Soviet 'Memoirs.' " *Russian Review* 25 (July 1966):285–96.

Blinov, S. I. "V. I. Lenin i nekotorye voprosy nachal'nogo etapa vneshnei politiki Sovetskogo gosudarstva." *Vestnik Moskovskogo universiteta.* Seriia IX, istoriia 3 (mai–iiun' 1972):3–22.

_____. *Vneshniaia politika Sovetskoi Rossii. Pervyi god proletarskoi diktatury.* Moskva: Mysl', 1973.

Blishchenko, I. P., and V. N. Durdenevskii. *Diplomaticheskoe i konsul'skoe pravo.* Moskva: Izdatel'stvo Instituta mezhdunarodnykh otnoshenii, 1962.

Bogush, E. Iu. *Mif ob "eksporte revoliutsii" i sovetskaia politika.* Moskva: Mezhdunarodnye otnosheniia, 1965.

Borisov, Iu. V. *Sovetsko-frantsuzskie otnosheniia (1924–1945 gg.).* Institut mezhdunarodnykh otnoshenii. Moskva: Mezhdunarodnye otnosheniia, 1964.

Borkenau, Franz. *The Communist International.* London: Faber and Faber, 1938.

Bradley, John. *Allied Intervention in Russia.* London: Weidenfeld and Nicolson, 1968.

Brailsford, H. N. "The Hope of Genoa." *New Republic* 30 (26 Apr. 1922):250–51.

Brandt, Conrad. *Stalin's Failure in China, 1924–1927.* Russian Research Center Studies, 31. Cambridge: Harvard Univ. Press, 1958.

Braunthal, Julius. *History of the International.* Vol. 2. *1914–1943.* Translated by John Clark. New York: Praeger, 1967.

Buriakov, V. A. "Lenin's Diplomacy in Action." *International Affairs* 5 (May 1972):92–97.

_____. "Missiia V. V. Vorovskogo v Italii v 1921 godu." *Voprosy istorii* 11 (noiabr' 1971 g.):131–42.

Buzinkai, Donald I. "The Bolsheviks, the League of Nations and the Paris Conference, 1919." *Soviet Studies* 19 (Oct. 1967):257–63.

———. "Soviet-League Disputes, 1920–1923." *East European Quarterly* 13 (Spring 1979):25–45.

———. "Soviet-League Relations, 1919–1939: A Survey and Analysis." Ph.D. diss., University of Chicago, 1961.

Calhoun, Daniel F. *The United Front: The TUC and the Russians, 1923–1928.* Soviet and East European Studies Series. Cambridge: Cambridge Univ. Press, 1976.

Carley, Michael J. "Anti-Bolshevism in French Foreign Policy: The Crisis in Poland in 1920." *International History Review* 2 (1980):410–31.

———. "The Origins of the French Intervention in the Russian Civil War, January–May 1918: A Reappraisal." *Journal of Modern History* 48 (Sept. 1976):413–39.

———. *Revolution and Intervention: The French Government and the Russian Civil War, 1917–1919.* Kingston and Montreal: McGill-Queen's Univ. Press. 1983.

Carr, Edward H. *German-Soviet Relations between the Two World Wars, 1919–1939.* Baltimore: Johns Hopkins Univ. Press, 1951.

———. *A History of Soviet Russia: Socialism in One Country, 1924–1926.* 3 vols. London: Macmillan, 1958–1964.

———. *A History of Soviet Russia: The Bolshevik Revolution, 1917–1923.* 3 vols. New York: Macmillan, 1951–1953.

———. *A History of Soviet Russia: The Interregnum, 1923–1924.* New York: Macmillan, 1954.

———. *International Relations between the Two World Wars, (1919–1939).* London: Macmillan, 1965.

———. *The October Revolution: Before and After.* New York: Alfred A. Knopf, 1964.

———. *The Russian Revolution: From Lenin to Stalin.* New York: Free Press, 1979.

———. *The Twenty Years' Crisis, 1919–1939: An Introduction to the Study of International Relations.* London: Macmillan, 1939; reprint ed., New York: St. Martin's Press, 1966.

———, ed. "Radek's 'Political Salon' in Berlin 1919." With a Note by M. Philips Price. *Soviet Studies* 3 (Apr. 1951):411–29.

Carsten, Francis L. *The Reichswehr and Politics, 1918 to 1933.* Oxford: Oxford Univ. Press, 1966.

———. "The Reichswehr and the Red Army." *Survey* 44–45 (Oct. 1962):114–32.

Cecil, Lamar. "The Kindermann Wolscht Incident: An Impasse in Russo-German Relations 1924–26." *Journal of Central European Affairs* 21 (July 1961): 188–99.

Chamberlin, William H. "Meet the Real Litvinoff." *American Mercury* 54 (Mar. 1942):273–83.

_____. *The Russian Revolution, 1917–1921.* 2 vols. New York: Macmillan, 1935.

_____. *Soviet Russia: A Living Record and a History.* Boston: Little, Brown, 1929.

Chester, Lewis, Stephen Fay, and Hugo Young. *The Zinoviev Letter.* Philadelphia: Lippincott, 1968.

Chossudovsky, E. M. *Chicherin and the Evolution of Soviet Foreign Policy and Diplomacy.* Geneva: Graduate Institute of International Studies, 1973.

_____. "Genoa Revisited: Russia and Coexistence." *Foreign Affairs* 50 (Apr. 1971):554–77.

_____. "Lenin and Chicherin: The Beginnings of Soviet Foreign Policy and Diplomacy." *Millennium* 3 (Spring 1974):1–16.

Chubar'ian, A. O. *Brestskii mir.* Institut istorii Akademii nauk SSSR. Moskva: Nauka, 1964.

_____. *Peaceful Co-existence and the Origin of the Notion.* San Francisco: 14th International Congress of Historical Sciences, 1975.

_____. *V. I. Lenin i formirovanie sovetskoi vneshnei politiki.* Institut istorii Akademii nauk SSSR. Moskva: Nauka, 1972.

_____. "V. I. Lenin i Genuia." *Istoriia SSSR* 2 (mart–aprel' 1970):36–50.

Clemens, Walter C., Jr. "Ideology in Soviet Disarmament Policy." *Journal of Conflict Resolution* 8 (Mar. 1964):7–22.

_____. "Lenin on Disarmament." *Slavic Review* 23 (Sept. 1964):504–25.

Coates, William P., and Zelda K. Coates. *Armed Intervention in Russia, 1918–1922.* London: Victor Gollancz, 1935.

_____. *A History of Anglo-Soviet Relations.* Vol. 1. *1917–1942.* With a Foreword by the Right Honorable David Lloyd George. London: Lawrence and Wishart, 1944.

_____. *A History of Anglo-Soviet Relations.* Vol. 2. *1943–1950.* London: Lawrence and Wishart, 1958.

Cohen, Stephen F. *Bukharin and the Bolshevik Revolution: A Political Biography, 1888–1938.* New York: Knopf, 1973.

Cowden, Morton H. *Russian Bolshevism and British Labor.* Boulder, Colo.: East European Monographs, No. 153; distributed by Columbia Univ. Press, 1984.

Craig, Gordon A., and Felix Gilbert, eds. *The Diplomats.* Princeton: Princeton Univ. Press, 1953.

Crowe, Sibyl. "The Zinoviev Letter: A Reappraisal." *Journal of Contemporary History* 10 (July 1975):407–32.

Dashin'skii, S., and Radopol'skii, Ian. *Podgotovka voiny protiv SSSR.* Moskva: Otdel voennoi literatury Gosudarstvennogo izdatel'stva, 1929.

Davies, Norman. "The Genesis of the Polish-Soviet War, 1919–20." *European Studies Review* 5 (Jan. 1975):47–67.

————. "The Missing Revolutionary War: The Polish Campaigns and the Retreat from Revolution in Soviet Russia, 1919–21." *Soviet Studies* 27 (Apr. 1975):178–95.

————. *White Eagle, Red Star: The Polish-Soviet War, 1919–20.* Foreword by A. J. P. Taylor. New York: St. Martin's Press, 1972.

Davis, Kathryn W. *The Soviet Union and the League of Nations, 1919–1933.* Geneva Special Studies, vol. 5, no. 1. Geneva: Geneva Research Center, 1934.

————. *The Soviets at Geneva: The USSR and the League of Nations, 1919–1933.* Geneva: Librairie Kundig, 1934; reprint ed., Westport, Conn.: Hyperion, 1977.

Debo, Richard K. "Dutch-Soviet Relations, 1917–1924: The Role of Finance and Commerce in the Foreign Policy of Soviet Russia and the Netherlands." *Canadian Slavic Studies* 4 (Summer 1970):199–217.

————. "George Chicherin: Soviet Russia's Second Foreign Commissar." Ph.D. diss., University of Nebraska, 1964.

————. "Litvinov and Kamenev—Ambassadors Extraordinary: The Problem of Soviet Representation Abroad." *Slavic Review* 34 (Sept. 1975):463–82.

————. "Lockhart Plot or Dzerzhinskii Plot?" *Journal of Modern History* 43 (Sept. 1971):413–39.

————. "The Making of a Bolshevik: Georgii Chicherin in England 1914–1918." *Slavic Review* 25 (Dec. 1966):651–62.

————. *Revolution and Survival: The Foreign Policy of Soviet Russia, 1917–1918.* Toronto: Univ. of Toronto Press, 1979.

de Palencia, Isabel. *Alexandra Kollontay: Ambassadress from Russia.* New York: Longmans, Green, 1947.

Deutscher, Isaac. *The Prophet Armed: Trotsky, 1879–1921.* London: Oxford Univ. Press, 1954.

————. *The Prophet Outcast: Trotsky, 1929–1940.* London: Oxford Univ. Press, 1963.

————. *The Prophet Unarmed: Trotsky, 1921–1929.* London: Oxford Univ. Press, 1959.

————. *Stalin: A Political Biography.* London: Oxford Univ. Press, 1949.

Dreiden, Sim. " 'U menia byli revoliutsiia i Motsart . . .' (Iz rukopisnogo naslediia G. V. Chicherina." *Nauka i zhizn'* 8 (avgust 1968):18–24.

Dyck, Harvey L. "German-Soviet Relations and the Anglo-Soviet Break, 1927." *Slavic Review* 25 (Mar. 1966):67–83.

————. *Weimar Germany and Soviet Russia, 1926–1933: A Study in Diplomatic Instability.* Studies of the Russian Institute, Columbia University. New York: Columbia Univ. Press, 1966.

Egorov, V. N. *Mirnoe sosushchestvovanie i revoliutsionnyi protsess.* Moskva: Mezhdunarodnye otnosheniia, 1971.

Elcock, H. J. "Britain and the Russo-Polish Frontier, 1919–1921." *Historical Journal* 12 (Mar. 1969):137–54.

Elwood, Ralph C. "Lenin and *Pravda*, 1912–1914." *Slavic Review* 31 (June 1972):355–80.

———. "Lenin and the Social Democratic Schools for Underground Party Workers, 1909–11." *Political Science Quarterly* 81 (Sept. 1966):370–91.

Farnsworth, Beatrice B. *William C. Bullitt and the Soviet Union*. Indiana Univ. International Studies. Bloomington: Indiana Univ. Press, 1967.

Fink, Carole. *The Genoa Conference: European Diplomacy, 1921–1922*. Chapel Hill: Univ. of North Carolina Press, 1984.

Fischer, Louis. *The Life and Death of Stalin*. New York: Harper, 1952.

———. *The Life of Lenin*. New York: Harper and Row, 1964.

———. "Litvinov's Diplomatic Year." *Fortnightly Review* 141 (Feb. 1934):129–34.

———. *Russia's Road from Peace to War: Soviet Foreign Relations, 1917–1941*. New York: Harper and Row, 1969.

———. *The Soviets in World Affairs: A History of the Relations between the Soviet Union and the Rest of the World, 1917–1929*. 2 vols. New York: Jonathan Cape and Harrison Smith, 1930; 2d ed., Princeton: Princeton Univ. Press, 1951.

Fischer, Ruth. *Stalin and German Communism: A Study in the Origins of the State Party*. With a Preface by Sidney B. Fay. Cambridge: Harvard Univ. Press, 1948.

Fisher, Herbert A. L. "Mr. Lloyd George's Foreign Policy, 1918–1922." *Foreign Affairs* 1 (15 Mar. 1923):69–84.

Fitzpatrick, Sheila, ed. *Cultural Revolution in Russia, 1928–1931*. Studies of the Russian Institute, Columbia University. Bloomington: Indiana Univ. Press, 1978.

———. *Education and Social Mobility in the Soviet Union, 1921–1934*. Studies of the Russian Institute, Columbia University. Soviet and East European Studies Series. Cambridge: Cambridge Univ. Press, 1979.

Florinsky, Michael T. *World Revolution and the USSR*. New York: Macmillan, 1933.

Fraiman, A. L. *Revoliutsionnaia zashchita Petrograda v fevrale–marte 1918 g.* Leningradskoe otdelenie Instituta istorii Akademii nauk SSSR. Moskva-Leningrad: Nauka, 1964.

Freund, Gerald. *Unholy Alliance: Russian-German Relations from the Treaty of Brest-Litovsk to the Treat of Berlin*. With an Introduction by J. W. Wheeler-Bennett. New York: Harcourt, Brace, 1957.

Fritz, Stephen E. "Lloyd George and Britain's Search for Peace, 1918–1922." *International Review of History and Political Science* 13 (Feb. 1976):31–70.

Fuller, C. Dale. "Lenin's Attitude Toward an International Organization for the Maintenance of Peace, 1914–1917." *Political Science Quarterly* 64 (June 1949):245–61.

Ganelin, R. Sh. *Sovetsko-amerikanskie otnosheniia v kontse 1917-nachale 1918 g.* Leningrad: Nauka, 1975.

Gankin, Olga H., and Harold H. Fisher, eds. *The Bolsheviks and the World War: The Origin of the Third International.* The Hoover Library on War, Revolution, and Peace Publication, No. 15. Stanford: Stanford Univ. Press, 1940.

Gasiorowski, Zygmunt J. "Poland's Policy towards Soviet Russia, 1921–1922." *Slavonic and East European Review* 53 (Apr. 1975):230–47.

——. "The Russian Overture to Germany of December 1924." *Journal of Modern History* 30 (June 1958):99–117.

——. "Stresemann and Poland after Locarno." *Journal of Central European Affairs* 18 (Oct. 1958):292–317.

——. "Stresemann and Poland before Locarno." *Journal of Central European Affairs* 18 (Apr. 1958):25–47.

Gatzke, Hans W., ed. *European Diplomacy between Two World Wars, 1919–1939.* With an Introduction by Hans W. Gatzke. Modern Scholarship on European History Series. Chicago: Quadrangle Books, 1972.

——. "Russo-German Military Collaboration During the Weimar Republic." *American Historical Review* 63 (Apr. 1958):565–97.

——. "Stresemann and Russia." *World Affairs Quarterly* 27 (Jan. 1957):344–55.

Gaworek, Norbert H. "From Blockade to Trade: Allied Economic Warfare Against Soviet Russia, June 1919 to January 1920." *Jahrbucher für Geschichte Osteuropas* 23 (1975):39–69.

Getzler, Israel. *Martov: A Political Biography of a Russian Social Democrat.* Cambridge: Cambridge Univ. Press, 1967.

Glasgow, George. "Preliminaries of Genoa." *New Republic* 30 (12 Apr. 1922):193–96.

Glenny, Michael V. "The Anglo-Soviet Trade Agreement, March 1921." *Journal of Contemporary History* 5 (1970):63–82.

Gorodetsky, Gabriel. *The Other "Zinoviev Letters": New Light on the Mismanagement of the Affair.* Slavic and Soviet Series, No. 3. Tel-Aviv: Russian and East European Research Center, Tel-Aviv Univ., Mar. 1976.

——. *The Precarious Truce: Anglo-Soviet Relations, 1924–27.* Soviet and East European Studies Series. Cambridge: Cambridge Univ. Press, 1977.

_____. "The Soviet Union and Britain's General Strike of May 1926." *Cahiers du Monde Russe et Sovietique* 17 (Apr.–Sept. 1976):287–310.

Gorokhov, I., L. Zamiatin, I. Zemskov. *G. V. Chicherin: Diplomat leninskoi shkoly.* Pod obshchei redaktsiei i s vstupitel'noi stat'ei V. S. Semenova. Moskva: Politizdat, 1966.

Govorchin, Gerald G. "The Voikov Affair." *International Review of History and Political Science* 9 (Feb. 1972):76–94.

Grant, Natalie, "The 'Zinoviev Letter' Case." *Soviet Studies* 19 (Oct. 1967):264–77.

Graubard, Stephen R. *British Labour and the Russian Revolution, 1917–1924.* Harvard Historical Monographs, 30. Cambridge: Harvard Univ. Press, 1956.

Gregor, Richard. "Lenin, Revolution and Foreign Policy." *International Journal* 22 (Autumn 1967):563–75.

Griffiths, Franklyn. *Genoa Plus 51: Changing Soviet Objectives in Europe.* Toronto: Canadian Institute of International Affairs, 1973.

_____. "Origins of Peaceful Coexistence: A Historical Note." *Survey* 50 (Jan. 1964):195–201.

Grigor'ev, L., and S. Olenev. *Bor'ba SSSR za mir i bezopasnost' v Evrope (1925–1933 gg.).* Moskva: Politizdat, 1956.

Gruber, Helmut. *International Communism in the Era of Lenin: A Documentary History.* Ithaca: Cornell Univ. Press, 1967.

_____. *Soviet Russia Masters the Comintern: International Communism in the Era of Stalin's Ascendancy.* Garden City, N.Y.: Anchor, 1974.

Hallgarten, George W. F. "General Hans von Seeckt and Russia, 1920–1922." *Journal of Modern History* 21 (Mar. 1949):28–34.

Haupt, Georges, and Jean-Jacques Marie, eds. *Makers of the Russian Revolution: Biographies of Bolshevik Leaders.* Translated from the Russian by C. I. P. Ferdinand. Commentaries translated from the French by D. M. Bellos. Ithaca: Cornell Univ. Press, 1974.

Heier, Edmund. "A Note on the Pashkovites and L. N. Tolstoy." *Canadian Slavonic Papers* 5 (1961):114–21.

Herwig, Holger H. "German Policy in the Eastern Baltic Sea in 1918: Expansion or Anti-Bolshevik Crusade? *Slavic Review* 32 (June 1973):339–57.

Heymann, Hans, Jr. "Oil in Soviet-Western Relations in the Interwar Years." *American Slavic and East European Review* 7 (1948):303–16.

Hiden, John W. "The Significance of Latvia: A Forgotten Aspect of Weimar *Ostpolitik.*" *Slavonic and East European Review* 53 (July 1975):389–413.

Himmer, Robert. "Harmonicas for Lenin? The Development of German Economic Policy toward Soviet Russia, December 1918 to June 1919." *Journal of Modern History* 49 (June 1977):IJ-00023.
_____. "Soviet Policy Toward Germany During the Russo-Polish War, 1920." *Slavic Review* 35 (Dec. 1976):665–82.
Holubnychy, Lydia. *Michael Borodin and the Chinese Revolution, 1923–1925.* Published for the East Asia Institute, Columbia University. Ann Arbor: University Microfilms International, 1979.
Hooker, James R. "Curzon and the 'Curzon Line.' " *Journal of Modern History* 30 (June 1958):137–38.
Hopper, Bruce C. "Narkomindel and Comintern: Instruments of World Revolution." *Foreign Affairs* 19 (July 1941):737–50.
Horak, Stephan M. "Lenin on Coexistence: A Chapter in Soviet Foreign Policy." *Studies on the Soviet Union* 3 (1964):20–30.
Hulse, James W. *The Forming of the Communist International.* Stanford: Stanford Univ. Press, 1964.
Iakushevskii, A. S. *Propagandistskaia rabota bol'shevikov sredi voisk interventov v 1918–1920 gg.* Akademiia nauk SSSR. Institut voennoi istorii Ministerstva oborony SSSR. Moskva: Nauka, 1974.
Ileshin, Boris. "Progulka po znakomoi ulitse." *Nedelia* 26 (1984):12.
Ioffe, A. E. "Ob usilenii zavisimosti Rossii ot stran Antanty v gody pervoi mirovoi voiny." *Voprosy istorii* 3 (mart 1957 g.):100–112.
_____. *Vneshniaia politika Sovetskogo Soiuza (1928–1932 gg.).* Institut istorii Akademii nauk SSSR. Moskva: Nauka, 1968.
Iroshnikov, M. P. "Iz istorii organizatsii Narodnogo komissariata inostrannykh del." *Istoriia SSSR* 1 (fevral'–mart 1964):105–16.
_____. *Sozdanie sovetskogo tsentral'nogo gosudarstvennogo apparata. Sovet Narodnykh komissarov i Narodnye komissariaty oktiabr' 1917–ianvar' 1918 g.* Izdanie vtoroe, ispravlennoe i dopolnennoe. Leningradskoe otdelenie Instituta istorii Akademii nauk SSSR. Leningrad: Nauka, 1967.
Iusupov, I. A. *Ustanovlenie i razvitie sovetsko-iranskikh otnoshenii (1917–1927 gg.).* Akademiia nauk Uzbekskoi SSR. Institut vostokovedeniia im. Beruni. Tashkent: Izdatel'stvo FAN Uzbekskoi SSR, 1969.
Jacobs, Dan N. *Borodin: Stalin's Man in China.* Cambridge: Harvard Univ. Press, 1981.
Jacobson, Jon. *Locarno Diplomacy: Germany and the West, 1925–1929.* Princeton: Princeton Univ. Press, 1972.
Jarausch, Konrad H. "Cooperation or Intervention?: Kurt Riezler and the Failure of German *Ostpolitik*, 1918." *Slavic Review* 31 (June 1972):381–98.

K. "Russia After Genoa and The Hague." *Foreign Affairs* 1 (15 Sept. 1922):133–55.

Kahan, Vilem. "The Communist International, 1919–43: The Personnel of Its Highest Bodies." *International Review of Social History* 21 (1976, Part 2):151–85.

Kapitsa, M. S. *Sovetsko-kitaiskie otnosheniia.* Moskva: Politizdat, 1958.

Kaplan, Jay L. "France's Road to Genoa: Strategic, Economic, and Ideological Factors in French Foreign Policy, 1921–1922." Ph.D. diss., Columbia University, 1974.

Kaplin, A. S. *V. I. Lenin: Osnovopolozhnik diplomatii sotsialisticheskogo gosudarstva.* Moskva: Znanie, 1970.

Kapur, Harish. *Soviet Russia and Asia, 1917–1927: A Study of Soviet Policy towards Turkey, Iran and Afghanistan.* Published for the Geneva Graduate Institute of International Studies. Geneva: Michael Joseph, 1966.

Karpova, R. F. *L. B. Krasin: Sovetskii diplomat.* Vydaiushchiesia diplomaty. Moskva: Sotsekgiz, 1962.

_____. "Zakliuchitel'nyi etap anglo-sovetskikh peregovorov 1920–1921 gg." *Vestnik Leningradskogo universiteta.* Seriia istorii, iazika i literatury, 14, vypusk 3 (1962):34–46.

Katkov, George. "The Assassination of Count Mirbach." *St. Anthony's Papers* 12 (1962):53–93.

Kelley, Robert F. "Soviet Policy on the European Border." *Foreign Affairs* 3 (15 Sept. 1924):90–98.

Kennan, George F. *American Diplomacy, 1900–1950.* Charles R. Walgreen Foundation Lectures. Chicago: Univ. of Chicago Press, 1951.

_____. "Peaceful Coexistence: A Western View." *Foreign Affairs* 38 (Jan. 1960):171–90.

_____. *Russia and the West under Lenin and Stalin.* Atlantic Monthly Press Book. Boston: Little, Brown, 1961.

_____. *Soviet-American Relations, 1917–1920.* Vol. 1. *Russia Leaves the War.* Princeton: Princeton Univ. Press, 1956.

_____. *Soviet-American Relations, 1917–1920.* Vol. 2. *The Decision To Intervene.* Princeton: Princeton Univ. Press, 1958.

_____. *Soviet Foreign Policy, 1917–1941.* Princeton: Van Nostrand, 1960.

Kennell, Ruth E. *Theodore Dreiser and the Soviet Union, 1927–1945: A First-Hand Chronicle.* New York: International, 1969.

Kessler, Harry. *Walter Rathenau: His Life and Work.* New York: Harcourt, Brace, 1930.

Keynes, John M. *The Economic Consequences of the Peace.* New York: Harcourt, Brace and Howe, 1920.

_____. *A Revision of the Treaty, Being a Sequel to "The Economic Consequences of the Peace."* New York: Harcourt, Brace, 1922.

Kharlamov, M. A., A. E. Ioffe, A. S. Kan, A. I. Konontsev, and A. S. Protopopov, eds. *Leninskaia vneshniaia politika Sovetskoi strany 1917–1924 gg.* Institut istorii Akademii nauk SSSR. Moskva: Nauka, 1969.

Kheifets, A. N. *Sovetskaia diplomatiia i narody Vostoka 1921–1927.* Akademiia nauk SSSR. Moskva: Nauka, 1968.

————. *Sovetskaia Rossiia i sopredel'nye strany Vostoka v gody grazhdanskoi voiny (1918–1920).* Institut narodov Azii Akademii nauk SSSR. Moskovskii gosudarstvennyi pedagogicheskii institut imeni V. I. Lenina. Moskva: Nauka, 1964.

Khinchuk, L. M. *K istorii anglo-sovetskikh otnoshenii.* Moskva: Gosudarstvennoe izdatel'stvo, 1928.

Khovratovich, I. M. *Georgii Vasil'evich Chicherin.* Partiinye publitsisty No. 1395. Moskva: Mysl', 1980.

————. "Neizvestnye psevdonimy G. Chicherina." *Zhurnalist* 6 (iiun' 1974):56–57.

Kirdetsov, G. "Desiatiletie Versalia." *Mezhdunarodnaia zhizn'* 6 (1929):3–19.

Kizel'shtein, G. B. " 'Muchitel'no zhazhdu vysokoi tseli.' Iz arkhiva G. V. Chicherina." *Ogonek* 48 (noiabr' 1963):18.

————. "O rukopisi G. V. Chicherina, posviashchennoi diplomaticheskoi deiatel'nosti A. M. Gorchakova." *Novaia i noveishaia istoriia AN SSSR* 4 (1966):129–31.

Kniazhinskii, V. B. *Proval planov "ob"edineniia Evropy." Ocherk istorii imperialisticheskikh popytok antisovetskogo "ob"edineniia Evropy" mezhdu pervoi i vtoroi mirovymi voinami.* Moskva: Politizdat, 1958.

Kobliakov, I. K. "Bor'ba Sovetskogo gosudarstva za normalizatsiiu otnoshenii s Germaniei v 1919–1921 gg." *Istoriia SSSR* 2 (mart–aprel' 1971):17–31.

————. "Bor'ba Sovetskogo gosudarstva za sokhranenie mira s Germaniei v period deistviia Brestskogo dogovora (mart–noiabr' 1918 g.)." *Istoriia SSSR* 4 (iiul'–avgust 1958):3–26.

————. *Ot Bresta do Rapallo. Ocherki istorii sovetsko-germanskikh otnoshenii s 1918 po 1922 g.* Moskva: Politizdat, 1954.

Kochan, Lionel. *Russia and the Weimar Republic.* Cambridge: Bowes and Bowes, 1954.

Korbel, Josef. *Poland between East and West: Soviet and German Diplomacy toward Poland, 1919–1933.* Princeton: Princeton Univ. Press, 1963.

Kornev, H. *Litvinov.* Moskva: Molodaia gvardiia, 1936.

Kovalev, I. "Neizvestnaia rukopis' G. V. Chicherina." *Neva* 5 (1964):220–21.

Krasil'nikov, A. N. *Politika Anglii v otnoshenii SSSR, 1929–1932 gg.* Moskva: Politizdat, 1959.

Kuznetsova, S. I. *Ustanovlenie sovetsko-turetskikh otnoshenii (K 40-letiiu Moskovskogo dogovora mezhdu RSFSR i Turtsiei).* Institut narodov Azii Akademii nauk SSSR. Moskva: Izdatel'stvo vostochnoi literatury, 1961.

Lahey, Dale T. "Soviet Ideological Development of Coexistence: 1917–1927." *Canadian Slavonic Papers* 6 (1964):80–94.

Lambert, Robert W. *Soviet Disarmament Policy, 1922–1931.* Research Report 64-2. Washington, D.C.: U.S. Arms Control and Disarmament Agency, 1964.

Lammers, Donald N. "British Foreign Policy, 1929–1934: The Problem of Soviet Russia." Ph.D. diss., Stanford University, 1960.

Lampert, Nicholas. *The Technical Intelligentsia and the Soviet State: A Study of Soviet Managers and Technicians, 1917–1928.* Studies in Soviet History and Society. New York: Holmes and Meier, 1979.

Laqueur, Walter. "Hitler and Russia 1919–1923." *Survey* 44–45 (Oct. 1962):89–113.

_____. "Russia and Germany." *Survey* 44–45 (Oct. 1962):3–11.

_____. *Russia and Germany: A Century in Conflict.* Encounter Book. Boston: Little, Brown, 1965.

Lazitch, Branko, and Milorad M. Drachkovitch. *Lenin and the Comintern.* Vol. 1. Hoover Institution Publications, 106. Stanford: Hoover Institution Press, Stanford Univ., 1972.

Lemin, I. M. *V. I. Lenin i voprosy vneshnei politiki SSSR.* Vsesoiuznoe obshchestvo po rasprostraneniiu politicheskikh i nauchnykh znanii. Seriia sed'maia mezhdunarodnaia, 16. Moskva: Znanie, 1959.

Lensen, George A. *The Damned Inheritance: The Soviet Union and the Manchurian Crisis, 1924–1935.* Tallahassee, Fla.: Diplomatic Press, 1974.

_____. *Japanese Recognition of the USSR: Soviet-Japanese Relations, 1921–1930.* Tokyo: Published by Sophia Univ. in cooperation with the Diplomatic Press, Tallahassee, Fla., 1970.

Leong, Sow-Theng. *Sino-Soviet Diplomatic Relations, 1917–1926.* Honolulu: Univ. Press of Hawaii and Research Corporation of the University of Hawaii, 1976.

Leonidov, A. "Socialism's First Diplomats." *New Times* 28 (12 July 1967):12–16.

Lerner, Warren. "The Historical Origins of the Soviet Doctrine of Peaceful Existence." *Law and Contemporary Problems* 29 (Autumn 1964):865–70.

_____. *Karl Radek: The Last Internationalist.* Stanford: Stanford Univ. Press, 1970.

————. "Poland in 1920: A Case Study in Foreign-Policy Decision Making under Lenin." *South Atlantic Quarterly* 72 (Summer 1973):406–14.

Libbey, James K. *Alexander Gumberg and Soviet-American Relations, 1917–1933.* Lexington: Univ. Press of Kentucky, 1977.

Librach, Jan. *The Rise of the Soviet Empire: A Study of Soviet Foreign Policy.* Praeger Publications in Russian History and World Communism, No. 146. New York: Praeger, 1964.

Lindeman, Albert S. *The 'Red Years': European Socialism versus Bolshevism, 1919–1921.* Berkeley and Los Angeles: Univ. of California Press, 1974.

————. "Socialist Impressions of Revolutionary Russia, 1920." *Russian History* 1 (1974):31–45.

Liubimov, N. N. "O V. V. Vorovskom." *Voprosy istorii* 10 (oktiabr' 1971 g.): 138–43.

Lungu, Dov B. "Soviet-Romanian Relations and the Bessarabian Question in the Early 1920s." *Southeastern Europe* 6, Part 1 (1979):29–45.

Macartney, C. A., and others. *Survey of International Affairs, 1925.* Vol. 2. Issued under the auspices of the Royal Institute of International Affairs. London: Oxford Univ. Press, 1928.

Macfarlane, L. J. "Hands Off Russia: British Labour and the Russo-Polish War, 1920." *Past and Present* 38 (Dec. 1967):126–52.

McKenzie, Kermit E. *Comintern and World Revolution, 1928–1943.* Studies of the Russian Institute, Columbia University. New York: Columbia Univ. Press, 1964.

Magerovsky, Eugene L. "The People's Commissariat for Foreign Affairs, 1917–1946." Ph.D. diss., Columbia University, 1975.

Mahaney, Wilbur L., Jr. "The Soviet Union, the League of Nations and Disarmament: 1917–1935." Ph.D. diss., University of Pennsylvania, 1940.

Maiorov, S. M. *Bor'ba Sovetskoi Rossii za vykhod iz imperialisticheskoi voiny.* Moskva: Politizdat, 1959.

Mann, Golo. "Rapallo: The Vanishing Dream." *Survey* 44–45 (Oct. 1962):74–88.

Marbor. "Sovetsko-angliiskie dogovory 1924 g." *Mezhdunarodnaia zhizn'* 11 (1929):63–76.

Marks, Sally. *The Illusion of Peace: International Relations in Europe, 1918–1933.* The Making of the 20th Century Series. New York: St. Martin's, 1976.

————. "The Myth of Reparations." *Central European History* 11 (Sept. 1978):231–55.

Martin, Thomas S. "The Urquhart Concession and Anglo-Soviet Relations, 1921–1922." *Jahrbucher für Geschichte Osteuropas* 20 (Dec. 1972):551–70.

Mayer, Arno J. *Political Origins of the New Diplomacy.* Yale Historical
    Publications, 18. New Haven: Yale Univ. Press, 1959.
_____. *Politics and Diplomacy of Peacemaking: Containment and Coun-
    terrevolution at Versailles, 1918–1919.* New York: Knopf, 1967.
Miller, A. "The Origin of Leninist Eastern Policy." *International Affairs*
    4 (Apr. 1972):68–75.
Minasian, N. M. *Pravovye osnovy leninskoi diplomatii.* Rostov-na-
    Donu: Izdatel'stvo Rostovskogo universiteta, 1970.
Mints, I. I., V. G. Trukhanovskii, A. F. Miller, N. I. Samorukov, and S. I.
    Iakubovskaia. *Sovetskaia Rossiia i kapitalisticheskii mir v 1917–
    1923 gg.* Moskva: Politizdat, 1957.
Molchanov, Iu. L. *Komintern: u istokov politiki edinogo proletarskogo
    fronta.* Moskva: Mysl', 1969.
Morgan, R. P. "The Political Significance of the German-Soviet Trade
    Negotiations, 1922–1925." *Historical Journal* 6 (1963):253–71.
Morley, James M. *The Japanese Thrust into Siberia, 1918.* Studies of
    the Russian Institute, Columbia University. New York: Columbia
    Univ. Press, 1957.
Morse, William P., Jr. "Leonid Borisovich Krasin: Soviet Diplomat,
    1918–1926." Ph.D. diss., University of Wisconsin, 1971.
Moulton, Harold G., and Leo Pasvolsky. *War Debts and World Prosper-
    ity.* Institute of Economics of the Brookings Institution, No. 46.
    Washington, D.C.: Brookings Institution, 1932.
_____. *World War Debt Settlements.* With the aid of the council and
    staff of the Institute of Economics. Investigations in International
    Economic Reconstruction. New York: Macmillan, 1926.
Mueller, Gordon H. "Rapallo Reexamined: A New Look at Germany's
    Secret Military Collaboration with Russia in 1922." *Military
    Affairs* 40 (Oct. 1976):109–17.
Narochnitskii, A. L., ed. *Leninskie traditsii vneshnei politiki Sovetskogo
    Soiuza.* Nauchnyi sovet AN SSSR po istorii vneshnei politiki SSSR
    i mezhdunarodnykh otnoshenii. Moskva: Mezhdunarodnye
    otnosheniia, 1977.
Nicholaevsky, Boris I. *Power and the Soviet Elite: "The Letter of an Old
    Bolshevik" and Other Essays.* Edited by Janet D. Zagoria. Pub-
    lished for the Hoover Institution on War, Revolution, and Peace of
    Stanford University. New York: Praeger, 1965; reprint ed., Ann
    Arbor: Ann Arbor Paperbacks, Univ. of Michigan Press, 1975.
_____. "Revoliutsiia v Kitae, Iaponiia i Stalin (Iz ocherkov po
    istorii vneshnei politiki Moskvy.)." *Novyi zhurnal* 6 (1943)
    :229–57; 8 (1944):346–84.
_____. "Russia, Japan, and the Pan-Asiatic Movement to 1925." *Far
    Eastern Quarterly* 8 (May 1949):259–95.
_____. "Sovetsko-iaponskoe soglashenie 1925 goda (Iz ocherkov po

istorii vneshnei politiki Moskvy.)." *Novyi zhurnal* 5 (1943):198–240.

_____. "Vneshniaia politika Moskvy." *Novyi zhurnal* 1; 3; 4 (1942): 230–46; 177–207; 302–31.

Nicolson, Harold. *Curzon: The Last Phase, 1919–1925; A Study in Post-War Diplomacy.* Boston: Houghton Mifflin, 1934.

Nikol'nikov, G. L. *Pobeda leninskoi strategii i taktiki po voprosam voiny, mira i revoliutsii.* Kiev: Izdatel'stvo Kievskogo universiteta, 1966.

Nikonova, S. V. *Antisovetskaia vneshniaia politika angliiskikh konservatorov 1924–1927.* Institut istorii Akademii nauk SSSR. Moskva: Izdatel'stvo Akademii nauk SSSR, 1963.

Nollau, Gunther. *International Communism and World Revolution: History and Methods.* With a Foreword by Leonard Schapiro. New York: Praeger, 1961.

North, Robert C. *Moscow and Chinese Communists.* Prepared and published under the auspices of the Hoover Institution on War, Revolution, and Peace of Stanford University. Stanford: Stanford Univ. Press, 1953.

North, Robert C., and Xenia J. Eudin. *M. N. Roy's Mission to China: The Communist-Kuomintang Split of 1927.* Documents translated by Helen I. Powers. Berkeley and Los Angeles: Univ. of California Press, 1960.

Northedge, F. S. *The Troubled Giant: Britain Among the Great Powers, 1916–1939.* Published for the London School of Economics and Political Science, New York: Praeger, 1966.

Northedge, F. S., and Audrey Wells. *Britain and Soviet Communism: The Impact of a Revolution.* London: Macmillan, 1982.

O'Connor, Timothy E. *The Politics of Soviet Culture: Anatolii Lunacharskii.* Studies in the Fine Arts: The Avant-Garde, No. 42. Ann Arbor: UMI Research Press, 1983.

Olenev, S. *Mezhdunarodnoe priznanie SSSR.* Moskva: Sotsekgiz, 1962.

Orde, Anne. *Great Britain and International Security, 1920–1926.* Royal Historical Society Studies in History. London: Royal Historical Society, 1978.

Oznobishin, D. V. *Ot Bresta do Iur'eva. Iz istorii vneshnei politiki Sovetskoi vlasti 1917–1920 gg.* Moskva: Nauka, 1966.

_____. *Politika partii v period mirnoi peredyshki 1918 g.* Moskva: Politizdat, 1973.

Page, Stanley W. *The Geopolitics of Leninism.* East European Monographs, No. 97. Boulder, Colo.: East European Monographs; distributed by Columbia Univ. Press, 1982.

_____. *Lenin and World Revolution.* New York: New York Univ. Press, 1959.

Pasvolsky, Leo, and Harold G. Moulton. *Russian Debts and Russian Reconstruction: A Study of the Relation of Russia's Foreign Debts to Her Economic Recovery.* With the aid of the council and staff of the Institute of Economics. Investigations in International Economic Reconstruction. New York: McGraw-Hill, 1924.

Petracchi, Giorgio. "Ideology and Realpolitik: Italo-Soviet Relations, 1917–1933." *Journal of Italian History* 2 (1979):473–519.

Pipes, Richard. *The Formation of the Soviet Union: Communism and Nationalism, 1917–1923.* Rev. ed. Russian Research Center Studies, 13. Cambridge: Harvard Univ. Press, 1964.

Pokrovskii, A. S. "K istorii zagovora R. Lokkarta (1918 g.)." *Istoricheskii arkhiv* 4 (iiul'–avgust 1962):234–37.

Pope, Arthur U. *Maxim Litvinoff.* New York: Fischer, 1943.

Popov, V. I. *Anglo-sovetskie otnosheniia (1927–1929).* Moskva: Izdatel'stvo Instituta mezhdunarodnykh otnoshenii, 1958.

_____. *Diplomaticheskie otnosheniia mezhdu SSSR i Angliei (1929–1932 gg.).* Moskva: Mezhdunarodnye otnosheniia, 1965.

_____., ed. *Dipkur'ery. Ocherki o pervykh sovetskikh diplomaticheskikh kur'erakh.* Moskva: Politizdat, 1970.

_____, gen. ed. *Leninskaia diplomatiia mira i sotrudnichestva (Ustanovlenie diplomaticheskikh otnoshenii mezhdu SSSR i kapitalisticheskimi stranami v 1924–1925 gg.)* Institut istorii Akademii nauk SSSR. Moskva: Nauka, 1965.

Pragmaticus. "The Lessons of Brest Litovsk." *Slavonic and East European Review* 15 (Jan. 1937):328–43.

Quigley, John. *The Soviet Foreign Trade Monopoly: Institutions and Laws.* Columbus: Ohio State Univ. Press, 1974.

Rigby, Thomas H. "The Birth of the People's Commissars." *Australian Journal of Politics and History* 20 (Apr. 1974):70–75.

_____. *Communist Party Membership in the USSR, 1917–1967.* Studies of the Russian Institute, Columbia University. Princeton: Princeton Univ. Press, 1968.

_____. *Lenin's Government: Sovnarkom, 1917–1922.* Soviet and East European Studies Series. Cambridge: Cambridge Univ. Press, 1979.

Roberts, James W. "Lenin's Theory of Imperialism in Soviet Usage." *Soviet Studies* 29 (July 1977):353–72.

Rosenbaum, Kurt. *Community of Fate: German-Soviet Diplomatic Relations, 1922–1928.* Syracuse: Syracuse Univ. Press, 1965.

_____. "The German Involvement in the Shakhty Trial." *Russian Review* 21 (July 1962):238–60.

Rosenberg, William G. *A. I. Denikin and the Anti-Bolshevik Movement in South Russia.* Amherst College Honors Thesis, No. 7. Amherst: Amherst College Press, 1961.

Rosenko, I. A. *Sovetsko-germanskie otnosheniia (1921–1922 gg.)*. Leningrad: Izdatel'stvo Leningradskogo universiteta, 1965.

Rosser, Richard F. *An Introduction to Soviet Foreign Policy*. Englewood Cliffs, N.J.: Prentice-Hall, 1969.

Rossow, Robert. "The Professionalization of the New Diplomacy." *World Politics* 14 (July 1962):561–75.

Rubinstein, Alvin Z., ed. *The Foreign Policy of the Soviet Union*. With Introductory Essays by Alvin Z. Rubinstein. 3d ed. New York: Random House, 1972.

Rubinshtein, N. L. *Sovetskaia Rossiia i kapitalisticheskie gosudarstva v gody perekhoda ot voiny k miru (1921–1922 gg.)*. Moskva: Politizdat, 1948.

———. *Vneshniaia politika Sovetskogo gosudarstva v 1921–1925 godakh*. Moskva: Politizdat, 1953.

Rudol'f. N. *Osnovy mezhdunarodnoi politiki Sovetskoi vlasti*. Moskva: Partizdat, 1933.

Ryzhikov, V. A. *Zigzagi diplomatii Londona (Iz istorii sovetsko-angliiskikh otnoshenii)*. Moskva: Mezhdunarodnye otnosheniia, 1973.

Schapiro, Leonard B. "Lenin's Heritage." *Encounter* 35 (July 1970):57–59.

———. *The Communist Party of the Soviet Union*. New York: Random House, 1960.

Scheffer, Paul. "Maxim Litvinov: An Intimate Study." *Current History* 34 (Aug. 1931):670–77.

Schinness, Roger T. "The Conservative Party and Anglo-Soviet Relations, 1925–27." *European Studies Review* 7 (Oct. 1977):393–407.

———. "The Tories and the Soviets: The British Conservative Reaction to Russia, 1917–1927." Ph.D. diss., State University of New York at Binghampton, 1972.

Schuker, Stephen A. *The End of French Predominance in Europe: The Financial Crisis of 1924 and the Adoption of the Dawes Plan*. Chapel Hill: Univ. of North Carolina Press, 1976.

Schulz, Gerhard. *Revolutions and Peace Treaties, 1917–1920*. Translated by Marian Jackson. London: Methuen, 1972.

Schurer, H. "Karl Moor: German Agent and Friend of Lenin." *Journal of Contemporary History* 5 (1970):131–52.

Semanov, S. N., ed. *Kommunisty. Sbornik*. Izdanie vtoroe. Zhizn' zamechatel'nykh liudei, vypusk 2 (559). Moskva: Molodaia gvardiia, 1977.

Senn, Alfred E. *Assassination in Switzerland: The Murder of Vatslav Vorovsky*. Madison: Univ. of Wisconsin Press, 1981.

———. *Diplomacy and Revolution: The Soviet Mission to Switzerland,*

1918. International Studies of the Committee on International Relations. Notre Dame: Univ. of Notre Dame Press, 1974.

_____. *The Great Powers, Lithuania and the Vilna Question.* Leiden: Brill, 1966.

_____. "The Rakovsky Affair: A Crisis in Franco-Soviet Relations, 1927." *Slavic and East-European Studies* 10, 3–4 (1965/66 Fall-Winter):102–17.

_____. *The Russian Revolution in Switzerland, 1914–1917.* Madison: Univ. of Wisconsin Press, 1971.

_____, ed. "The Politics of *Golos* and *Nashe Slovo.*" *International Review of Social History* 17 (1972, Part 3):675–704.

_____, ed. *Readings in Russian Political and Diplomatic History.* Vol. 2. *The Soviet Period.* Dorsey Series in European History. Homewood, Ill.: Dorsey, 1966.

Service, Robert. *The Bolshevik Party in Revolution: A Study in Organizational Change, 1917–1923.* New York: Harper and Row, 1979.

Shane, Theodore K. "British Reaction to the Soviet Union, 1924–1929: A Study of Policy and Public Opinion." Ph.D. diss., Indiana University, 1953.

Sheviakov, A. A. "Ustanovlenie diplomaticheskikh otnoshenii SSSR so stranami Tsentral'noi i Iugo-Vostochnoi Evropy." *Voprosy istorii* 1 (ianvar' 1975 g.):32–48.

Shishkin, V. A. "Oktiabr'skaia revoliutsiia i ekonomicheskie otnosheniia Sovetskogo gosudarstva s kapitalisticheskim mirom (1917–1918 gg.)." *Voprosy istorii* 11 (noiabr' 1966 g.):3–19.

_____. *Sovetskoe gosudarstvo i strany Zapada v 1917–1923 gg. Ocherki istorii stanovleniia ekonomicheskikh otnoshenii.* Leningradskoe otdelenie Instituta istorii Akademii nauk SSSR. Leningrad: Leningradskoe otdelenie Izdatel'stva Nauka, 1969.

Shtein, B. E. "V. I. Lenin i Genuezskaia konferentsiia 1922 goda." *Vestnik Moskovskogo universiteta.* Seriia 9, istoricheskie nauki 2 (mart–aprel' 1960):15–39.

Shub, David. "Kamo: The Legendary Old Bolshevik of the Caucasus." *Russian Review* 19 (July 1960):227–47.

Silverlight, John. *The Victors' Dilemma: Allied Intervention in the Russian Civil War.* New York: Weybright and Talley, 1970.

Silverman, Dan P. *Reconstructing Europe after the Great War.* Cambridge: Harvard Univ. Press, 1982.

Skaba, A. D. *Parizhskaia mirnaia konferentsiia i inostrannaia interventsiia v Strane Sovetov (ianvar'–iiun' 1919 goda).* Institut istorii Akademii nauk Ukrainskoi SSR. Kiev: Naukova dumka, 1971.

Slusser, Robert M., and Jan F. Triska. *A Calendar of Soviet Treaties, 1917–1957.* With the Assistance of George Ginsburgs and Wilfred

O. Reiners. Hoover Institution on War, Revolution, and Peace Documentary Series, No. 4. Stanford: Stanford Univ. Press, 1959.

Smirnov, Iu. P. *Leninskii printsip mirnogo sosushchestvovaniia*. Minsk: Belarus', 1965.

Smith, Arthur L. "The German General Staff and Russia, 1919–1926." *Soviet Studies* 8 (Oct. 1956):125–33.

Solov'ev. O. F. "Iz istorii bor'by Sovetskogo pravitel'stva za mirnoe sosushchestvovanie s Angliei." *Voprosy istorii* 2 (fevral' 1965 g.): 54–64.

Sonkin, M. E. *Kliuchi ot bronirovannykh komnat*. Moskva: Politizdat, 1966.

_____. *Okno vo vneshnii mir. Ekonomicheskie sviazi Sovetskogo gosudarstva v 1917–1921 gg.* Moskva: Mysl', 1964.

Sontag, John P. "The Soviet War Scare of 1926–27." *Russian Review* 34 (Jan. 1975):66–77.

Sontag, Raymond J. *A Broken World, 1919–1939.* The Rise of Modern Europe Series, vol. 19. New York: Harper and Row, 1971.

Sonyel, Salahi R. *Turkish Diplomacy, 1918–1923: Mustafa Kemal and the Turkish National Movement.* Sage Studies in 20th Century History, vol. 3. Beverly Hills, California: Sage, 1975.

Stepanov, A. I. "Diplomatic Practice: Forms and Methods." *International Affairs* 12 (Dec. 1972):43–49.

_____. "The Historical Experience of Co-operation Between the USSR and Germany: The 1926 Berlin Treaty." *International Affairs* 8 (Aug. 1963):91–96.

_____. "Leninskie printsipy partiinogo rukovodstva vneshnei politiki i tvorcheskoe razvitie ikh KPSS na sovremennom etape." *Voprosy istorii KPSS* 12 (1976):57–69.

Stepanov, G. "Pervoe torgovoe soglashenie." *Vneshniaia torgovlia* 2 (1967):12–14.

Strakhovsky, Leonid I. *Intervention at Archangel. The Story of Allied Intervention and Russian Counter-Revolution in North Russia, 1918–1922.* Princeton: Princeton Univ. Press, 1944.

_____. *The Origins of American Intervention in North Russia (1918).* With a Foreword by James B. Scott. Princeton: Princeton Univ. Press, 1937; reprint ed., New York: Fertig, 1972.

Struger, Marlene. "Nikolai Nikolaievich Krestinsky and Soviet-German Relations 1921–1930." Ph.D. diss., University of Wisconsin, 1973.

Suprunenko, N. I. *Ocherki istorii grazhdanskoi voiny i inostrannoi voennoi interventsii na Ukraine (1918–1920).* Moskva: Nauka, 1966.

Tang, Peter S. H. *Russian and Soviet Policy in Manchuria and Outer Mongolia, 1911–1931.* Introduction by Philip E. Mosely. Durham: Duke Univ. Press, 1959.

Taracouzio, T. A. *The Soviet Union and International Law: A Study Based on the Legislation, Treaties and Foreign Relations of the Union of Socialist Soviet Republics.* New York: Macmillan, 1935.

————. *War and Peace in Soviet Diplomacy.* New York: Macmillan, 1940.

Tarasov, V. V. *Bor'ba s interventami na Severe Rossii (1918–1920 gg.).* Moskva: Politizdat, 1958.

Tarulis, Albert N. *Soviet Policy Toward the Baltic States, 1918–1940.* Notre Dame: Univ. of Notre Dame Press, 1959.

Thompson, John M. *Russia, Bolshevism, and the Versailles Peace.* Studies of the Russian Institute, Columbia University. Princeton: Princeton Univ. Press, 1966.

Thornton, Richard C. *The Comintern and the Chinese Communists, 1928–1931.* Far Eastern and Russian Institute Publications on Asia, No. 20. Seattle: Univ. of Washington Press, 1969.

Tiutiukin, S. V. "Stranitsa biografii G. V. Chicherina (1914–1917 gg.)." *Istoricheskie zapiski AN SSSR* 79 (1966):243–58.

Toynbee, Arnold J. *Survey of International Affairs, 1920–1923.* Published under the auspices of the British Institute of International Affairs. London: Oxford Univ. Press, 1925; reprint ed., Johnson, 1965.

————. *Survey of International Affairs, 1924.* With a Preface by the Right Honorable H. A. L. Fisher. Published under the auspices of the British Institute of International Affairs. London: Oxford Univ. Press, 1926; reprint ed., Johnson, 1965.

————. *Survey of International Affairs, 1926.* Issued under the auspices of the Royal Institute of International Affairs. London: Oxford Univ. Press, 1928.

————. *Survey of International Affairs, 1927.* Issued under the auspices of the Royal Institute of International Affairs. London: Oxford Univ. Press, 1929.

————. *Survey of International Affairs, 1928.* Assisted by V. M. Boulter. Issued under the auspices of the Royal Institute of International Affairs. London: Oxford Univ. Press, 1929.

————. *Survey of International Affairs, 1929.* Assisted by V. M. Boulter. Issued under the auspices of the Royal Institute of International Affairs. London: Oxford Univ. Press, 1930.

————. *Survey of International Affairs, 1930.* Assisted by V. M. Boulter. Issued under the auspices of the Royal Institute of International Affairs. London: Oxford Univ. Press, 1931.

Trani, Eugene P. "Woodrow Wilson and the Decision to Intervene in Russia: A Reconsideration." *Journal of Modern History* 48 (Sept. 1976):440–61.

Treadgold, Donald W., ed. *Soviet and Chinese Communism: Similarities and Differences.* Seattle: Univ. of Washington Press, 1967.

Triska, Jan F., and David D. Finley. *Soviet Foreign Policy.* New York: Macmillan, 1968.

Triska, Jan F., and Robert M. Slusser. *The Theory, Law, and Policy of Soviet Treaties.* Stanford: Stanford Univ. Press, 1962.

Trofimova, L. I. "Genuezskaia konferentsiia." *Novaia i noveishaia istoriia* 5 (sentiabr'–oktiabr' 1977):109–34.

———. "Moskva i Parizh obmenivaiutsia poslami (50 let ustanovleniia diplomaticheskikh otnoshenii mezhdu SSSR i Frantsiei)." *Novaia i noveishaia istoriia* 6 (noiabr'–dekabr' 1974):86–95.

———. "Pervye shagi sovetskoi diplomatii." *Novaia i noveishaia istoriia* 6 (noiabr'–dekabr' 1971):37–52; 1 (ianvar'–fevral' 1972): 63–79.

———. "Stranitsa diplomaticheskoi deiatel'nosti G. V. Chicherina." *Voprosy istorii* 2 (fevral' 1972 g.):114–23.

Trush, M. I. "Diplomat leninskoi shkoly (K 100-letiiu so dnia rozhdeniia G. V. Chicherina)." *Mezhdunarodnaia zhizn'* 11 (1972):88–96.

———. "A Diplomat of the Leninist School. For the 100th Anniversary of the Birth of G. V. Chicherin." *International Affairs* 12 (Dec. 1971):66–72.

———. *Vneshnepoliticheskaia deiatel'nost' V. I. Lenina 1917–1920. Den' za dnem.* Institut marksizma-leninizma pri TsK KPSS. Moskva: Institut mezhdunarodnykh otnoshenii, 1963.

Tucker, Robert C. "The Emergence of Stalin's Foreign Policy." *Slavic Review* 36 (Dec. 1977):563–89.

———. "Several Stalins." *Survey* 17 (Autumn 1971):165–78.

Ulam, Adam B. *The Bolsheviks: The Intellectual and Political History of the Triumph of Communism in Russia.* New York: Macmillan, 1965.

———. *Expansion and Coexistence: The History of Soviet Foreign Policy, 1917–1967.* New York: Praeger, 1968.

———. "Lenin: His Legacy." *Foreign Affairs* 48 (Apr. 1970):460–70.

———. "Lenin's Last Phase." *Survey* 21 (Winter-Spring 1975):148–59.

———. *Stalin: The Man and His Era.* New York: Viking, 1973.

Uldricks, Teddy J. *Diplomacy and Ideology: The Origins of Soviet Foreign Relations, 1917–1930.* Sage Studies in 20th Century History, vol. 9. Beverly Hills, Calif.: Sage Publications, 1979.

———. "Russia and Europe: Diplomacy, Revolution, and Economic Development in the 1920s." *International History Review* 1 (Jan. 1979):55–83.

———. "The Soviet Diplomatic Corps in the Cicerin Era." *Jahrbucher für Geschichte Osteuropas* 23 (1975):213–24.

Ullman, Richard H. *Anglo-Soviet Relations, 1917–1921.* Vol. 1. *Intervention and the War.* Princeton: Princeton Univ. Press, 1961.

_____. *Anglo-Soviet Relations, 1919–1921*. Vol. 2: *Britain and the Russian Civil War, November 1918–February 1920*. Princeton: Princeton Univ. Press, 1968.

_____. *Anglo-Soviet Relations, 1917–1921*. Vol. 3. *The Anglo-Soviet Accord*. Princeton: Princeton Univ. Press, 1972.

Unterberger, Betty M., ed. *American Intervention in the Russian Civil War*. With an Introduction by Betty M. Unterberger. Problems in American Civilization. Lexington, Mass.: Heath, 1969.

_____. *America's Siberian Expedition, 1918–1920: A Study of National Policy*. Durham: Duke Univ. Press, 1956.

Ushakov, V. B. *Vneshniaia politika Germanii v period Veimarskoi respubliki*. Institut mezhdunarodnykh otnoshenii. Moskva: Izdatel'stvo IMO, 1958.

Valerin, R. "Ot razryva do vosstanovleniia anglo-sovetskikh otnoshenii." *Mezhdunarodnaia zhizn'* 11 (1929):47–62.

Vasiukov, V. S. *Predistoriia interventsii, fevral' 1917–mart 1918*. Moskva: Politizdat, 1968.

_____. *Vneshniaia politika Vremennogo pravitel'stva*. Moskva: Mysl', 1966.

Volkov, F. D. *Anglo-sovetskie otnosheniia, 1924–1929 gg*. Moskva: Politizdat, 1958.

_____. *Krakh angliiskoi politiki interventsii i diplomaticheskoi izoliatsii Sovetskogo gosudarstva (1917–1924 gg.)*. Moskva: Politizdat, 1954.

Von Laue, Theodore H. *Why Lenin? Why Stalin? A Reappraisal of the Russian Revolution, 1900–1930*. 2d ed. Critical Periods of History. Philadelphia: Lippincott, 1971.

Von Riekhoff, Harald. *German-Polish Relations, 1918–1933*. Baltimore: Johns Hopkins Univ. Press, 1971.

Vygodskii, S. Iu. *Leninskii Dekret o mire*. Leningrad: Lenizdat, 1958.

_____. *U istokov sovetskoi diplomatii*. Moskva: Politizdat, 1965.

_____. *V. I. Lenin: rukovoditel' vneshnei politiki Sovetskogo gosudarstva (1917–1923 gg.)*. Leningrad: Lenizdat, 1960.

_____. *Vneshniaia politika SSSR: politika mira i mezhdunarodnogo sotrudnichestva*. Moskva: Politizdat, 1958.

_____. *Vneshniaia politika SSSR 1924–1929 gg*. Moskva: Politizdat, 1963.

Wade, Rex A. "Argonauts of Peace: The Soviet Delegation to Western Europe in the Summer of 1917." *Slavic Review* 26 (Sept. 1967):453–67.

_____. *The Russian Search for Peace: February–October 1917*. Stanford: Stanford Univ. Press, 1969.

_____. "Why October? The Russian Search for Peace in 1917." *Soviet Studies* 20 (July 1968):36–45.

Wandycz, Piotr S. *France and Her Eastern Allies, 1919–1925: French-Czechoslovak-Polish Relations from the Paris Peace Conference to Locarno*. Minneapolis: Univ. of Minnesota Press, 1962.

_____. "French Diplomats in Poland, 1919–1926." *Journal of Central European Affairs* 23 (Jan. 1964):440–50.

_____. *Soviet-Polish Relations, 1917–1921*. Russian Research Center Studies, 59. Cambridge: Harvard Univ. Press, 1969.

Warth, Robert D. "The Acros Raid and the Anglo-Soviet 'Cold War' of the 1920's." *World Affairs Quarterly* 29 (July 1958):115–51.

_____. *The Allies and the Russian Revolution: From the Fall of the Monarchy to the Peace of Brest-Litovsk*. Durham: Duke Univ. Press, 1954.

_____. *Joseph Stalin*. Twayne's Rulers and Statesmen of the World Series, TROW 10. New York: Twayne, 1969.

_____. *Leon Trotsky*. World Leaders Series, TWLS 72. Boston: Twayne, 1977.

_____. "The Mystery of the Zinoviev Letter." *South Atlantic Quarterly* 49 (Oct. 1950):441–53.

_____. *Soviet Russia in World Politics*. New York: Twayne, 1963.

Weissman, Benjamin M. "The After-effects of the American Relief Mission to Soviet Russia." *Russian Review* 29 (Oct. 1970):411–21.

_____. *Herbert Hoover and Famine Relief to Soviet Russia: 1921–1923*. Hoover Institution Publications, 134. Stanford: Hoover Institution Press, Stanford Univ., 1974.

_____. "Herbert Hoover's 'Treaty' with Soviet Russia: August 20, 1921." *Slavic Review* 28 (June 1969):276–88.

Wesson, Robert G. *Soviet Foreign Policy in Perspective*. Dorsey Series in Political Science. Homewood, Ill.: Dorsey, 1969.

Wheeler-Bennett, John W. *Disarmament and Security since Locarno, 1925–1931, Being the Political and Technical Background of the General Disarmament Conference, 1932*. With an Introduction by Sir Neill L. Malcolm. Information Series No. 7. New York: Macmillan, 1932.

_____. *The Forgotten Peace: Brest-Litovsk, March 1918*. Studies in Modern History. New York: William Morrow, 1939.

_____. *Information on the Reduction of Armaments*. With an Introduction by Sir Neill L. Malcolm. Information Series No. 2. London: George Allen and Unwin, 1925.

_____. *Information on the Renunciation of War, 1927–1928*. With an Introduction by Philip H. Kerr. Information Series No. 4. London: George Allen and Unwin, 1928.

_____. *The Pipe Dream of Peace: The Story of the Collapse of Disarmament*. New York: n.p., 1935; reprint ed., Fertig, 1971.

_____. "Twenty Years of Russo-German Relations: 1918–1939." *Foreign Affairs* 25 (Oct. 1946):23–43.

_____. *The Wreck of Reparations, Being the Political Background of the Lausanne Agreement, 1932.* With an Introduction by Sir Walter Layton. New York: William Morrow, 1933.

Wheeler-Bennett, John W., and Hugh Latimer. *Information on the Reparation Settlement, Being the Background and History of the Young Plan and the Hague Agreements, 1929–1930.* With a Foreword by Sir Charles Addis. Information Series No. 6. London: George Allen and Unwin, 1930.

White, John A. *The Siberian Intervention.* Princeton: Princeton Univ. Press, 1950.

White, Stephen. " 'Anti-Bolshevik Control Officers' and British Foreign Policy, 1918–1920." *Co-existence* 13 (Oct. 1976):144–56.

_____. *Britain and the Bolshevik Revolution: A Study in the Politics of Diplomacy, 1920–1924.* New York: Holmes and Meier, 1980.

_____. "Colonial Revolution and the Communist International, 1919–1924." *Science and Society* 40 (Summer 1976):173–93.

_____. "Communism and the East: The Baku Congress, 1920." *Slavic Review* 33 (Sept. 1974):492–514.

Whiting, Allen S. *Soviet Policies in China, 1917–1924.* Studies of the Russian Institute, Columbia University. New York: Columbia Univ. Press, 1954.

Williams, Robert C. "Collective Immortality: The Syndicalist Origins of Proletarian Culture, 1905–1910." *Slavic Review* 39 (Sept. 1980):389–402.

_____. *Culture in Exile: Russian Emigres in Germany, 1881–1941.* Ithaca: Cornell Univ. Press, 1972.

Wilson, Joan H. *Ideology and Economics: U.S. Relations with the Soviet Union, 1918–1933.* Columbia: Univ. of Missouri Press, 1974.

Wise, E. F. "Anglo-Russian Trade and the Trade Agreement." *Empire Review* 28 (Sept. 1923):995–1004.

Wish, Harvey. "Anglo-Soviet Relations During Labour's First Ministry (1924)." *Slavonic and East European Review* 17 (Jan. 1939):389–403.

Wolfe, Bertram D. "Dress Rehearsals for the Great Terror." *Studies in Comparative Communism* 3 (Apr. 1970):1–24.

_____. *An Ideology in Power: Reflections on the Russian Revolution.* Introduction by Leonard Schapiro. Published in conjunction with the Hoover Institution on War, Revolution, and Peace of Stanford University. New York: Stein and Day, 1969.

_____. "Nationalism and Internationalism in Marx and Engels." *American Slavic and East European Review* 17 (Dec. 1958):403–17.

_____. *Three Who Made a Revolution: A Biographical History.* Beacon

Contemporary Affairs Series. Boston: Beacon, 1948; reprint ed., New York: Dell, 1964.

Yassour, Avraham. "Lenin and Bogdanov: Protagonists in the 'Bolshevik Center.' " *Studies in Soviet Thought* 22 (Feb. 1981):1–32.

Zarkhi, Aleksandr, and Vladlen Loginov. "Revoliutsiia i Motsart." *Iskusstvo kino* 4; 5 (1984):161–92; 159–92.

Zarnitskii, S. V., and A. N. Sergeev. *Chicherin*. Zhizn' zamechatel'-nykh liudei. Seriia biografii, vypusk 8 (423). Moskva: Molodaia gvardiia, 1966.

Zarnitskii, S. V., and L. I. Trofimova. *Sovetskoi strany diplomat*. Moskva: Politizdat, 1968.

Zhukovskii, N. P. *Na diplomaticheskom postu*. Moskva: Politizdat, 1973.

Zorin, V. A. *Osnovy diplomaticheskoi sluzhby*. Moskva: Mezhdunarodnye otnosheniia, 1964.

Index

AEG, *See* Allgemeine Eletritsitaets Gesellschaft

Afghanistan
crucial to British interests in India, 143
Treaty of Friendship (1921) with Soviets, 142
treaty with Soviets, 109

Afghan-Persian Treaty of Neutrality and Nonaggression (1927), 144

Afghan-Soviet Treaty of Neutrality and Nonaggression (1926), 144

Afghan-Turkish Treaty of Neutrality and Nonaggression (1928), 144

Aksel'rod, P. B., led Liquidators, 27

Aleksandr II
A. M. Gorchakov reaction to internal reforms, 9
Tsar, 4

Aleksandr III, Tsar, 4

Allgemeine Elektrische Gesellschaft, 20

Allgemeine Elektritsitaets Gesellschaft, engineers arrested by Soviets, 160

Allies, affirm reparation rights of Russia, 88

All-Russian Union of Consumer and Cooperative Societies, 116–18

American Civil War, Russian-United States relations, 10

Anglo-Soviet agreement signed (1920), 118

Anglo-Soviet Commercial Treaty (1921), 142

diplomatic immunity assured, 154–55

Anglo-Soviet Economic Treaty, not ratified, 130

Anglo-Soviet rapprochement and Chamberlain, 130

Antimilitarist propaganda, 36

Aristocratic heritage, Chicherin renounces, 12

Arkos
British police search, 154
Soviet Trading Company in London, 119

Armenia and Soviet issues with Turkey (1921), 142

Asia
British as obstacle to socialistic revolution, 115
capitalism vs. socialism competition, 134

Austria
de jure recognition to Soviet government (1924), 127
prisoner-of-war agreement with Soviet Russia (1920), 67

Azerbaidzhan and Soviet settlement of issues with Turkey (1921), 142

Baldwin, Stanley, as British prime minister, 126–27, 130

Baltic states
Chicherin

wanted credit and trade with
the West, 83
wanted revenue for arms, 21
Les Prisons Russes, published by V. N.
Figner, 31
Levin, L. G., (chief of Kremlin
medical staff), sent to see
Chicherin, 162
Liberation of Labor Group, Switzerland, 11
Liebknecht, Karl, 13
Liquidators
condemned by Chicherin, 29
renounced revolution within the
party, 27
repudiated, 27–28
Lithuania
Chicherin negotiating peace (1919–
1920), 64
neutrality and nonaggression pact
with Soviet Union, 111
peace treaty with Soviet Russia
(1920), 67, 109
Litvinov, M. M.
in Berlin with Chicherin (1922), 70f
Commissariat of Foreign Affairs
(1926–1927), 154
Chicherin disagreed on Rapallo
Treaty, 158
coveted Chicherin's position, 154
delegate to Genoa Conference
(1922), 82
as deputy commissar of collegium
(1918), 57
diplomacy emphasized disarmament,
161
discussed prisoner exchange with
British (1919), 118
entertained foreign dignitaries for
Chicherin, 53
leader on LKRE, 42
rivalry with Chicherin, 57
signed German-Soviet Commercial
Treaty (1925), 108
succeeded Chicherin at Commissariat of Foreign Affairs, 170
urged acceptance of Briand-Kellogg
Pact, 163
"Liutsifer," Chicherin pseudonym, 57
LKRE. *See* London Committee for the
Repatriation of Emigrants
Locarno, Switzerland
Chicherin saw pact as London-Paris
antagonism, 103–4

diplomatic conference (1925), 103
Stresemann met with Western pow-
ers, 107
Locarno Treaty (1925)
Chicherin sought to undermine, 109
demilitarization of Rhineland, 107
Soviet government
anxious over ramifications, 153
criticized Locarno Treaty, 108
Soviets need defensive allies in
Central Asia, 143
Weimar Republic agreed on western
frontier, 107
Lockhart, R. H. Bruce
described Chicherin (1918), 52
described Chicherin in bad health
(1929), 161–62
London, Chicherin 1917 arrest, 44
London Committee for the Repatria-
tion of Emigrants, 42
Chicherin as secretary, 42
*Londonskii Komitet po repatriatsii
emigrantov,* 42
Lunacharskii, A. V., Chicherin's
Mozart writings, 167

MacDonald, J. Ramsay, 127–28, 129,
130
Maiskii, I. M.
Chairman of London Committee for
the Repatriation of Emigrants, 42
lectured with Chicherin, 30
Maltzan, Baron Ago von (chief of
Eastern Section, German Foreign
Ministry), 87
"Marko Polo," Chicherin Pseudonym,
57
Martov, Iu. O., Menshevik leader, 18
Marxist socialism trend, 13
Marxist study of Mozart, 167
Maurice Conradi
acquittal, 125
assassinated Vorovskii (1923), 125
Mediterranean Sea, free from Soviet
penetration, 123
Mehring, Franz, trustee for factional
funds, 27
Meiendorf, Baron Rudol'f
Kazimirovich (cousin to Baroness
Meiendorf), 5
Meiendorf, Baroness Zhorzhina
Egorovna, taught her children, 6